A CERTAIN FAITH

A CERTAIN
FAITH

The Catholic Alternative

BARRY R. PEARLMAN

Angelico Press

First published as *A Certain Faith:*
Analogy of Being and the Affirmation of Belief
by the University Press of America in 2012
Angelico Press edition 2021
Copyright © Barry R. Pearlman 2021

All rights reserved:
No part of this book may be reproduced or transmitted,
in any form or by any means, without permission

For information, address:
Angelico Press, Ltd.
169 Monitor St.
Brooklyn, NY 11222
www.angelicopress.com

ppr 978-1-62138-741-1
cloth 978-1-62138-742-8

Book and cover design
by Michael Schrauzer

CONTENTS

PREFACE ix

PART ONE: REALITY 1
   CHAPTER 1. A Certain Idea 3
   CHAPTER 2. Creation 31
   CHAPTER 3. Good and Evil 67

PART TWO: WISDOM 93
   CHAPTER 4. Son of God 95
   CHAPTER 5. Lamb of God 127
   CHAPTER 6. Christ the King 153

PART THREE: SPIRIT 195
   CHAPTER 7. Purgation 197
   CHAPTER 8. Illumination 217
   CHAPTER 9. Union 243

BIBLIOGRAPHY 277
INDEX 287

PREFACE

IT HAS BEEN THE PERENNIAL TEACHING OF the Church that, by means of our natural reason reflecting upon creation, we can attain certain knowledge of the existence of God. The Church has also affirmed that, insofar as our faith rests upon the revelation of God in Jesus Christ, faith too is certain since it is established upon the authority of the one revealing, namely God. Such a contention that any beliefs, let alone faith, can be certain is utterly anathema to the postmodernist thinking that permeates our current, Western, secular culture. Reacting against the overconfidence of the modernist-rationalist tendencies inherited from the *optimisme* of the Enlightenment, postmodernism has proclaimed the relativity of all knowledge and values, emphasizing instead: dissimilarity, plurality, contextuality, and skepticism. This has propagated a culture plagued by either individualism and despair or an overweening and autocratic political correctness. Philosophy has degenerated into an introverted obsession with analytics, while religion is dismissed as a private myth. Our intention is to correct this postmodernist idea that truth is merely subjective and that faith is but an artificial edifice erected as some kind of wish fulfillment.

This book builds upon a certain idea: that there is an intrinsic principle within thought, namely being. This truth will be of value not only to anyone seeking a clear and certain foundation for belief, but also to those desiring an introduction to the idea of being and its applications (ontology). In order to do so, it will be most profitable to start with what is evident and certain in human thought. Therefore, the first chapter introduces the idea of being in general and, after some basic and very brief analyses, applies this idea of being to the question of the existence of God as naturally understood by the intellect.

By "naturally understood" is meant nothing more than the common-sense idea underlying all proper science that there is always to be postulated some causal principle behind any natural object of investigation. Too often arguments for the existence of God are either purely formal, relying upon deduction alone; or they are empirical, arguing inductively from the beauty and order of nature or from some historical, miraculous event. However, formally proven propositions still need to be shown to relate to reality, while empirically derived propositions can only produce probable truths. Therefore, contemporary rational belief requires both formal reason and empirical evidence. Neither alone is sufficient. Accordingly, in chapter two we examine the evidence gleaned from cosmology and quantum physics to support the deductions, already made in chapter one, that there is a first cause behind the cosmos itself. At the same time, we eliminate the postmodernist argument that the mind is somehow trapped inside itself and unable to extend its thoughts to extramental objects. In short, we try to ground our formal arguments upon objective evidence wherever possible and throughout.

Chapter three argues that there need be no contradiction between the idea of the existence of God and the fact of evil. On the contrary we shall show that evil (understood as a lack or distortion of the good) actually supports the argument that God exists.

Believing merely in the *existence* of God belongs to natural philosophy. Therefore, the first three chapters, which comprise part one, constitute a natural understanding of God. Such natural belief is not yet faith, certainly not religion. It is necessary to circumscribe the view popularized by the media and other detractors of religion that merely to believe in the existence of God makes one religious or even that belief is the product of faith. We argue the opposite: that faith follows rational belief. For we take belief simply to be the assent to the truth of a proposition: e.g., one can believe in the existence of black holes without putting one's faith in them.

Rather, faith adds to belief the quality of trust. One puts one's faith in an individual because one can trust in that person's authority. Founders of religion, such as Moses, Jesus, Muhammad, Zoroaster, Lao Tse, or Gautama Buddha, were trusted as authorities for their various religions. Therefore, in order to prepare for the possibility of faith, we examine in the three chapters of part two the person of Jesus, who, it will be argued, proclaimed himself to be the Son of God, offering salvation in his name, and that he came to establish the Church with a definite apostolic and sacramental structure. If Jesus's claim is true, it elevates our natural conception of God from that of an impersonal, deistic Being or Principle, to the Christian view that God intentionally orchestrated salvation history — a history which also encompasses the Church.

Religion, in turn, adds to faith the quality of devotion — expressed through rituals, sacraments, prayer, and meditation — leading to some end: wisdom, mystical union, or eternal life. Having already concluded in part two that Jesus is who he claimed to be, we proceed in part three to explain the life of devotion: first its morality, then its spirituality, and finally its supreme end — union with God. The latter is accomplished by considering the lives of five saints.

The entire book implicates the notion of analogy of being briefly introduced in the first chapter and more fully presented in the second. This idea continues to make its appearance in parts two and three, all the time expanding its meaning and variety of applications, until in the final chapter it is employed to elucidate the principle constituting the prayer of union. The procedure herein is mainly intuitive — introducing the minimal of metaphysical concepts — since it is not our intention to create yet another philosophical or theological system. (Such would be neither desirable nor possible for this author.) Rather the purpose of this book is to foster faith. But in order to do this it is essential first to settle upon a few evident truths. To this end a stepwise approach has been adopted — more like the steps of an escalator than of a staircase — since, like the steps of an escalator, the ideas of each subsequent chapter emerge from those of the previous one. Thus, the reader may find it helpful to follow the argument of the book simply by reviewing the introductory sections and the concluding comments of each chapter.

The content, structure, and varying styles of this volume endeavor to appeal to the whole person; to take one from a situation of doubt, through faith and the understanding of virtue, to the threshold of contemplation. The perspective of this text is that of mainstream Christian belief, whose deposit fully represents the teaching and mind of Jesus as expressed in the Gospels. There is nothing herein that should displease anyone who respects the Holy Scriptures. So it is hoped the reader will find the abundant scriptural references helpful. This book is written for the inquiring general reader open to the possibilities of faith in Jesus Christ and especially those who may be interested in the Catholic faith, either from the inside or the outside.

A Certain Faith

* * *

The immediate inspiration for the thematic idea behind this book is Charles Morerod, O.P., in his *Ecumenism and Philosophy* (Ann Arbor: Sapientia Press, 2006), for it was he who identified for me the essential error which underlies our postmodern culture. Therefore, I would like to thank Professor Joseph Pearce of Ave Maria University for his kind permission to quote from Fr Morerod's timely publication.

My appreciation also to Megan K. T. Bless, contract manager for Ignatius Press, for permission to include citations from the appendix to Rod Bennett's *Four Witnesses: The Early Church in Her Own Words* (San Francisco: Ignatius Press, 2002). Thanks also to Tom DeVries, international rights manager of Wm. B. Eerdmans Publishing, for permission to quote from Richard Bauckham, *Jesus and the Eyewitnesses: The Gospels as Eyewitness Testimony* (Grand Rapids: Wm. B. Eerdmans, 2006); to Alexandra McDonald, rights and special sales manager for SPCK Publishing, to quote from N. T. Wright, *The Resurrection of the Son of God* (London: SPCK, 2003); and especially to Diane Flynn, editorial assistant at Paulist Press, for her permission to cite from R. P. Phillips, *Modern Thomistic Philosophy*, vol. II (Westminster, MD: The Newman Press, 1957). My thanks also to Dr. J. J. Haldane, FRSE, professor of philosophy at University of St Andrews, for identifying the Paulist Press as the current owner of The Newman Press.

Finally, I would also like to express my sincere gratitude to John Riess, editor of Angelico Press, for publishing this volume. It is an honor to be associated with this esteemed publishing house. My thanks also to Professor Peter Kwasniewski for his valuable suggestions and timely corrections to the manuscript; as well as my compliments to Michael Schrauzer for his imaginative and handsome cover design.

Old Testament quotations are from *The New Jerusalem Bible* (London: Darton, Longman, and Todd, 1985). New Testament quotations are from *The Revised Standard Version* (New York: Thomas Nelson, 1971). Any alterations to these are my own translations. Every effort has been made to ensure that whatever has been written herein is based upon peer-respected authorities: I make no claim to originality. However, any errors in explicating their ideas are mine alone.

... and if I were to say,
"I do not know Him,"
I should be a liar...
                    John 8:55

PART ONE

REALITY

I am who am.
Exodus 3:14

CHAPTER I

A Certain Idea

*For whoever would draw near to God
must believe that he exists...*[1]

TO THINK OF ANYTHING, ANYTHING AT all, is to conceive of some being. For example, we can think of a human being, an angelic being or a Supreme Being; or we could think of the condition of being happy, virtuous, or holy. Of course, we can also conceive of ideal beings such as justice, truth, beauty, or the number pi. Even something that can be sensed or imagined is some being—the color red, the beat of one's heart, the object of one's hope, heaven. These are ideas of something, not nothing. For to think of nothing is the same as not thinking, just as to speak of nothing is not to say anything at all (or to do nothing at all is but not to act). Therefore, all thought presupposes that we are thinking of some being, some *thing*. The word being denotes anything that exists or possibly exists: any*thing* of which we can conceive. The words being and thing are one and the same, substitutable one for the other. Since everything of which we can conceive is some being, it follows as a truism that to think is to have some being as a mental object. In other words, being, or more correctly being in general, merely signifies whatever is noted when the mind apprehends its object—whatever can be thought.

Now since the words *being* (*ens*) and *thing* (*res*) are convertible, interchangeable, with one another, it follows that being (or thing) is the simplest, most elementary, of ideas. By "simple" we mean *not compounded of parts*. For if we assumed the idea of being to be compounded of parts, then there could be only two possibilities: either those parts can exist or they cannot. But if they *cannot* exist, then there *are no* parts within being, and we have our thesis.

---

[1] Heb 11:6b.

If, however, we should assume the alternative, that being is compounded of parts which do exist, then the idea of any "part" is also an idea of some being or of some thing. To think of a part is to give it existence—at least in our minds. If we assume that the idea of being consists of parts which *themselves* have being (otherwise there are no parts) then to conceive of such a "part" is to presuppose that being already belongs to it formally, i.e., in principle. For these reasons, the idea of being is logically prior to the idea of a part. Consequently, it is false to assert that the *idea of being* is compounded of parts. Rather it is simple, as we have said. It is irreducible...except to nothing. St Thomas Aquinas regards this notion of being in general as "*ens abstractissimum*," the thinnest and shallowest of concepts, denoting the barest removal from nothingness.[2]

In fine, this elemental, atomic idea of being simply denotes an object of thought: of what actually exists or can possibly exist. What cannot possibly exist, because its existence is absurd (self-contradictory), is inconceivable. It does not exist for us. It is *non-being*, no-thing. Its mental conception is logically repugnant like a false truth, a square circle, or a saintly demon. Only a possible being (virtual or actual) is conceivable.

Implicit within thinking, then, is the idea of being in general. Truly, being makes thought possible, for without being we could not conceive of any*thing*. If there were only nothing, nothing could be thought—for indeed there would be no one there to think. What does not exist cannot act![3] And thinking is an act presupposing a subject of the action *and* an object towards which the act of thought is directed. As such the idea of being is the very formative principle of all thought, including all demonstrable knowledge (*scientia, episteme*): such as the formal sciences of logic,

---

2 *Summa Contra Gentiles* II.25. A note to this passage by Joseph Rickaby reads: "There is always ambiguity in this term [by Aquinas] of 'mere existence,' *ipsum esse*.... Either it means *ens abstractissimum*, the thinnest and shallowest of concepts, denoting the barest removal from nothingness: or it is *ens plenissimum*, being that includes (virtually at least) all other being.... In this latter sense the term is predicable of God alone." Cf. II.26.
3 The contrapositive is also certain: whatever acts exists.

mathematics, and metaphysics; as well as the empirical sciences of physics, chemistry, biology, forensics, etc.[4] Let us see how the idea of being in general enters into some of these disciplines.

LOGIC

For example, in (symbolic) logic we often find in textbooks the assertion:[5]

$$p$$

This stands for any proposition, axiom, term, etc.—in other words, anything *p*osited by the mind—i.e., being in general. Next is found the statement

$$p \equiv p$$

which means p is identical with p. This is the principle of identity, stipulating that any being or object of thought is identical with itself.

Now if an object of thought *is* identical with itself, then it is not the case that it is *not* identical with itself, or it is not the case that p is identical with anything that is *not* (~) *p*. Thus it follows that being cannot both be itself and not be itself formally or properly determined. By "formally or properly determined" we simply mean that one cannot at once both affirm and deny of a particular being the same definite property or state. This is the *principle* of contradiction[6] which in symbols reads:

$$\sim (p \cap \sim p)$$

or one can *not* posit *both* p and not p. Stated by Aristotle it reads: "The same attribute cannot both belong and not belong to [any] being

---

[4] Formal thought is deduced *a priori* from first principles, self-evident ideas, or axioms. Empirical thought is inferred *a posteriori* from interactive observation of beings in act. From each of these, theoretical systems are then logically derived.

[5] See Elliot Mendelson, *Introduction to Mathematical Logic* (New York: D. Van Nostrand, 1979); Robert Neidorf, *Deductive Forms: An Elementary Logic* (New York: Harper & Row, 1967); Theodore Sider, *Logic for Philosophy* (Oxford: Oxford University Press, 2010).

[6] It is also called the rule of non-contradiction. Since the conjunction of a proposition and its denial is logically impossible, its intellectual repugnance gives the principle (*ratio*) for its rejection. The principle then generates the rule.

formally regarded as the same."[7] For example, if we affirm of some object of thought something that is in fact true, we cannot then say that it is false.[8] Being cannot both be and not be. From these three rules it is possible to construct the whole of logic from *modus tollens* (the rule that if a proposition p implies some consequent q, then if q is false, p is false) to Gödel's undecidability principle that all formal systems (such as mathematics) will contain some propositions whose truth cannot be determined from *within that system alone*. These and many more propositions have been proved from these first principles and constitute the foundation of the vast corpus of logic and mathematics. Deny these fundamental principles, and logic and mathematics — and therefore jurisprudence, forensics, physics, etc. — collapse!

CRITERIOLOGY

In the discipline of criteriology these three first principles of being, identity, and contradiction also form the first criteria in the process of judgment. In this discipline, for example, we find the same three first logical principles of thought, but expressed in the following form:

> (A) Being is: i.e., some possible thing exists (viz., being in general as anything which is simply and immediately apprehended).

This is the foundational, formative principle (or simply form) of thought.

> (B) Being is what it is: a thing is what it is.

This is the *principle* of identity once again. Note: postulate (B) presupposes postulate (A), that something is first noticed and discerned as some possible existent (*ens, res*).

> (C) Being cannot both be and not be.

---

[7] *On Interpretation*, 24b7, vol. 8 in *The Great Books* (London: Encyclopaedia Britannica, 1952).
[8] That is, a proposition (*propositum*, p) must implicate something (q*uiddam*, q), p → q, for it to be a true statement of logic. Cf. Sider, *Logic for Philosophy*, sec. 2.1, sec. 2.4.

This latter criterion, as we have seen, is the principle of contradiction which in turn requires one of two further mental operations to that of simple identification — viz., either the division of some being from every other determinate being or the negation of that being. For example, *division*: "The cover of this book is either entirely red or entirely green." Or *negation*: "This book is entirely red or it is not *entirely* red." Moreover, contradiction presupposes that one has already identified the object as being what it is (in the examples, being the color red or green). Of course it must be understood that the rule of contradiction is not conditioned by time. One hears it said that a thing cannot both be and not be the case at *the same time*. But it should be understood that what is intended is that at no given moment can an object ever receive contradictory attributes. The focus of contradiction is directed to the identity of the object, not to the circumstance of time. A thing cannot now or at any other time receive *contradictory* attributes.[9] A contradictory state of affairs cannot be.

It follows that the principle of contradiction itself cannot be denied. For to deny it is to invoke it. Either we accept the principle of contradiction or we contradict it. In the latter case we appeal to the very principle that we are denying. We appeal to it as the formal authority to legitimate the act of denial. The principle of contradiction is certain — cannot be doubted — and is the basis of all rational thought. Therefore, if anyone wishes to contradict the idea that we think of being, then, having accepted the principle of contradiction, one must also accept those principles assumed within it such as the principle of identity which it presupposes and the idea of being which in turn underlies that. It is apparent that this is just the rule of *modus tollens* introduced above. If the principle of contradiction entails (logically implicates necessarily) the idea of being, then, if the idea of being is false, the principle of contradiction is false. But the *principle* of contradiction cannot be false. And, therefore, neither is the idea of being. It is demanded by the principle of contradiction for without the mind's apprehension of being we could never form that principle.

---

9 See Cardinal Mercier, *A Manual of Modern Scholastic Philosophy* (London: Kegan Paul, 1938), 473–75.

The idea of being is, therefore, certain and is *the* criterion of truth and all skepticism about this is *de facto* excluded.

> Our primary intellectual cognition is of being, and in knowing it we know its identity with itself and the impossibility of its being contradictory. This we know immediately, and we cannot have any doubt about the truth of these primary principles, and we shall only know whether a proposition is true or false when we have discovered whether it is so necessarily linked with the first principles which immediately express the notion of being.[10]

Therefore, the fundamental criterion of truth is the demonstration that a particular judgment can be resolved analytically into those primary or first principles *which express the notion of being.*

One should not assume that all beings apprehended by the mind are real in the sense of having some substantial, extramental reality. We have not got that far yet! Everything we have been asserting up to now treats being as a formal concept and as the means through which (*medium quo*) every other thing is known. However the external world is made known to us, it is through the idea of being in general that we come to understand it as some existent thing, i.e., as a (conceptualized) object expressed in and by the mind. This thing is properly and immediately known, but it is represented in and through the formal idea. Thus there is immediate objective knowledge even though the idea of being is a medium of cognition, because our minds are enabled through that idea to apprehend the perceived object as this actual (or virtual) identifiable thing. We must not confuse the idea of being with Being. The first is ideal or formal, while the second is real or substantial.

> Now this objective concept of being is a thing of a most general kind, which is predicable of all things which are, or can be. The simple and direct concept of being is a very imperfect and confused one, and is first both in the logical order and in that of time. For that is first in the logical

---

10 R. P. Phillips, *Modern Thomistic Philosophy* (Westminster, MD: Newman Press, 1957), 2:128–29.

order, or first known, which is included in every other concept, and this is the case with respect to the simple concept of being, since every concept is of some being, or of some determination of being. Similarly it is first in the order of time, for the first idea to be acquired is, as we saw, the most general one, and this is the idea of being. The case is, however, different with regard to the metaphysical concept of [B]eing, which can only be acquired as the result of a long process of thought, and so cannot be first.[11]

This is the order we have followed thus far. It is important to respect this order since there is some confusion in modern philosophy with such contraries as real vs. ideal, objective vs. subjective, and concrete vs. abstract. In short, there is a tendency to identify the ideal with the real to the extent that attacks on any form of "logocentrism" become normative. This is the postmodernist error. But there is no attempt here to deny the ineffability of the substantial since we only know form, not substance. Neither the substance of a stone, a tree, an animal, an angel, or God is retained in our minds as such.[12] Beneath all our thoughts lies being, and this idea "has no idea that represents it. It has no archetype that contains all its intelligible reality. It is its own archetype, and it contains in itself the archetype of all beings."[13] Being thus subsumes within itself a note of the infinite; so it is without restriction, and therefore does not confine the world or us within a logocentric prison where we are bound by the meaning of a word. It is living persons who think, not "dead texts." We are open to being in general and though it is the thinnest and shallowest of concepts so that it is hardly a concept at all, nonetheless as the *terminus a quo* of all knowledge it is very powerful in the disciplines it generates, as we have already seen, and, as we shall see next, truly elegant.

---

11 Phillips, *Modern Thomistic Philosophy*, 2:160.
12 "Therefore, of a substance no quidditive concept can be had naturally that is immediately caused by the substance. One can have only a concept that is caused or abstracted from accidents first, and that is only the concept of being." John Duns Scotus, *Ordinatio* 1.3, q. 3, n. 145.
13 Nicolas Malebranche, *Dialogues on Metaphysics*, trans. Willis Doney (New York: Abaris Books, 1980), II, v.

Part One: Reality

METAPHYSICS

A third area in addition to logic and criteriology in which these first principles find application is the discipline of metaphysics. To save time we will assume the common-sense understanding found in all the empirical disciplines (not to mention our own everyday experiences) that we have conscious sense experiences, for example the process of reading this book. It should be clear by now that these sensory percepts when they enter consciousness are also considered beings in the manner described above.

However, we must avoid the error of assuming that these sensory percepts have the same mode of existence in our minds and outside them as pantheism and ontologism do. For if being in general were found in things formally as *their* organizing principle then the pantheistic conclusion that all things are one Being would be unavoidable. Or, on the other hand, we would conclude that the world was but Idea and that in *knowing the idea* of being in general we would know the world (idealism) and God besides (ontologism). In fact, we might say that this is also the postmodernists' misconception, namely that since (as they imagine) thought attributes extramental reality to its *ideas*, so those ideas must be eschewed. It should be clear that we do not so attribute. Pantheism, idealism, ontologism, and postmodernism betray the identity fallacy by either mistaking the ideal for the real, or the real for the ideal.

Furthermore, we must avoid another error (made by nominalists, conceptualists, and subjectivists) that being is anything but objective: a sheer concoction of the mind. This too is false, for in all things there is something that refers or relates to reality. "If this were not so, real and logical being would be on the same footing; but they are not, for *the mind cannot confer on logical being a capacity for real existence.*"[14] Merely thinking of something, however consistent (or beautiful), does not render it real. We are not God.

We cannot, therefore, like Descartes, doubt that there is a real world behind our sensations. Even he had to admit that something, some demon at least, had to be responsible for his sensory experiences.

---

14 Phillips, *Modern Thomistic Philosophy*, 2:161. Italics added.

> I shall suppose, not that God who is supremely good and the fountain of truth, but some evil genius not less powerful than deceitful, has employed his whole energies in deceiving me; I shall consider that the heavens, the earth, colors, figures, sound, and all other external things are nought but the illusions and dreams of which this genius has availed himself in order to lay traps for my credulity; I shall consider myself as having no hands, no eyes, no flesh, no blood, nor any senses, yet falsely believing myself to possess all these things; I shall remain obstinately attached to this idea.... [15]

How full this text is of ideas of beings in general: earth, colors, sound, dreams, evil genius (*malin génie*), flesh, blood, etc. Yet Descartes missed this point and thereby set the subjectivist pattern for the philosophers who followed. If only he had seized upon the general idea he could have assuaged his doubts more easily.

Few philosophers these days deny the common-sense, real world especially given the achievements of empirical scientists. To believe that a demon (or computer) is programming us is an assumption too far. We apply Ockham's razor that entities must not be multiplied beyond necessity. The explanations of physics and neurophysiology reinforce one another and serve to provide an adequate foundation for the origins of our sensations. Therefore, we shall take the real world for granted as the common-sense understanding shared by most reasonable inhabitants of this world including those skeptical philosophers who manage to lecture and publish while deconstructing the fundamental principles of the intellect.

Cause and substance

A fundamental principle of metaphysics is called the Reason of Being (*raison d'être*): *every being must either possess its intelligible sufficiency in itself, a se, or derive it from some other being, ab alio.* The only possible alternative — that a being derives its reason for

---

[15] René Descartes, *Meditations*, in *The Great Books* (London: Encyclopaedia Britannica, 1952), 31:77.

being from nothing at all, i.e., that there *is no* reason for being—is absurd since what does not exist cannot act. If there is nothing there, nothing is done. Thus from nothing only nothing can come (*ex nihilo nihil fit*).[16]

This reason of being is either intrinsic or extrinsic. It is intrinsic if a thing is what it is from something belonging to its own nature such as a circle, consciousness, or God. To contradict this is impossible, since that would deny that its nature is its *nature*, i.e., deny that a thing is what it is because of what it is—a clear violation of the principle of identity. On the other hand, reason of being is extrinsic if a thing derives its properties or its existence from another. Again, the third alternative—that *nothing can be* a reason for being—is not an option. "Every being has the reason of being of that which belongs to it either in itself or in some other: in itself, if that which belongs to it is a constituent of it in itself; in another, if that which belongs to it does so without being a constituent of it in itself."[17]

This idea is self-evident so it cannot be deduced from the idea of identity. However, it can be proved by a *reductio ad absurdum*. For if this principle is denied one must then hypothesize that whatever *exists* does *not possess its existence* either of itself or from any other. Since *ex hypothesi* it does exist, it must have existence as its own proper possession (any other thing already having been excluded); and therefore it both exists of itself and yet does not exist of itself—a clear violation of the principle of contradiction, and therefore an absurdity. Of course, if its existence is neither from itself nor from some other, then it cannot exist at all.

That the idea of being is the directive (formative) principle behind every intellection is therefore inescapable: analysis is incomplete and without foundation until it comes to rest in this principle. For it can be directly observed that the self-evident (and therefore certain) nature of the principle of reason of being arises when the *idea of being* divides itself into "two objects of thought conceptually different whose real identity we perceive immediately, namely being itself and an object of thought 'grounded in existence' or intelligibly

---

16 Recall that by nothing, we mean: *not anything that can be thought.*
17 Phillips, *Modern Thomistic Philosophy*, 2:236.

determined or 'apt (in virtue of itself or of something else) to perfect the movement of intelligence.'"[18] Whatever is has that whereby it is.

From this truth it is only a short step to the notion of causality since it is just a special application of the principle of reason of being to concrete objects of perception. In fact, Maritain shows that the first principles of the human intellect along with the principle of reason of being already have their counterpart in the real world.[19] The perdurance of objects over time and the obstinacy or resistance objects have in opposition to us illustrate respectively the principles of identity and of contradiction. Objects exhibit a stable identity and will painfully contradict our intentions if we *act as though they are not there*: e.g., walking into a glass door.

Thus the principle of reason of being has a real counterpart: the principle of causality. The formal and material reasons for this are the phenomena of change or motion in things which involve the cessation and coming to be of certain qualities or properties in time. To observe change is to observe differences in things either spatially or temporally. A thing's identity is felt to be under pressure for some reason, intrinsically or extrinsically. When a thing loses its identity entirely then we say it has changed into something else: it has ceased to be what it is and has become something other than what it was — or has utterly perished.

However, we also observe that more often the same identifiable thing does not lose its identity. There may be differences in location, attitude, or appearance, yet something of its identity perdures. That which perdures or subsists is denoted substance and refers only to that permanent reality which survives and supports those qualities which can change in a thing without affecting what it is. Those changeable attributes are called accidents, appearance, or phenomena. We cannot say that these accidental phenomena depend upon nothing at all, so we postulate substance as that which grounds those accidental features.

For example, an object can change color, position, attitude, or size without ceasing to be what it is. Or an animal goes through zygote, embryo, fetus, infant, and adult without ceasing to be that

---

18   Jacques Maritain, *A Preface to Metaphysics* (London: Sheed and Ward, 1945), 102. Italics added.
19   Ibid. Following Leibniz and Wolff, he calls it the principle of sufficient reason.

animal substantially. In all these changes some organizing principle subsists.[20] In other words, from the moment of conception there exists in every generated *suppositum* an *entelechial haecceity*: i.e., a unique incommunicable individuality acting towards a specific end (in this case, the fruit of that conception) which belongs to any entity that has its ultimate actuality in itself. And if it should also be either virtually or actually rational, then it is a person.[21]

Again, in physics the underlying constituent of everything physical is matter — a primitive stuff which is capable of receiving different forms through some extrinsic formative energy or force. Everything physical is conceived to be a substantial form of matter with more or less complexity. Thus substance simply applies the reason for being to a thing's intrinsic constitution. The entire thrust of empirical science is to discover what the intrinsic underlying principle is which renders something the intelligible thing that it is. Science succeeds in its explanations only when this substance is formally identified. For example, the spacetime singularity preceding the Big Bang is one such substance, or substantial form. Whatever underlies spacetime would be another substantial form.

It should be reiterated at this point that we do not receive a thing's substance into our intellects as *substance*. It is obvious that one does not receive the substance of a black hole into one's mind when one conceives it — only its formal principle. Neither do we apprehend its appearance. By nature a black hole has no appearance for no information can escape from it.[22] We grasp its substance in principle as explaining the collapse of a super-massive star and serving to ground the explanation of its subsequent behavior and properties. That is all

---

20 This is what Duns Scotus refers to as an essentially ordered cause consisting of three properties: (1) regulation in the sense that the second cause depends upon the first precisely in the act of causing, and consequently (2) a higher cause is more perfect than those dependent causes which follow, and finally (3) that all essentially ordered causes are simultaneously directed to produce the final effect. Cf. *De Primo Principio* 3.11.

21 *Quodlibetal Questions* 9.7, 19.41 and *Ordinatio* 2, d. 3, pars I, nn. 5–65, n. 169. See also Thomas Williams, *The Cambridge Companion to Duns Scotus* (Cambridge: Cambridge University Press, 2003), 118–21.

22 Black holes were predicted long before any quantum fringe effects were discovered.

that substance has ever meant, namely, that underlying immanent act which serves to ground our explanations of the nature of a thing. The alternative would be to say that nothing so grounds them which would necessitate the death of all scientific explanation, formal and empirical.

There is, therefore, nothing mystical in the *idea* of substance. It is only the intrinsic application of the principle of the reason for being, while the extrinsic application of that principle is the conventional idea of causality empirically understood.[23] The *mystery* of substance, however, comes from the fact that we cannot know substance as substance, only as form. Substance is postulated as that which subsists in itself but is not known in itself. Substance whether material or immaterial will always retain an ineffable quality, and any knowledge of it always ought to be open to further possible revelations or discoveries.

NATURAL THEOLOGY

It should be apparent that metaphysics is little more than the formal science of thought and its applications. Its ambition is no more than to determine which concepts are suitable when one reflects upon the world.[24] And the concept it uses is the concept of Being, where the uppercase distinguishes it from being in general. The former is real being, the latter ideal being; the former grounds reality, while the latter is the principle of thought. The idea of being in general becomes Being when one seeks to account for the thing which underlies extramental objects. As we have seen, this is substance and Being simply carries the notion of substance to its limit: Ultimate Reality or the Absolute.

Why does one postulate such a thing? The reason is that it is eminently natural to do so. To think of anything is to think of being in general and through continued application of this idea one ascends to the ultimate question: why is there something rather than nothing?

---

23 It is not necessary here to distinguish between Aristotle's material, efficient, formal, and final causes. Indeed, when creation is regarded as an integrated system of laws, all such laws need only implicate but one, infinite, universal, providential Cause. See Malebranche, *Dialogues on Metaphysics*, VII, ix–x; X, xiii–xiv; XII, x, xiv.

24 Thomas A. F. Kelly, *Language, World and God* (Blackrock: Columba Press, 1996).

Initially when we posed the question "of what do we think?" we found the answer to be "of being in general." From this followed definite principles of thought which facilitated the construction of a consistent system of logical rules. Moreover, in criteriology the same idea authorized the avoidance of faulty judgments by constantly referring one's conclusions back to these first principles: being, identity, and contradiction. When applied to extramental objects, the idea yielded the notions of cause and of substance, which answered the question of what determined or lay under the changing states of these objects. Finally, when the world as a whole was considered, the same problem arose. The world is thoroughgoingly contingent and demands an explanation. The persistent and dogged pursuance of the answer to this question has driven science, philosophy, and theology. And the answer must be something rather than nothing, since what does not exist cannot be the cause or substance of anything, let alone Creation. This question is simply a reiteration of the question of being: in fact, it is but to think it. The idea of Being is the form of this question addressed to World. It is the intellect noting its object and enquiring whence is its reality or reason for being.

The discoveries of modern empirical science have only reinforced this tendency, since it is now believed that the whole of spacetime had a beginning, i.e., there was a state of affairs in which there was nothing we could call spacetime followed ontologically by a state of affairs which we do call spacetime. We say "followed ontologically" because it did not occur *in* time, since time too came to be along with space, and because one reality proceeded from another — not from nothing at all. Whatever is the origin of time is *de facto* non-temporal or eternal, since time cannot be the cause of itself — or it would have to precede itself or exist before it ever existed, which is absurd. Whatever was the origin of space is also not limited by space (or anything else) and is, therefore, infinite. And changeable matter, consisting perhaps of quantum units of spacetime, came similarly from something immaterial since matter too had a beginning. Finally, energy as ordered forces must have come from something all powerful. Clearly, some unchanging, all-powerful, infinite, eternal, and immaterial Reality must be the *first* principle of all that is.

A Certain Idea

Now nothing can be, as it were, "firster" than first. For, indeed, if there is a creative, explanatory principle (i.e., *Explanans*) behind everything that is to be explained (the *explananda*) then it must have existed eternally. It cannot come from nothing, as we have seen, nor can it create itself, for then it would have had to precede its own existence, which is absurd. And it cannot be created by anything else since it is hypothesized to be first. *It* is the creator. Therefore it is eternal; for there is nothing otherwise to create it. And if it can exist, then being all powerful, it *must* exist.[25] How natural to wonder at the universe and how equally natural to seek a unifying Principium behind it all; and how fruitless it is arbitrarily to stifle this spirit of wonder.

It is precisely in this spirit that St Thomas constructed his five ways[26] to demonstrate the existence of such a Being, which St Thomas repeatedly calls God at the end of each demonstration, e.g.: "And this everyone understands to be God"; or "To which everyone gives the name of God"; or "This all men speak of as God"; or "This being we call God." Note that he does not say *is* God, rather *understands,* or *speaks of,* or *calls.* The reason for this follows from St Thomas's use of the word "demonstration." This he makes clear in his preceding article, where he responds to the objection that the middle term in a demonstration is the essence of a thing; and since we cannot know what God's essence (substance) consists of, then we cannot demonstrate what we cannot know. St Thomas's rebuttal of this objection is that the proof of God's existence should be understood as a proof of some cause from its effects. "This is especially the case in regard to God, because, in order to prove the existence of anything, it is necessary to accept as a middle term the meaning of the name, and not its essence, for the question of its essence follows on the question of its existence. Now the names given to God are derived from his effects.... Consequently, in demonstrating the existence of God from his effects,

---

25 This is essentially the point of the modal argument given in the *De Primo Principio*. Duns Scotus demonstrates that there cannot be an infinite regression of essentially ordered causes, nor even in the accidental causes sustained by them. He then proves that the first principle is necessarily of infinite perfections (as required by the second property of essentially ordered causes). And what is of infinite perfections (modes of being), if it can exist, must necessarily exist.
26 *Summa Theol.* I, q. 2, a. 3.

Part One: Reality

we may take for the middle term the meaning of the word 'God.'"[27] What he means here is that we gain an idea of the cause from our understanding of its effects, because something of the cause is somehow communicated to the effects.

For example, in the impressionist piece *Claire de Lune,* Debussy conveys the dynamics of water revealed through the play of moonlight on waves splashing and surging in a cove, and through this he is able to evoke an intimation of movement and light. This is what St Thomas would call knowledge of analogy of being (*analogia entis*). For just as one can suggest in music an analogy between the surge of the ocean's tide and the heart's passions, so one can attribute in an analogous way the meaning of the effects to their cause. The reason is that they share between them a common idea — not exactly, but proportionally. The idea evoked is not the same in each, but similar enough to intimate to us something of the cause through our notion of the effect. If this difference in the ideas evoked were absolute, then the analogy would break down and the ideas would be equivocal. In other words, the analogous idea presents us with a unifying concept. This is just the unity which a univocal thing has; and provided that the common idea does not contain any differences essentially, it will be perfectly one in sense and meaning. So when Thomas says, for example, in his First Way, that we signify by "God" the meaning attributed to that of first mover *per se*, he is merely saying that God is normally understood to have this perfection. If a first mover exists, and God is a first mover, then God exists. This is the principle of identity again. In St Thomas's demonstration of the term, God is simply identified with that Cause which is proved in each respective demonstration.

> The term 'God' indicates the mediated knowledge that we naturally (spontaneously) have of God as the ultimate cause of the being of things. In this sense, natural and spontaneous knowledge of God (the idea, the name) is not only a premise of the proof of his existence, but also its proper object. In fact, the proof concludes that God is precisely that cause which our intellect had identified and

---

27 *Summa Theol.* I, q. 2, a. 2, obj. 2.

named, and so it does nothing other than reflectively make explicit the cognitive path upon which we had already spontaneously embarked.[28]

Therefore, the objection that these proofs do not prove what they intend to, namely, the God of Judeo-Christian faith, for example, misses the point by demanding too much. Thomas's demonstrations are less presumptuous. But they do not exclude the possibility of future revelations or expansions of our understanding of his Being. Every cause is greater than its effect[29] so that God's Being remains forever ineffable, but something of that nature is communicated through his acts just as it is with all other beings,[30] or science is a futile enterprise.

The Five Ways of St Thomas Aquinas

We proceed directly to present the five ways in St Thomas's own words.

> *First way*: The existence of God can be proved in five ways. The first and more manifest way is the argument from motion. It is certain, and evident to our senses, that in this world some things are in motion. Now whatever is in motion is put in motion by another, for nothing can be in motion unless it is in potency to that towards which it is in motion. But a thing moves in so far as it is in act. For motion is nothing else than the reduction of something from potency to act. But nothing can be reduced from potency to act except by something in a state of act. Thus that which is actually hot, as fire, makes wood, which is potentially hot,

---

28 Fulvio Di Blasi, *God and the Natural Law* (South Bend, Indiana: St Augustine's Press, 2006), 113.
29 For if the effect were the greater, then something which is neither a cause nor the effect conspired in the effect; but something cannot come from nothing. Neither can they be of equal potency, for then the cause would have nothing *ad extra* to give to produce the effect.
30 The laws of nature are such that a cause communicates through its action a capacity which is transferred from agent (*terminus a quo*) to patient (*terminus ad quem*) as a formative or organizing energy or principle. Classical Hamiltonian mechanics relates this total energy to the change in all the positions and momenta in a system independently of time. This energy is conserved. See B. P. Cowan, *Classical Mechanics* (London: Routledge & Kegan Paul, 1984), 91–98.

to be actually hot, and thereby moves and changes it. Now it is not possible that the same thing should be at once in act and potency in the same respect, but only in different respects. For what is actually hot cannot simultaneously be potentially hot, though it is simultaneously potentially cold. It is therefore impossible that in the same respect and in the same way a thing should be both mover and moved, that is, that it should move itself. Therefore, whatever is moved must be moved by another.[31] If that by which it is moved be itself moved, then this also must be moved by another, and that by another again. But this cannot go on to infinity, because then there would be no first mover, and, consequently, no other mover, seeing that subsequent movers move only because they are moved by the first mover,[32] just as the staff moves only because it is moved by the hand. Therefore it is necessary to arrive at a first mover which is moved by no other. And this everyone understands to be God.

Second way: The second way is from the notion of efficient cause.[33] In the world of sense we find there is an order of

---

31 It cannot as a whole move itself as a whole, since it would have to be both active and passive in the same way and under the same conditions. Therefore, if a whole is moved (changed), it is moved by another.

32 There cannot be an infinite regress of motor causes for there would be no starting point (*terminus a quo*) in the non-finite sequence and therefore no final concrete effect; and it would take an infinity of causes before the effect is realized, but the effect has been realized (for here we all are!): there has to be a locomotive first in a series of cars, a candelabrum cannot suspend from nothing however long the chain, a potentially infinite mathematical series requires a formula to generate it, and even subatomic particles received their energy from the initial Big Bang. We must not confuse mathematical infinity with metaphysical infinity. Mathematical infinities are produced by algorithmic operators or formulae which generate them, whereas in metaphysical infinites, their properties or perfections are categorematically predicated of them. Indeed, they are opposites: Mathematical infinities are actually finite and only potentially infinite; while the metaphysical infinite is actually infinite and never finite, no matter how diffusive of itself. They are categorically different concepts.

33 What natural science normally understands as a cause — as opposed to formal or substantial causes. This argument was refined by Duns Scotus in *De Primo Principio* — an argument which is still being studied by scholars.

A Certain Idea

efficient causes. There is no case known (nor indeed, is it possible) in which a thing is found to be the efficient cause of itself,[34] because in that case it would be prior to itself, which is impossible. Now in efficient causes it is not possible to go on to infinity, because in all efficient causes following in order, the first is the cause of the intermediate cause, and the intermediate is the cause of the ultimate cause, whether the intermediate cause be several, or one only. Now to take away the cause is to take away the effect. Therefore, if there be no first cause among efficient causes, there will be no ultimate, nor any intermediate cause. But if in efficient causes it is possible to go on to infinity, there will be no first efficient cause, neither will there be an ultimate effect, nor any intermediate efficient causes, all of which is plainly false. Therefore, it is necessary to admit a first efficient cause, to which everyone gives the name God.[35]

Third way: The third way is taken from possibility and necessity,[36] and runs thus. We find in nature things that are possible to be and not to be, since they are found to be generated, and to be corrupted, and consequently they are possible to be and not to be. But it is impossible for these to exist always, for that which is possible not to be at some time is not. Therefore, if everything is possible not to be, then at one time there could have been nothing in existence.[37] Now if this were true, even now there would be nothing in existence, because that which does not exist only begins to exist by something already existing.

---

34 Since it would have to precede its own existence.
35 Imagine a bomb with an infinite fuse, sheathed so that it can only be lit at its tip. The fuse, not being finite, has no starting point—for its tip recedes infinitely. Therefore, the bomb can never be ignited, will never explode, and will never produce a big bang. For if there is no initial cause, there can be no succeeding causes and no final effect—unless some eternal Reality, outside the infinite succession, should sustain the entire series.
36 This is the argument from contingency.
37 Why is there something rather than nothing, especially since everything taken as a whole eventually corrupts or runs down?

Therefore, if at one time nothing was in existence, it would have been impossible for anything to have begun to exist; and thus even now nothing would be in existence — which is clearly false. Therefore, not all beings are merely possible, but there must exist something the existence of which is necessary. But every necessary thing either has its necessity caused by another, or not. Now it is impossible to go on to infinity in necessary things which have their necessity caused by another, as has already been proved in regard to efficient causes.[38] Therefore we must admit the existence of some being having of itself its own necessity, and not receiving it from another, but rather causing in others their necessity. This all men speak of as God.

Fourth way: The fourth way is taken from the gradation to be found in things. Among beings there are some more and some less good, true, noble, and the like. But "more" and "less" are predicated of different things, according as they resemble in their different ways something which is the maximum, as a thing is said to be hotter according as it more nearly resembles that which is hottest. There is then, something which is truest, something best, something noblest, and, consequently, something which is most being; for those things that are greatest in truth are greatest in being.... Now the maximum in any genus is the cause of all in that genus; as fire, which is the maximum of heat, is the cause of all hot things.... Therefore there must also be something which is to all beings the cause of their being, goodness, and every other perfection.[39] And this we call God.

Fifth way: The fifth way is taken from the governance of things. We see that things which lack knowledge, such as

---

38 Thus each Way builds upon the previous one.
39 There must be something which is the extrinsic reason for that sublimity or beauty which everything has, taken as a whole, including human intelligence. Multiplicity of perfections can only come from a unitary, all-perfect, highest (or ontologically first) source.

natural bodies, act for an end, and this is evident from their acting always, or nearly always, in the same way, so as to obtain the best result. Hence it is plain that they achieve their end not by chance, but by design. Now whatever lacks knowledge cannot move towards an end, unless it be directed by some being endowed with knowledge and intelligence, as the arrow is directed by the archer. Therefore some intelligent being exists by whom all natural things[40] are ordered to their end; and this being we call God.

The subtlety of these classical arguments for the existence of God ought not to escape us. They attribute to the First Being five qualities which are proper to God: *primum movens, primum efficiens, primum necessarium, primum et maxime ens, primum gubernans intelligendo.*[41] Attributes such as these demand a Being who exists of his own nature. Thus the proof of the existence of God remains incomplete until God's essence and existence have been shown to be one.

If we take the fourth way (which contains the most subtle truth) first, it is evident that the Supreme Being cannot be composite, since the assertion that whatever of itself is diverse can, of itself, also be one, leads to the contradiction of the principle of identity. Just as we argued above that the idea of being must be simple, so also with the unitary Being whose existence multiplicity demands. For if one and the same property is found in several beings, it is impossible that each of them should possess it of itself, and therefore, they must receive it from some other, which is Unity. As St Thomas says, "If any one thing is found as a common characteristic in many things, it must be caused in them by some one cause; for it is impossible that it should belong to each of them *of itself*, since each as it is in itself is distinct from any other, and the diversity of causes produces diversity of effects."[42] Multiple creatures exhibiting the same property must

---

40   Again taken as a whole, the cosmos cannot write into itself its own laws: they must be given to the cosmos by that from which it came—order comes from order, and great order from greater order. This is the principle of the Second Law of Thermodynamics.
41   Phillips, *Modern Thomistic Philosophy*, 2:292.
42   Quoted in ibid., 2:288. Italics added. A quality cannot be both uniquely proper *and* pervasive.

receive that property from a common source or ancestor. It cannot be the other way around since diverse causes produce diverse effects. Therefore, since the gradation of various perfections found throughout reality demands a unitary (non-multiple) cause which is the source of all such perfections, then there must be some all-perfect, single Reality as their cause. Now since this Reality is unitary (non-multiple), then it cannot have a share of existence, but its existence must be constitutive of it, so its essence *is* its existence.

Thus, with the first mover, since it is unmoved, it must be actually so and not potentially so, since there is nothing else in act to reduce it from potency to act, otherwise it would not be the *first* mover. What is itself unmoved, but moves, is pure act, or reality in action. Therefore, as the first mover exists it does so essentially — from its own nature (because there is no other) — and thus its existence will be *ipso facto* identical to its essence. As in the fourth way, "wherever there is diversity and composition we are in the presence of the conditioned and not the unconditional: this is only arrived at where there is pure identity."[43]

Similarly with the second way: the first cause, itself being uncaused, must possess in itself its own reason for being. It cannot cause itself, neither can it receive existence from another (being first cause), therefore it is itself its own existence. Also, in the third way, a Being whose existence is necessary, because all contingent beings must depend for their existence upon such a being or they could not be,[44] necessarily has existence as its essential property, or it would also be contingent (upon nothing) and would have immediately ceased to be, and then nothing could ever come to be.

Finally, the perfection of intelligence found throughout creation must be supplied by a first cause which is also intelligent. Now intelligence implies order and order can only decrease in closed systems. "This means that if the degree of order of any system is to increase, it must receive energy and order from outside."[45] The remarkable order which is found throughout the cosmos came from some initial

---

43 Phillips, *Modern Thomistic Philosophy*, 2:292.
44 See Germain Grisez, *God? A Philosophical Preface to Faith* (South Bend: St Augustine's Press, 2005). The entire book is devoted to proving this point.
45 A. Ya. Lerner, *Fundamentals of Cybernetics* (New York: Plenum, 1975), 264.

A Certain Idea

conditions set by something of maximum order, since it is the source of all other order and compositions of order. This order or intelligibility must exist of itself in that which is a maximum, since maximum order cannot come from less. However, given what has been established in the preceding ways, it follows that we are referring to an infinite perfection here and not a limited maximum, because that which is first and whose existence is necessary has nothing to limit it.

The same argument can be made from another aspect: that of simplicity. To say that a real being is without parts is to say it is without intrinsic boundaries or limits. Also since such a being is the first cause, there is nothing extrinsic that can limit it. Now what is unbounded is all-inclusive, since, having no peripheries, nothing is excluded. Therefore, God's existence entails his essence. Furthermore, God being simple, all perfections belong to him from whom all other necessarily finite beings obtain their delimiting perfections. Given that intelligence and rationality are manifest in the universe, it follows that they must be properties of God also.[46]

At this point the intelligibility of material order makes it possible to infer a personal God. By personal, we mean free. Nothing binds the Creator but his own nature, which as we have seen is infinite in power, operation, and perfection. We will not attempt to prove the personal nature of God,[47] but will leave that to revelation when we turn to look at the question of faith. It is enough from the vantage of reason to observe that whatever is infinitely perfect spontaneously inspires awe and adoration. This invokes us to reflect upon the transcendental properties of God.

The transcendental properties of God

These qualities will be introduced briefly, since they have been alluded to or implicit in our discussion of Being thus far. In this context, by transcendental we simply mean those qualities which transcend any genus or class. The concept of being is not a universal

---

46 *Summa Contra Gentiles* I.43, nn. 2–7. Cf. Bernard Lonergan, *Insight* (Toronto: University of Toronto Press, 1992), 695–97.
47 For proof of this see Duns Scotus, *De Primo Principio* 4.1–4.7; 4.12–4.15; 4.41–46. See also Di Blasi, *God and the Natural Law*, 128–42.

class nor does it belong to a universal class, since *every* idea can only be the idea of *some* being. In short, being cannot be a set or subset of being: being is simply itself. Since being transcends any genus and these qualities are those belonging to being—and therefore not accidental to being—they are transcendental too. There are six possible transcendental properties of universal predication which follow immediately upon the concept of Being as such: being, thing, otherness, one, true, and good. However, being (*ens*) cannot be a property of itself so is excluded as a transcendental. Thing (*res*) is convertible with being adding only the idea of name, and can also be excluded. Otherness from being can only mean non-being (non-existence) so cannot be a property either. This leaves three transcendental properties which can be predicated of every Being.

God is one. God is one in two senses: uniqueness and simplicity of essence. God is unique because if there were more than one God they would be distinct and would have to differ in some manner. Each would have to have perfections distinct from the other. Each would possess and lack various perfections; else they would be the same Being (what differs is not the same). But in lacking perfections none would be God. But a God of infinite perfections exists (as we have seen in the fourth way); therefore multiplicity is not possible in God. Moreover, if there were several gods each would have its own distinct essence or nature, but each would also have existence (or they would not be). Therefore, essence and existence would not be the same in these several gods.

God is simple because every compound presupposes a cause which unifies the parts. But God is uncaused. The only reality in God is his undivided essence which is his existence: and this essence is one substance which is pure act (actuality) for there is no potency (potentiality) in God. Change can only be from what one is into what one is not, but God lacks nothing. Therefore, there is no becoming in God, "no alteration, no shadow caused by change."[48] God is constant; and therefore trustworthy and faithful.

God is true. God is true because God is one: he is selfsame, unchangeable Being. He cannot deny himself or be in conflict with

---
48 Jas 1:17 (NJB); cf. Mal 3:6.

himself. In God, ontological and logical truth (logos) are one and the same essence. Also, whatever is in act (at a specific time) acts for a given end. For either a *particular* action does nothing at all, in which case it does not act; or the action does everything possible, in which case it would be in perpetual self-contradiction; or it acts for a determinate end.[49] Furthermore, everything acts according to its nature, since a thing cannot do what does not belong to itself to do or what it is not able to do. Therefore, insofar as Being acts, it acts out of its own formative principle and so is expressive of that form. It acts according to and is expressive of its own rationale (logos). Otherwise there would be no coherent principle behind the act, and therefore no coherent act. Because there is one substance in God, all his acts are expressive of his nature or logos or wisdom.

> For Wisdom is quicker to move than any motion;
> She is so pure; she pervades and permeates all things,
> She is the breath of the power of God,
> Pure emanation of the glory of the Almighty;
> So nothing impure can find its way into her.
> For she is a reflection of the eternal light,
> Untarnished mirror of God's active power, and image of
>   his goodness.
> Although she is alone, she can do everything;
> Herself unchanging, she renews the world,
> And, generation after generation, passing into holy souls
> She makes them into God's friends and prophets.[50]

God is good. Goodness follows upon perfection and as God is infinitely perfect so God is infinitely good. And what is good is desirable so that every person is by nature inclined to love God, in one's own way more than oneself, simply because of who he is ... because of the excellence of his perfections. From this arises the natural determination to seek God and to possess Him; and not only the natural determination, but the right to do so. Nothing, no government, no

---

49 This is the principle of finality. Here we are speaking of a definite manner of producing. See Duns Scotus, *Quodlibetal Questions* 2.31.
50 Wis 7:24–26. See also Col 1:15–20.

ideology, no power or state or minority is above God. Since all things must be ordered to their proper end and there is nothing more perfect than God, it would be idolatry to give to a mere creature the devotion owed to God. Furthermore, since God is a Being who gives Being, it follows that all goodness, truth, and beauty come from him since all perfection is in him. And since to give to another the fullness of Being — for God does all things well — is what is meant by love, the essence of God is love.[51]

Finally, what is one, true, and good — and loving — is also beautiful, lovely.[52] A thing is beautiful according to St Thomas when it includes: "integrity or perfection ... due proportion or harmony; and lastly splendor, or clarity."[53] Such resplendence of form is attractive and delightful, transporting the beholder by degrees to joy, even ecstasy. We are reminded of the words of Plato:

> He who has been instructed thus far in the things of love, and who has learned to see the beautiful in due order and succession, when he comes toward the end will suddenly perceive a nature of wondrous beauty — a nature which in the first place is everlasting, not growing and decaying, or waxing and waning; secondly, not fair in one point of view and foul in another ... but beauty absolute, separate, simple, and everlasting, which without diminution and without increase, or any change, is imparted to the ever-growing and perishing beauties of all other things. He who from these ascending under the influence of true love, begins to perceive that beauty, is not far from the end.... But what if man had eyes to see the true beauty — the divine beauty, I mean, pure and clear and unalloyed, not clogged with the pollutions of mortality and all the colors and vanities of human life — thither looking, and holding converse with the true beauty simple and divine?[54]

---

51 1 Jn 4:16.
52 *Summa Theol.* I-II, q. 27, a. 1, obj. 3.
53 *Summa Theol.* I, q. 39, a. 8, obj. 5.
54 *Symposium*, in *The Great Books* (London: Encyclopaedia Britannica, 1952), 7:167.

Such intimations of the transcendent are the wellspring of religious sensibilities found universally in all peoples in all cultures and eras. This should not surprise us given that all humanity thinks being as their first-order concept. It is remarkable that research into the nature of language confirms that all languages have a deep structure, which is the same as that of logic and is related to the intentionality of linguistic behavior.[55] Operators, objects, qualifiers, quantifiers, and particles are not only to be found in both spoken language and logical strings, but the deeper structure of semantics and syntax is similar for all languages. This fact is sufficient to explain the universality, across cultures and throughout history, of the unfolding of the religious dimension within human experience. It is our human nature to think being: it gives us our *sensus communis*[56] and unites us as one family.

* * *

We have, therefore, established the following **proposition**: *The existence of God, in the sense of an infinite, all-powerful, eternal, and immaterial First Being, is a certain conviction of the human mind such that to doubt it is to deny the first principles of the intellect.* In this Being (one, true, good, and beautiful) thought comes finally to rest. The fact that we think being ushers one naturally to this proposition, as we have demonstrated.

It follows that it is repugnant to reason to *deny* the existence of God as First Principle: *For reason seeks Being, not nothing*! Moreover, to dispute this proposition compels one by a huge *modus tollens* argument to reject the foundational idea of being along with all that implicates it: identity, contradiction, reason for being, criterion of truth, etc.; for in denying the conclusion one denies the antecedents.

---

55 Jonathan Bennett, *Linguistic Behaviour* (Cambridge: Cambridge University Press, 1976). See also John Lyons, *Chomsky* (Glasgow: Collins Fontana, 1979); Robert C. Berwick and Noam Chomsky, *Why Only Us: Language and Evolution* (Cambridge: MIT Press, 2016).

56 This Latin term is technical and refers to that capacity of uniting all our other senses (exteroceptive, proprioceptive, or interoceptive) under a common faculty: *coenaesthesia* (Aristotle's κοινη αισθεση). It does not mean the idea of naïve or practical "common sense." Rather, it subtends our senses providing the foundation for our ontological perception of ourselves. It is this ontological awareness that we have in common.

Because of this it is not surprising that we constantly witness atheism generating moral and philosophical relativism, nihilism, surrealism, acedia, and despair.[57] Since there is no grounding for truth, truth no longer has authority, for in a godless universe, only matter remains. We are just clever apes, after all, reason having evolved merely to serve the will — the will to power — as Nietzsche portended. Therefore, persuasion by rational appeal to an immutable truth becomes incongruous and can no longer convey credibility. And since (it only requires nerve) one can always choose to reject human opinions or political ideologies — or choose to deconstruct them — the only option for the secular state is to enforce conformity through either indoctrination or force. Thus atheist regimes cannot but become totalitarian. The twentieth century (and this one) has witnessed the profusion of such atheistic totalitarian regimes where power, not truth, is the only authority.

We have shown how all-embracing this idea of being in general is: in generating logic, serving as the analytic criterion for judgment, founding the metaphysical principles of thought, encompassing within its infinity all that is finite, even to demonstrating the existence of an unlimited Reality. But we have also noted how humble a concept it is, for it only enables us to penetrate to the principle of things — to their form, not to their substance. Our all-too-human knowledge, however, is never complete, and although we can postulate a particular substance and learn its principles through its effects, we must always expect something new. We admit what we do not know, but we must not deny what we do know. Surely that is what is required by authenticity.

In the next chapter we shall address the Kantian critique that our minds are designed to think in fixed *a priori* categories so that our ideas cannot reflect reality, and at the same time we shall also provide astonishing physical evidence in support of our proposition. And in the third chapter we will address the aporia of how a good God can permit evil. Then we shall explore the certainties that are revealed through faith.

---

[57] Alister McGrath, *The Twilight of Atheism* (London: Rider, 2004).

CHAPTER 2

Creation

*If charmed by their beauty, they have taken these for gods,
Let them know how much the Master of these excels them,
Since he was the very source of beauty that created them.
And if they have been impressed by their power and energy,
Let them deduce from these how much mightier is he that
   has formed them,
Since through the grandeur and beauty of the creatures
We may, by analogy, contemplate their Author.*[1]

IN THE PRECEDING CHAPTER WE DEMONstrated the existence of a First Being in answer to the question of what ultimately lay behind the cosmos as its first cause and necessary reality. Since this demonstration proceeded simply by expanding the reiterated use of the idea of being, which is an undeniable form of the intellect,[2] it was argued that to deny the existence of a First Being (Principium, Ultimate Reality, Supreme Being, etc.) would mean relinquishing the first principles of the mind, viz.: being, identity, and contradiction. Such a resolve would, of course, make life impossible given that these principles have their counterpart in the real world.

For example, let us imagine a postmodernist professor of philosophy who denies these three first principles. The professor asks a prized graduate assistant if the paper for the seminar is ready and the student replies:

"I might have done it, and if so it could be on your desk."
Then adding in an undertone: "But then again it might not."

---

1   Wis 13:3–5.
2   "I say the first object of our intellect is being because in it lies a twofold primacy — namely, not only one of commonness but also one of virtuality. Everything that is *per se* intelligible either includes essentially the idea of being (*entis*) or is virtually or essentially contained in what includes essentially the notion of 'being.'" Scotus, *Ordinatio* 3.1, q. 3, n. 137. To deny being is to invoke it — precisely the point missed by the "children of the enlightenment."

"Nooo..." says the professor after searching, "it is definitely not here."

"How would you know?" asks the student, "after all you do not accept the principle of identity. It could be there and you would never recognize it."

"Are you sure you typed it for me?" the professor asks, losing patience.

"I both typed it and did not type it," the student retorts.

"That's absurd!"

"Only if you accept the principle of contradiction," the assistant sings, raising an index finger.

"Ah! At last!" Relieved to have found the paper, the professor betrays a chuckle: "Alright—you should know that such theories only apply in the classroom and in learned monographs." Then exasperated: "Now I can't find the keys to the seminar room!"

"What do you need the keys for, seeing as how you don't accept the principle of causality either? Perhaps you should look in the student union building."

"I have never even been in the student union."

"Immaterial—since the keys could have moved themselves there for no reason whatsoever." Then, falling back in the chair: "Do not tell me you require an extrinsic reason for their being there!"

Although seemingly frivolous, the preceding conversation might not seem so after considering the following quotes emanating from an influential postmodernist thinker.[3]

> He denies that language has a fixed meaning connected to a fixed reality or that it unveils definitive truth.
>
> There is no ultimate grounding for our systems of thought and language.

---

3 Jacques Derrida quoted in Stanley J. Grenz, *The Named God and the Question of Being* (Louisville: Westminster John Knox Press, 2005), 122–29, passim. Italics added.

> There is no "signified" (i.e., no mental concept) that exists apart from the "signifier" (i.e., the word that we attach to that thought).... Through language and concepts, we *impose the sense of objective meaning on the flux of experience*.... I *claim* to see a mug on a desk in a room. Our tendency is to assume that this is an objective, given occurrence. *Yet there is no single correct statement that objectively describes the experience.* On the contrary, I could offer many possible descriptions of it, and each description would actually *alter* and color the experience itself.
>
> Writing has no extralinguistic referent.
>
> The origin of language lies with writing (the "sign of a sign") and not with some assumed immediate experience of the correspondence of thought with object.

There are several criticisms to be made of this point of view. In violation of the principle of identity, he confuses the mental idea with the objective sensory experience. He seems unaware that behind phenomena are the organizing principles (forms) of things. The writer also ignores contemporary research into comparative linguistics, paleontology, cosmology, particle physics, forensics, etc. (Do the writings about dinosaur fossils refer to nothing? Do neutron stars not exist? Was there no dead body at the murder scene?) Moreover, he overlooks that there is a common core experience shared by everyone witnessing a given phenomenon even though their perspectives differ. Also, there are several self-contradictions in these quotes. For example, does the phrase "writing has no extralinguistic referent" mean that these writings of the author also refer to nothing? Is the writer the only one *not* imposing his sense of objective meaning on the flux of experience? Just how did he manage the hundreds of detailed tasks necessary to publish, such as dealing with his editor, bank manager, and tax official, for example, while at the same time denying the fundamental principles of the human mind?

How did philosophy fall into this imbroglio? When did it lose sight of its object? Although the origins of this state of affairs can be traced back to Ockham and the nominalists, the main precursor was Immanuel Kant.

Part One: Reality

KANTIANISM

Of all *les philosophes*, the one most often regarded as epitomizing the achievement of the (so-called) Enlightenment was Immanuel Kant (1724–1804).[4] For it was he who assigned boundaries to empirical knowledge, who restricted human thought within categories, who declared the *a priori* rules for understanding, and who banished pure reason and ethics to realms of their own beyond the phenomenal world. Never travelling more than sixty miles from his birthplace in East Prussia, the philosopher of Königsberg lived a remarkably uneventful life. Born into a Pietist Lutheran family, he studied theology and the classics at the Collegium Fredericianum. Anecdotes about his life reveal little more than various disruptions to his bachelor routine such as: the consternation of his neighbors when one day he missed taking his customary constitutional at the precise hour, or the crisis occasioned by the burgeoning poplars which obstructed his view of the church steeple upon which he was wont to gaze.[5]

Kant was unfamiliar with the history of philosophy, especially that of scholasticism. Even so, he had acquired from Leibniz's philosophy the belief that the mind possessed its own innate ideas, while Locke's empiricism had also convinced him that knowledge did have its source in sense experience. However, Hume's devastating attack upon Locke's reduction of reality into matters of fact and relations between ideas persuaded Kant to differentiate the world of sense from the mind's innate capacity to organize that world. He was also impressed by the coherence of Newton's mathematical system, especially its description of nature in terms of Euclidean geometry as well as such categories as space, time, motion, and causality (contra Hume). It was from wrestling with the problem of how the certainties supplied by mathematics and physics could be reconciled with the fact that knowledge was derived from sense experience that Kant produced his *Critique of Pure Reason*. His purpose was to erect the infrastructure for a genuine science by...

---

4 Norman Hampson, *The Enlightenment* (Harmondsworth: Penguin Books, 1990), 196; cf. Frederick Copleston, *A History of Philosophy: Wolff to Kant* (New York: Paulist Press, 1977), 6:54–55.
5 R. I. Watson, *The Great Psychologists* (Philadelphia: J. B. Lippencott, 1963), 203.

substituting the certainty of scientific method for *that random groping after results without the guidance of principles, which has hitherto characterized the pursuit of metaphysical studies.*[6] It will render an important service to the inquiring mind of youth, by leading the student to apply his powers to the cultivation of genuine science, instead of wasting them ... on speculations which can never lead to any result, or on the idle attempt to invent new ideas and opinions.[7]

For Kant, the basis of all knowledge was the synthetic act whereby the impressions from sense experience were unified by the mind. This process was explicable neither in terms of pure thought (which Kant believed was primarily analytical), nor in terms of the effects upon our mental faculties of externally sensed elements. As far as the former was concerned, analysis could only treat objects of knowledge *already given* in synthetic *forms*. As far as the latter was concerned, external elements of experience could only produce isolated disordered effects (as Hume had indicated), since sense data did not seem to contain within themselves the principles for synthetic combination. Yet the fact remained that such notions as, for example, causality, time, and space provided the fundamental conditions for the organization of experience prior to any experiential act. They were not formed *a posteriori*, i.e., subsequent to experience, as Locke had originally maintained, but they existed *a priori*, i.e., prior to experience.

Consciousness, therefore, comprised various mental components prior to any experience of the individual. These were: the dimensions of perception, i.e., space and time; the forms of thought, i.e., the categories;[8] and the ultimate agent for knowing, i.e., the ego. It was

---

[6] This is more of a comment on Hume and Locke, since he was unfamiliar with the system of the scholastics. Italics added.

[7] "Preface" to *Critique of Pure Reason* in *The Great Books* (London: Encyclopaedia Britannica, 1952), 42:10.

[8] The twelve categories were: quantitative categories of unity, plurality, and totality; qualitative categories of reality, negation, and limitation; relational categories of substance and accident, cause and effect, and reciprocity of agent and recipient; and modal categories of possibility/impossibility, existence/non-existence, and necessity/contingency. Cf. *Pure Reason*, 42:43.

by virtue of these *a priori* constituents that reason could process the raw data of experience. Reason, through its various forms, created and synthesized knowledge. That is, it made sense of the world by organizing it into a meaningful whole through the categories operating upon raw sense data against the dimensions of space and time. Kant's obvious intention was to give mathematics an *a priori* basis. But by doing so he also made empiricism the only acceptable rational approach to knowledge. He also elevated Euclidean geometry and Newton's laws of motion to an *a priori* pre-eminence within the human mind.

This phenomenal world of pure experience was the only world we could know and was the proper domain of science. The noumenal world was still the realm of things in themselves (substances) which, though unknowable, could merely be postulated upon the exercise of what was called the "transcendental dialectic."[9] Just three things could be posited by this dialectic: the freedom of the will, the immortality of the soul, and the existence of God. However, because of their transcendental nature, they *"cannot be employed as immanent principles* in relation to the objects of experience; they are, consequently, of no use to us in this sphere, *being but the valueless results of the severe but unprofitable efforts of reason."*[10] The unavoidable conclusion was that these concepts (God, the soul, substance, etc.) can have no epistemic (knowable) reality. Thus Kant's *Critique* resulted in the banishment from science of all metaphysical ideas and their replacement by mathematical concepts instead. It marked the end of theology as a science.

There are fundamental defects in Kant's understanding of cognition, not least of which are his categories, which virtually no one accepts today.[11] In fact, Rosmini has demonstrated that all the categories of Kant can be resolved into the single idea of being in general

---

9 Kant divided transcendental knowledge into two areas: the transcendental aesthetic (intuition, sensibility) and transcendental logic (reason, understanding). The latter was further subdivided into analytic and dialectic. Transcendental analytic involved the discernment of the categories and the transcendental ego. Transcendental dialectic comprised hyperphysical postulates. Ibid., 42:37.
10 Ibid., 42:236. Italics added.
11 Bernard d'Espagnat, *On Physics and Philosophy* (Princeton: Princeton University Press, 2006), 286–87. How can non-existence be a category of being?!

as the fundamental form of thought.[12] In order to generate Kant's categories, Rosmini theorizes, one has only to unite this idea to some external stimulus perceived as a modification of our fundamental feeling — our accustomed, characteristic, homeostatic state. The intellect objectifies this felt modification to our habitual state by apprehending the stimulus as something (*quiddam*) through this idea of being. For example, the notion of extension is formed *a posteriori* from the visual and tactile sensations of the surface continuity of bodies. Extension together with movement, when united with the idea of being, gives our concept of three-dimensional space. Or our conception of a color is merely the impression of various objects sharing the same visual spectrum, and then identifying it as this (accidental) being — and so with other feelable qualia. Again, the notion of time is also derived *a posteriori* from the perception of change in finite things. This sensed succession of states, when transmitted to the intellect, is then conjoined synthetically to the idea of being, giving rise to the notion of duration. And as we turn to reflect upon our operative role in all these faculties, so we apprehend our own existence: i.e., we know ourselves as agent (an *ens*). We may also recall how the various metaphysical concepts of contingency, substance, accident, and action and passion were also shown to implicate this idea. *In fine*, Rosmini treats possible being as the sole *a priori* synthetic idea in the intellect, thereby rendering Kant's twelve categories, including his elaborate transcendental logic, superfluous.

However, our purpose here is not to propound Rosmini's theory, but simply to observe that the Kantian categories *per se* have not been proved to possess any *a priori* existence within the intellect. Yet we have already seen how the idea of being in general enables us to apprehend the formative principle of things (such as the principles of potential energy, of motion, of intrinsic or extrinsic cause, and of prime matter). Kant's assertion, that the intellect *only* discerns phenomena, is simply wrong — and his need for the categories becomes redundant.

Nevertheless, Kant did retain the idea of substance or the noumenal. But how could he identify the noumenal while claiming that

---

12 Antonio Rosmini, *The Origin of Thought* (Durham: Rosmini House, 1989).

we can only know phenomena and his categories? If the noumenal (the thing in itself) is unknowable, how can we know that it exists? Furthermore, it is a contradiction to assert both that it exists and underlies the causes of sense impressions, while denying that mental categories such as existence and causality can apply to it. In other words, giving existence to the noumenal or substantial while denying its own existence as a mental category betrays his dependence upon the idea of being in general. This was the thrust of our first chapter: *to think of anything is to think of it as some possible or actual being.* For Kant to conceive of substance as an object of thought already necessitates his thinking of some actual or possible being. This he disavowed because he was incapable of conceiving of two modes of being: one which is subjective and supplied to our cognition by the senses, and the other which is objective and contributed by the intellect. Because ideal being possesses an analogous identity in both these modes, its intelligibility does not alter the external thing as *thing (ens)*: it simply makes it visible to the understanding; and so the aporia Kant felt over the subject-object diremption dissolves.

> All real things, therefore, are known through *ideas*, without which nothing is known. In other words, real things need two conditions if they are to be known positively: 1. they operate upon feeling and thus render themselves sensible; 2. after they are rendered sensible, the intelligent subject must apply the idea to this sensible thing and see it in the idea, or in ideal being. In other words, the subject sees the relationship of (formal) identity between the real, sensible thing and the ideal object. The real thing, therefore, remains unknown until it is *object*; the idea [i.e., being], however never ceases to be the object of the mind, and would not even exist unless contemplated by some mind.[13]

The real needs illumination if it is to be made known. It receives this light through the intelligible idea (i.e., being in general), which

---

13 Antonio Rosmini, *Essence of the Human Soul* (Durham: Rosmini House, 1999), 358.

is prior to every perception and therefore universally applied. By this cognitive act we discover in each felt reality its unique particularity and posit it as this actual (named) existent.[14] Because Kant was unable to distinguish between ideal existence and the particular thing perceived by means of that idea, he was also unable to grasp that all creatures (mental or extramental) could be conceived of as participating in transcendent Being, and thereby communicating its effects. The following quotations[15] exemplify this inability:

> If the Supreme Being forms a link in the chain of empirical conditions, it must be a member of the empirical series, and, like the lower members which it precedes, have its origin in some higher member of the series.
>
> If the empirical law of causality is to conduct us to a Supreme Being, this being must belong to the chain of empirical objects—in which case it would be like all phenomena, itself conditioned.
>
> I can never *complete* the regress through the conditions of existence, without admitting the existence of a necessary being; but, on the other hand, I cannot make a *commencement* from this being.
>
> But if all that we perceive must be regarded as conditionally necessary, it is impossible that anything which is empirically given should be absolutely. It follows from this that you must accept the absolutely necessary as *out of* and beyond the world, inasmuch as it is useful only as a principle of the highest possible unity in experience, and you cannot discover any such necessary existence in the *world*. . . .
>
> The transcendental idea of a necessary and all-sufficient being is so immeasurably great, so high above all that is empirical, which is always conditioned, that we hope in vain to find materials in the sphere of experience

---

14 I.e., the first principle of the intellect applied to an apprehended *quiddam*. Antonio Rosmini, *The Origin of Ideas* (London: Forgotten Books, 2015), 323.
15 *Critique*, 184–91, passim.

sufficiently ample for our conception, and in vain seek the unconditioned among things that are conditioned....

These few quotations suffice to establish a fundamental philosophical bias in Kant which he inherited from his Lutheran background and education, viz.: a peculiar univocal conception of being such that it was impossible for him to conceive that there was a cooperative relationship between God and his creatures: viz., that God can be principal cause while man is ancillary cause of the same act. Like someone using a tool, both perform the action, but the second cannot act without the first which works through the instrument. Neither could he conceive that there could even be participation by creatures in the Divine Wisdom from which traces of divinity could have been discerned.

In his book *Ecumenism and Philosophy*, Charles Morerod follows this error from Luther through Calvin to Hobbes, Kant, Marx, Nietzsche, and Barth. He shows how Luther in turn received it from Scotus who (Morerod believes) had misconceived St Thomas's analogy of being.[16]

> Not being outside time and culture, Luther was not immune to the philosophy which permeated his formation. In the deep recesses of his mind was a univocal idea of being which came to him from a globally Scotist heritage, assimilated all the more poorly for being unconscious (which would lead him to developments foreign to Scotus himself). In perceiving God and man univocally

---

16 Scotus states: "I call a concept univocal if it is one in such a way that its unity is sufficient for a contradiction to arise when it is affirmed and denied of the same thing. Its unity is also sufficient for its use as a middle term in a syllogism so that we may conclude without committing a fallacy of equivocation..." Scotus, *Ordinatio* 1.3, q. 2, n. 26. While Aquinas requires that perfections attributed to God do retain their meaning although their mode is unbefitting to the divine essence since they are derived from limited creatures, Scotus also insists that these terms do indeed preserve their original logical signification, but can become fitting of God only when they are joined to the notion of infinitude, a truth which Aquinas himself accepted. For reconciliation between Aquinas and Scotus on the issue of univocity, see Alexander W. Hall, *Thomas Aquinas and John Duns Scotus: Natural Theology in the High Middle Ages* (New York: Continuum, 2007).

as beings of the same kind, the Reformer was led to see their actions in terms of concurrence. In fact, when one and the same action is performed by two beings at the same level, since neither of the two can accomplish it 100 percent, they mutually overshadow each other: "second causes obscure first causes." Under such conditions, it was necessary to exclude human action from the realm of salvation in order to safeguard divine majesty, at the risk of leaving man his autonomy in "profane" life. Calvin would inherit these philosophical pre-suppositions from Luther's great theological themes.[17]

For Luther the only possible relationship between individuals and God is that of forensic justice (*simul justus et peccator*), leaving them with no alternative but to sin: "Free will cannot by its own power will anything good, and ... *of necessity* serves sin."[18] Behind this was Luther's assumption that man and God possessed being univocally and so were in essential competition: "It would be a difficult question indeed, nay, an impossibility, I confess, if you should attempt to establish both the *prescience* of God and the *Free-will* of man.... This Omnipotence and prescience of God, I say, utterly abolishes the doctrine of 'free will.'"[19] So in order to protect God's absolute sovereignty, the unconditioned God was relegated to be unequivocally beyond the conditioned world. "Free-will is plainly a divine term, and can only be applicable to none but the divine Majesty.... Whereas, if it be ascribed unto men, it is not more properly ascribed than the divinity of God would be ascribed unto them: which would be the greatest of all sacrilege."[20]

This dilemma of Luther's also persists through the Scholastic dispute about the analogy of being — from Aquinas through Henry of

---

17 Charles Morerod, *Ecumenism and Philosophy* (Ann Arbor: Sapientia Press, 2006), 167–68.
18 Martin Luther, *The Bondage of the Will* (Grand Rapids: Baker Book House, 1976), 75. See also chs. 80, 84, 85.
19 Ibid., chs. 92–93.
20 Luther, *Bondage of Will*, ch. 26. Clearly Luther conceives free will univocally in God and man, so that if God has it then man cannot.

Ghent, and Duns Scotus to Cajetan. It originates from the failure to separate two distinct meanings of analogy as either proportional predication or participatory likeness. The difficulty arises when an attribute is used univocally of both creatures and God: either God's transcendence ceases to exist, as Kant (and Luther) feared, or it becomes noetically inaccessible, as Kant maintained. For if one speaks univocally of any quality in *creatures* then God becomes unknowable, since all language is then concretized or operationalized, while at the same time restricted to creatures. Transcendence is then either a concept emptied of content, as the logical positivists claimed; or God's name is nothing more than an expression of mere subjective significance, as the postmodernists maintain. Alternatively, if names or properties are predicated univocally of *God*, then, although God's transcendence is saved, reality becomes devoid of substance since such perfections can have meaning only when applied to God. This dilemma was the basis for Kant's *Critique of Pure Reason* and why he abandoned formal knowledge in favor of inherent ideas, with idealism as the natural result.

It is also the reason why postmodern thinking has opted for the equivocal nature of language. However, this attempt to avoid the issue through flight into equivocation has its own insuperable problems, for it shatters forever any unity in being or in nature, and leaves existence without any (ultimate) explanation. Knowledge is fragmented, being is ruptured, and relativity holds sway. One finds oneself abandoned in a cosmos of infinite regressions, left with only one's will and one's praxis. This is the postmodern experience.

Nevertheless, the principle of analogy is fundamental to how we speak not only of God but of any being whose existence is inferred from its effects. This is characteristic of all science (*scientia*). Indeed, science could not progress without it. The basic principle involved in speaking about inferred entities or hypothetical constructs is the due proportion or likeness between a cause and its effects, as the fossilized teeth of a dinosaur preserve evidence of its diet, or the elements comprising a distant star can be determined from its spectroscopic banding. Again, when a physicist detects a fundamental particle tracing a trajectory in a bubble chamber with a definite curve and gradient, the physicist then quite rightly identifies the particle which has the particular mass, velocity, spin, and energy that would produce such a trajectory. The particle, say a pi meson, would be the only thing (being) that could produce these effects. The particle is not the trace in the bubble chamber, nor is it the effects, but rather the cause of those effects. We may know nothing more about a particle than its properties, which in this case are formally, though analogously, expressed in a mathematical model, but we do know something of its existence — not its substance but its *form*, i.e., its principle, as the perduring cause of its (reproducible) effects. As Ernest Nagel put it: "The real is that which is invariant under some stipulated set of transformations, changes, projections, or perspectives.... In an analogous manner, physical reality has been attributed to theoretical entities like atoms, electrons, mesons, probability waves, and the like because they satisfy some indicated condition of invariance."[21] This is like the relation between substance and accidents that we observed in the previous chapter, except that in the empirical world these entities are only tentatively understood: further understanding could change our opinions about them, but not their postulated existence.

The fundamental criterion, which gives us the authority to speak analogically, is that the unity which being possesses rests ultimately upon the unity of God, who is Being in act. God is immanent to all beings not as their *form* but as their *cause*. This immanence must be understood as a continuously creative, all-sustaining presence. And in as much as this is an eternal activity, then God, as First Principle, is preeminently related to all creatures as a cause is to its effect. Since God is the ultimate cause of all perfections, the creature receives of them through God's activity, for whatever does not belong to a being essentially, i.e., intrinsically, is caused *ab alio*.

Because these perfections exist in God *per essentiam*, but in the creature *per participationem*, there is no danger of univocity, since there is a distinction between what is given and how it is received. It is no contradiction to speak of creatures as having, or participating in, a certain quality or perfection in common with God in a proportional, albeit limited, manner while also recognizing that that perfection

---

21 Ernest Nagel, *The Structure of Science* (London: Routledge & Kegan Paul, 1971), 150–51.

exists in God in an eminent manner. This is because, while God is infinite perfection, the creature receives perfections according to its limited capacity and form. For what is there in the creature that it has not received, since all good things come from God? And as we receive so we are: for it is precisely these qualities or properties that give the creature its identity or nature. But their mode and limitation make them only relatively like the attributes of God, which in him are of absolute and infinite perfection.

The patterns of analogy and those of participation correspond as the ideal and real aspects of the unity of being. These should not be confused. Analogy of being is not intended to conflate the proportional unity of a general concept (genus) with the real diversity (species) of beings. This is to misunderstand the nature of analogy. Yet this unity and order, of both the general concept and the real diversity, connect each of the latter with their Principle, albeit in different ways.[22]

Thus, the cardinal difficulty with Kant's understanding of cognition was his misunderstanding of the analogy of being (*analogia entis*). He did not see that what makes analogical predication possible is the likeness of creatures to God, but at differentiated degrees of being. It is precisely because perfection can come in degrees that what is an infinite plenitude of being in God is limited in the creature. We can affirm the goodness of God because God's effects are manifested in his creatures, and because the good is a transcendental perfection belonging to God.[23] Clearly creatures, being limited in their perfections, are only imperfectly like God. This means creatures are both like and unlike God: they are alike insofar as they share a certain identifiable quality or perfection with him (and more so if they may willingly receive of his Being); and they are unlike in their deficiency and nature (especially if they separate themselves from his grace). Therefore, analogical predication lies between univocal and equivocal predication:[24] between identity of meaning and difference between

---

22 See Bernard Montagnes, *The Doctrine of the Analogy of Being according to Thomas Aquinas* (Milwaukee: Marquette University Press, 2004), 91.
23 *Summa Theol.* I, q. 13, a. 2, obj. 3.
24 *Summa Theol.* I, q. 13, a. 5, obj. 3.

meanings. There is some positive content which can be attributed to God, and some negative content which cannot.

> The statement, therefore, that God is wise ("wise" meaning infinitely more than wise in the human sense) has a positive content. To demand that the content of analogical ideas should be perfectly clear and expressible, so that they could be understood perfectly in terms of human experience, would be to misunderstand altogether the nature of analogy.... The infinity of the object, God, means that the finite human mind can attain no adequate and perfect idea of God's nature; but it does not mean that it cannot attain an imperfect and inadequate notion of God's nature. To know that God understands is to know something positive about God, since it tells us at the very least that God is not irrational like a stone or a plant, even though to know what the divine understanding is in itself exceeds our power of comprehension.[25]

Because Kant (like Luther) regarded God as restrictively transcendent, he could not *abstract the likeness* between God's Being and his creatures *from the perfections they shared* in different, yet commensurate, forms.[26] This overemphasis on God's absolute transcendence to the exclusion of his immanence became *de rigueur* for those who followed these thinkers. The eventual divorce of God from his creation (which then became reduced to a machine) led finally to the denial of his even being necessary for its existence. It was but a short step to atheism, and to the neurosis of our age.

However, even though in attaining knowledge of God we do not comprehend his essence, for that is truly beyond us, yet through the artistry of his creation, we can understand abstractly, but in a proportional manner, something of the nature of the Supreme Artisan: "For we know by certain knowledge, more certain than that of

---

25 Frederick Copleston, *A History of Philosophy*, vol. 2, *Augustine to Scotus* (New York: Paulist Press, 1977), 395–96.
26 The mental form is not a sense-image, but a meaning abstracted from it. *Summa Theol.* I, q. 76, a. 2, obj. 6.

Part One: Reality

mathematics, that God is simple, one, good, omniscient, all-powerful, free.... We are more certain of the divine perfections than of the beating of our own hearts."[27] The universe is so extraordinarily beautiful, so precisely balanced, and formed with such exquisite intricacy and intrinsic unity, that it cannot fail to inspire awe and raise the soul to contemplate the Artist who lies behind it all. Had Kant known what physicists and cosmologists now know, he could never have asserted that our ideas can have no referent to an objective ultimate Reality. To be convinced of this, and to lay Kantianism finally to rest, one need only take a glance at what has been discovered by modern science.

THE GRAND DESIGN

> You, however, ordered all things by
> measure, number and weight.[28]

Cosmic wonder[29]

When we survey some of the discoveries made by physicists and cosmologists we are astounded by the sheer number of minute "coincidences" and exact, predictive confirmations to the extent that it is impossible to accept that we know nothing of reality. Nor is it any longer possible to accept that we are imposing some kind of *a priori* order upon the scheme of things. Indeed, as we shall see in this section and the next, it is certain that we discern the organizing principle or form of things which to a remarkable degree strengthens our confidence in our affirmation that an underlying "something" sustains it all.

Consider the bewildering structures we encounter from the tiniest constituents of the atom to the organization not only of galaxies, but on the colossal scale of hyper-galactic structure, even to the curvature

---

27 Jacques Maritain, *The Degrees of Knowledge* (London: Centenary Press, 1937), 282.
28 Wis 11:20.
29 The works of the following physicists were consulted in this and the next section: John D. Barrow, David Bohm, Paul Davies, Bernard d'Espagnat, Harald Fritzsch, Martin Gardner, Robert Mills, and Roger Penrose (see bibliography). The current Standard Model has been followed.

of spacetime itself. Yet all these structures are governed by a few constants such that if they varied only slightly the universe would be remarkably different from its present form.[30]

The smallest structures in the universe are governed by the Planck length, which is about 10^{-35}m (i.e., a decimal point followed by thirty-four zeros and the number one). This is unimaginably minute, yet at this level, where the structure of reality seems to resemble a fine foam, violent fluctuations are thought to occur in the curvature of spacetime itself. At these limits of smallness, gravity, it would seem, exists in a quantum unit called a graviton, which can have a spin that is twice the spin of photons (particles of light).[31] Because the mathematical formalism treats these two types differently, there appears to be a basic right-left asymmetry to their spin behavior. This is rather strange since there is no evidence of such left- or right-handedness in the gravitational field itself. Yet the left-right asymmetry, or *chirality*, of nature has been established for the weak nuclear force.[32] As Penrose puts it: "We may take the view that a quantum gravity theory is aimed at something much more than merely gravitation; it is laying the basic framework for all of physics, where the current framework of classical spacetime is to be viewed as a convenience or approximation to something more fundamental."[33] This is an example of that attitude described by d'Espagnat as open realism, and is typical of the posture we have suggested which postulates a reality whose features are constantly being refined. But the essential point to be

---

30 John D. Barrow, *The Constants of Nature: From Alpha to Omega* (London: Jonathan Cape, 2002).
31 Spin (angular momentum) is an intrinsic and defining property of quantum particles and cannot be resolved into anything else. Fermions such as leptons and quarks have spin in odd ½ multiples of Planck's constant h, while bosons such as photons, gluons, and other field disturbances like the Higgs, have whole multiples of h. Fermions constitute matter; bosons produce fields in which the fermions move. The Higgs inertia-producing boson has 0 spin. It was discovered on 4 July, 2012, having a mass of approximately 125.7 Giga electron volts, with a 1 in 3 million probability that this result was due to chance. See Jonathan Allday *Quarks, Leptons and the Big Bang* (Boca Raton, FL: CRC Press, 2017), 353.
32 There are four fundamental "forces" in the universe: the strong and weak nuclear forces, electromagnetism, and the (gravitational) geometry of spacetime.
33 Jonathan Penrose, *The Road to Reality* (London: Jonathan Cape, 2004), 938.

noted here is that it is impossible either to confine such discoveries or descriptions to a limited set of Kantian categories on the one hand or to deny that there is something being referred to on the other.

Ascending one scale to the nucleus, we find another constant. Known as the Compton wavelength (about 10^{-15}m for a proton) it sets the minimum sizes for nuclear particles (such as protons and neutrons). Coincidentally, the average separation between the protons and neutrons is also specified by the Compton wavelength. The reason for this coincidence arises from the exchange of "messenger" particles between the protons and neutrons. These messenger particles are likewise governed by a Compton wavelength that gives them a rest mass similar to the protons. These have been identified by experiment to be pi mesons and it turns out that they have the same relative mass as the nuclear particles; and they are constructed of the same quarks.

Now quarks are fundamental constituents which come in six flavors with the evocative names of: *u*p, *d*own, *s*trange, *c*harm, *b*ottom and *t*op. Moreover, these constituents, which cannot exist apart, combine in twos or threes to form respectively the mesons and the heavier baryons (protons, neutrons, etc.). The surprising thing is that, since a proton, for example, is made of uud quarks, and has an integral charge of +1,[34] then each quark contributes only a fraction of the charge: in this case of the order +⅔, +⅔, −⅓ respectively. Furthermore, quarks decay. The b quark decays to produce a c quark and a virtual W⁻ boson which itself decays. In the summer of 1980, physicists at Cornell University while studying the decay of B mesons observed that the decay of b quarks results mostly in c quarks. The mass of the B mesons was worked out to be about 5.26×10^{-10} J *in agreement with theoretical predictions.* This is in the order of twelve decimal places!

When we climb to the next level to consider atoms and molecules, the electromagnetic forces come into play. There is an interesting relation between the strength of the electromagnetic force and gravity:

$$\alpha_G \geq \alpha^{12} (m_e/m_p)^4$$

---

[34] Actually it is 1.6×10^{-19} coulombs, but for calculations it is made unitary and designated as *e*. Tetraquarks and pentaquarks have also been discovered.

The term, α_G, on the left represents the force of gravity while the α on the right is the electromagnetic fine-structure constant. This equation compares the strength of gravity with the strength of electromagnetism multiplied by the ratio of electron mass m_e to proton mass m_p. Because α is raised to the twelfth power it is very sensitive to values of m_e. When numbers are inserted we get 5.9×10^{39} on the left and 2.0×10^{39} on the right. The difference between these numbers is infinitesimal to forty decimal places! Yet if gravity were only slightly weaker or electromagnetism slightly stronger, or if the mass of the electron was barely less, relative to the mass of the proton, all stars would be red dwarfs. Similarly, if all these respective differences were slightly opposite, the stars would all be blue giants. Moreover, if gravity were even minutely weaker there might be no planets formed to orbit these stars. The point to be appreciated here is the precise balance and interconnectedness between the very small (the masses of electrons and protons) and the very large (the size of stars). Paul Davies calls this "truly astonishing."[35]

We live in an expanding universe, which expansion has been continuing since the Big Bang generated it some 13.8 billion years ago relative to our inertial frame.[36] There are several parameters involved

---

35 Paul Davies, *The Accidental Universe* (Cambridge: Cambridge University Press, 1982), 73.

36 See Allday, *Quarks, Leptons and the Big Bang*, 230–33. This can be calculated from the analysis of the cosmic microwave background (CMB) data from COBE, WMAP, and Planck Surveyor where the Hubble rate of expansion has a value of 21.8 km/sec. A galaxy in our region at a distance of 1 million light years (9.461×10^{18} km) would take $d/H = 4.34 \times 10^{17}$ seconds or 13.8 billion years for the expansion of space to remove it to that distance. Of course, the expansion of the universe has not been uniform. Moreover, in the region of Schwarzschild objects (super-massive stars, black holes, or singularities) their immense gravities would severely reduce that number. The possibility to transform space and time coordinates from one inertial system to another shows that we are not privileged observers in the universe: there is no universal clock. All our standards of "time" are divisions of *our* heliocentric cycle in *our* local gravitational field which constitutes *our* inertial frame. That the visible universe has feasibly existed for the equivalent of some 13.8 billion *earth-revolutions* is all that (so far) can be inferred from our frame of reference. Since Newton's presupposition of time invariance is wrong, the dispute between ancient and recent creationists about fixed days of creation is incongruous, anachronistic, and theologically pointless. Cf. Ps 90:4; 2 Pet 3:8.

in the calculation of the rate of cosmic expansion: the gravitational constant G, Planck's constant h, and the speed of light c. In particular, one can compute the critical energy density of matter ρ_{crit}, for which the universe is spatially flat and the actual energy density of matter ρ at that early time. If ρ exceeds ρ_{crit} then spacetime will curve back in on itself and be spatially closed, resulting in the eventual contraction of the universe. On the other hand, if ρ is somewhat less than ρ_{crit} then the universe will rapidly expand. These dynamics were determined at the initial moment of creation called the Planck time where the ratio between the energy density of matter and the critical density was set to be an almost infinitesimal 10^{-60}. Davies comments that "we know of no physical reason why ρ is not a purely arbitrary number. Nature could have chosen any value at all. To choose ρ so close to ρ_{crit}, fine-tuned to such stunning accuracy, is surely one of the great mysteries of cosmology.... If this crucial ratio had been 10^{-57} rather than $< 10^{-60}$, the universe would not even exist, having collapsed to oblivion after just a few million years."[37] The difference between an infinitely diffused, structureless universe on the one hand and a short-lived expansion followed by an immediate crunch on the other is so meticulously determined that in order for the universe to achieve its present structure, the bang that occurred must have been such as to lie *precisely on the boundary* between these two possible outcomes.

If this is not astonishing enough, the Nobel Laureate Roger Penrose reveals that for our universe to have the entropy (a measure of the disorder, or dissipation of unusable energy) which it has today, the initial thermodynamic conditions of the Big Bang had to be accurate to one part in $10^{10^{123}}$—a staggeringly minute figure! Penrose states that this entropy value "would have been a possibility for a spacetime singularity constituting the initial state of the universe"... which "gives us some idea of the utterly extraordinary *precision* that was involved in the creation of the universe, as we presently understand it."[38] There is

---

37 Paul Davies, *The Accidental Universe* (Cambridge: Cambridge University Press, 1982), 90.

38 Roger Penrose, *Fashion, Faith and Fantasy in the New Physics of the Universe* (Princeton: Princeton University Press, 2016), 274–75. Because Boltzmann's equation for entropy is a logarithm, the number 10^{123} is the *logarithm* of the volume of the total phase-space at the creation of the universe.

not enough time in the life of the universe to obtain such a result by chance. Yet this result had to be selected within the limits of Planck time $t_p = 10^{-43}$ of a second! These precise thermodynamic conditions are required for all those energy-dependent processes necessary to life, "from the shining of the sun to the muscular and mental activities of our bodies and minds, and that give us the framework of directed time in which alone we are able to think and act."[39]

Of all the possible universes, ours is the only one that satisfies these exacting parameters. Even if one merely compares the velocity of the receding galaxies with the velocity required to escape mutual gravitational attraction, one finds that only our universe has the ratio required for life to exist. C. B. Snow and Stephen Hawking have indicated that "from an ensemble of infinitely many universes having all possible ratios of recessional velocity to escape velocity, the only universe in which life could emerge is the actual universe, where the velocities are equal."[40] And R. P. McCabe points out that "if the charge in the electron had been slightly different; if the reaction between two protons had been different; if the constant of gravity had been different then the universe, as we know it, would certainly not exist. Hydrogen would have turned into inert helium—no water, no life.... Our universe is an event of zero probability."[41] Yet it exists.

Indeed, when considering the facts that some large numbers (such as 10^{40}) keep repeating themselves in various contexts (gravitational fine structure, total number of protons, number of protons in a star, ratio of the age of the universe to that of the atomic nucleus, etc.) and the question of why fundamental constants (such as the gravitational constant, the fine structure constant, Planck's constant, Hubble's constant for retreating galaxies) have the precise values they do, which when brought together reveal such unexpected agreements, the point should be taken that clearly something is going on here! "The laws which enable the universe to come into being spontaneously seem themselves to be the product of exceedingly ingenious design.

---

[39] Roger Mills, *Space, Time and Quanta* (New York: W. H. Freeman, 1994), 251.
[40] George Gale, "The Anthropic Principle," *Scientific American*, December 1981, p. 164. Quoted in Thomas Dubay, S. M., *The Evidential Power of Beauty* (San Francisco: Ignatius Press, 1999), 216.
[41] Quoted in Dubay, *Evidential Power of Beauty*, 216–17.

If physics is the product of design, the universe must have a purpose, and the evidence of modern physics suggests strongly to me that the purpose includes us."[42]

This latter conclusion has been reached by several physicists (Whitrow, Dicke, et al.) who put forward the weak anthropic cosmological principle that the physical and cosmological quantities are restricted to values permitting of life. But some (Carter) have gone further to proffer the strong anthropic principle that the universe *must* have those properties conducive to life if human observers are to emerge.[43] In the words of physicist Stanley Jaki: "We see the same story: the story of one cosmic specificity leading to another, and in staggeringly exact and specific quantitative terms. In the matter-antimatter states, for instance, ordinary matter particles must outnumber antimatter particles in the specifically exact ratio of one part in ten billion to let subsequent physical interactions issue in processes characteristic of our actually observed universe... at any stage, the slightest departure from the specificity as postulated would prevent the formation of galaxies and certainly the emergence of man."[44]

Of course, one could go on elaborating these cosmic coincidences and exquisitely fine tunings.[45] However, it is precisely such facts as these involving parameters such as time, gravity, density, speed of light, ratio of protons to photons, etc., that negate any belief that we can know nothing of reality — only phenomena. And the reason is simply that in order to arrive at these extraordinarily elegant and meticulously exact proportions we are impelled to expound an explanatory theory that predicts them. The Big Bang theory is just such a theory which

---

42 Paul Davies, *Superforce* (London: Heinemann, 1985), 243.
43 See John D. Barrow and Frank J. Tipler, *The Anthropic Cosmological Principle* (Oxford: Oxford University Press, 1989).
44 Dubay, *Power of Beauty*, 215.
45 See Barrow and Tipler, *Anthropic Cosmological Principle*, 295–356. Some thirty separate universal constants are recounted which require precise calibration necessary to generate a universe capable of sustaining life. For the myriad coincidences necessary to make our Earth a suitable planet for complex life — such as our solar system's location in the galaxy, the masses of the sun and earth and moon, a Jupiter-sized planet, earth's magnetic field, plate tectonics, carbon cycle, carbon to oxygen resonance, sun's photonic spectrum, etc. — see Guillermo Gonzalez and Jay Richards, *The Privileged Planet* (Washington, DC: Regnery, 2004); Peter Ward and Donald Brownlee, *Rare Earth* (New York: Copernicus, 2004).

involves our discovering certain physical *principles* which involve the notion of *form*, not phenomena. To penetrate beyond phenomena to discern the organizing principle behind things, is non-Kantian; simply because Kant had no knowledge of St Thomas's tenet that, although our knowledge comes to us through our senses, nevertheless we are able to abstract the formal principles which account for them.[46] We perceive form and from that we discern as from a distance the faint outlines of something wonderfully sublime.

The choice, therefore, is not just between the univocity which insists that our propositions must exactly describe reality and the equivocity which, because we cannot do the former, requires our withdrawing into a state of radical idealism. Rather there is a middle way whereby we can produce proportional or analogous propositions which lie between univocity and equivocity. This is termed analogy of being because it refers us to something which we can know approximately and with some likeness reflective of the nature of the thing, because our ideas are *conditioned* by our putting the question to reality and seeing the answer that comes back when we do our experiments or observations. Moreover, these observations are repeatable and objective. We cannot believe that every time corroborations of these results are independently verified, God works a miracle to ensure that everyone comes up with the same precise answer. Neither do they come from nothing—i.e., from *not anything* that can be thought—simply because they are heuristic and lead to further advances in knowledge of... *something*, always of something more, with greater compass, explanatory power, predictability, elegance, and heurism again! Kant, in his time, could never have appreciated this.

Quantum weirdness

However, when we turn to the quantum world, any claim that our knowledge is delineated by *a priori* categories is dashed as is our natural common-sense understanding gained from our experience of the macroscopic world. Kant's categories just do not apply. The quantum world is so strange that it bears no resemblance or likeness to anything to which we are accustomed. For example, atoms (or

---

46 *Summa Theol.* I, q. 12, a. 12, obj. 3; also, I, q. 84, a. 6.

photons, electrons, etc.) acquire definite positions only when one actually observes them. A measurement on one of a pair of particles which puts one of them into a definite state (of charge or polarization) simultaneously puts its twin, although distantly removed, into a corresponding definite state (of charge or polarization) in accordance with the conservation laws. Known as quantum entanglement or wave superposition, this means one cannot really speak of an objective separation between quantum pulses of energy.

An electron, when it approaches an energy barrier with a stopping potential, will sometimes recoil or will sometimes simply disappear only to rematerialize on the other side! Surrounding these electrons are virtual particles which, ghostlike, flicker in and out of existence spontaneously. Not existing long enough to violate any conservation laws, they function as information transmitters during interactions. Protons also have their cloud of virtual particles called pi mesons which mediate the strong force that binds them together. This force is only effective within 10^{-12} cm. Even in a vacuum, particles and anti-particles indeterminately appear as though from nothing, interact with each other, and then disappear all within the uncertainty interval of the Heisenberg time. And chargeless and (virtually) massless neutrinos penetrate the earth and you and me without so much as a "by your leave!" Does this lack of resemblance to our experience imply that we can know nothing of reality or that we are wrong to believe there is anything underlying that reality? Does radical idealism win out? Or does realism still obtain?

In order to answer these questions it will suffice if we first sketch the main differences between the quantum world and our own empirical reality. There are several concepts which must be given up when examining the quantum world. One is the notion that something can be localized in space. In the quantum world there is no empty space in which any particle can be placed and there is no definite particle either. This is because the formalism that is used to predict quantum events *does not depend upon either of these discrete concepts*. The formulation simply follows the propagation history of a wave function over time, the results of which cannot be said to be independent of the experimental setting, or apparatus, or even the conscious observers making the final calculations. This wave, or rather probability density function (known as ψ),[47] expresses the statistical probability of finding a certain density of energy within a specified region at a given time — much like a crime wave expresses the likelihood of there being a concentration of crime in a given area. The crime wave is real insofar as the given area is in fact prone to crime, but the actual statistical function itself is only an ideal representation of the event's likely occurrence. Just as one would have to make an observation to determine if a certain crime did in fact take place in a particular location and time, so one would have to make an observation to determine if a definite quantum event took place. But the difference at the quantum level is that our observation affects the result.

For instance, an observation could involve determining through which of two open slits a photon passed before striking a screen. One cannot know the result until the observation is performed. Everything in the quantum world, including the experimental apparatus, remains in a probable state until the observer looks at the recording device. Then, according to one (the Copenhagen) interpretation of the facts, the observer is said to cause the probability wave to collapse — as though it travelled as a wave but collided like a particle.[48] This is because the quantum world is so minute that any attempt at observation interferes with that world. In our macroscopic world we observe objects from reflected light received upon our retinas. But in the microscopic world of quantum physics any attempt to shine photons or electrons upon energy quanta in order to observe them results in interactions between the former and the latter. At this point the quantum world interacts with the macroscopic world giving a reading on some measuring apparatus or detection device, but only when the actual measurement is done.

---

47 This function is often squared when it functions as a non-commutative complex state vector. Its function is to transition the quantum world into our classical Newtonian world: the so-called wave collapse. See Alexandre Zagoskin, *Quantum Mechanics: A Complete Introduction* (Hachette, UK: Teach Yourself Books, 2015), 136–39.
48 Mills, *Space, Time, and Quanta*, 383. Professor Robert Mills, along with Chen Ning Yang, was the developer of non-Abelian (i.e., non-commutative) Gauge Theory.

At a time when you're not observing the system, it's incorrect to talk about the positions of the particles, about their momenta, or even how many particles there are; this is because particles are quanta, and states corresponding to different numbers of quanta can be superposed. It's not just that you don't *know* what the system is doing, it's that it can't be said to be *doing anything*. All the different things the system *might* be doing can interfere with each other and are therefore all part of the reality of the situation: All the possible histories play a role in determining the final probability distribution. The only thing that you can rightly say describes the state of the system is the wave function, and what the wave function does is to keep track of all the different interfering histories and provide a way of predicting statistical correlations among different possible observations at different times.[49]

Because of the interconnectedness of these wave functions, the notion of localized events has to be abandoned. Rather, we speak of a quantum entanglement within the quantum world, and between it and the world of our gross experiences. Because we and all the objects with which we are familiar are, as it were, convoluted hyper-densities of these superposed energy potentials within an interconnected energy field, the concept of discrete objects must be abandoned along with the idea of empty space.[50] This holistic view is entirely different from the image of discrete objects that we normally utilize. Indeed, "an atomistic materialism reducing the whole world to a set of atoms, particles and so on, interacting through distance-decreasing forces, is an experimentally disproved conception . . . *such materialism is just simply false.*"[51]

---

49 Mills, *Space, Time, and Quanta*, 366.
50 And the classical idea of chance! In order for chance events to occur, two conditions must be necessary according to probability theory: the events must be independent of each other and they must be repeatable. But the evidence from quantum physics is that every quantum event is entangled and unique. Therefore, quantum potentials notwithstanding, "God does not play dice." Darwinism has still not caught up with this.
51 Bernard d'Espagnat, *On Physics and Philosophy*, 268. Italics added. See also Paul Davies and John Gribben, *The Matter Myth* (London: Penguin Books, 1992).

If the materialism of the Cartesian-Newtonian type (i.e., the idea of extended matter with properties of permanence, solidity, impenetrability, discreteness, etc., located in real absolute space and time) is false, what then *is* real? These probability waves do not seem to describe anything that exists, but only a tendency that exists *in potentia*. As Heisenberg put it, "It meant a tendency for something. It was a quantitative version of the old concept of 'potentia' in Aristotelian philosophy. It introduced something standing in the middle between the idea of an event and the actual event, a strange kind of physical reality just in the middle between possibility and reality."[52] This is the *hylomorphic* theory which postulated that physical reality comprised some kind of primeval stuff (primal matter) which was entirely passive with only a capacity for action, but which had to be organized by something which was in act, namely an organizing principle or form. The quantum world is *thoroughgoingly contingent and requires something in act to give it form*. The implications of this are immense. At first sight it might appear that underlying physical reality there is a sort of sea or field of potentials which are actualized to manifest form or energy quanta only when acted upon in the gross world. But it is not just one-way, since these potentials cannot take *any* value or form. The law of counter-factuality ensures that the quantum world can contradict us when we theorize wrongly.

Does all this support Kant's proposal that space and time are concepts we impose on this state of affairs? Does it contradict the perspective of scholasticism? The answer is no to both questions. The idea of space as a necessary *a priori* category simply did not belong to scholasticism. On the contrary, St Thomas understood space (and time for that matter) to be but the measurement of distance: concerning space, merely the distance between the boundaries of extended bodies; concerning time, the distance between events with regard to before and after. In both these cases our knowledge of space and time comes from an *a posteriori* observation and measurement performed upon the extramental world received through our senses. As such, space and time were thought by St Thomas, Bl. Duns Scotus, and all the scholastics following them to possess

---

52 Werner Heisenberg, *Physics and Philosophy* (London: Penguin Books, 1989), 29.

only a logical or relational existence, but no absolute existence of their own[53]—neither extramentally, as with Descartes and Newton, nor within mental categories, as with Kant. The point here is that it would be incongruous to include the scholastics within this critique of Kant's theory which had embraced the Cartesian-Newtonian or classical paradigm. Therefore, insofar as quantum physics undermines the classical paradigm, it undermines Kant also, but not the scholastics, who took a position similar to that of quantum physics where the formulations include the observers making the measurements.

A final question arises about the contingency of the quantum world. If the neurons of our own brains are composed of such potential states rather than individual particles, how can our brains synthesize the discrete phenomena we experience from such an indefinite quantum-entangled matrix? The notions of discrete particles located in space are, according to Kant, ultimately reducible to the *a priori* structures of the mind. "But then the thesis . . . that thought emanates from brains which are themselves composed of atoms becomes inconsistent. Within it, the objects that are supposed to explain thought turn out to only [*sic*] exist relatively to thought!"[54] It is apparent that there is a higher, more inclusive, and, therefore, simpler order that grounds human consciousness together with these state vectors. Because of this, physicist David Bohm was led to propose:

> that the more comprehensive, deeper, and more inward actuality is neither mind nor body, but rather a yet higher-dimensional actuality, which is their common ground and which is of a nature beyond both. . . . So we do not say that mind and body causally affect each other, but rather that the movements of both are the outcome

---

53 Phillips, *Modern Thomistic Philosophy*, 1:96. It is often forgotten that the time axis has an imaginary component (*ict*) whereas only space coordinates are real numbers. See D. F. Lawden, *An Introduction to Tensor Calculus, Relativity and Cosmology* (New York: John Wiley & Sons, 1982), 9–14. According to physicist Julian Barbour, the concept of time is no longer necessary to explain the universe. See Julian Barbour, *The End of Time* (London: Phoenix, 2003). For a penetrating physical, philosophical, and theological discussion, also see Shahn Majid, ed., *On Space and Time* (Cambridge: Cambridge University Press, 2008).
54 D'Espagnat, *On Physics and Philosophy*, 268.

of related projections of a common higher-dimensional ground.... So it will be ultimately misleading and indeed wrong to suppose, for example, that each human being is an independent actuality who interacts with other human beings and with nature. Rather, all these are projections of a single totality.[55]

This ground of things, which Bohm calls implicate order, d'Espagnat prefers to term "veiled reality":

> Beyond Kantian causality, which underlies empirical causality and whose importance, of course, is considerable, I believe in the existence of an "extended causality" that acts, not between phenomena but *on* phenomena *from* "the Real."... Of course, it does not involve events like efficient causes (in Aristotle's sense) since such efficient causes bring time in. But it may involve structural causes and the latter, in this approach do not boil down to mere regularities observed within sequences of phenomena. In fact the structural "extended causes" — which vaguely bring to mind Plato's Ideas — are structures of "the Real." And we saw that, in my eyes, they constitute the ultimate explanation of the fact that physical laws — hence physics — exist.[56]

Because we cannot reduce Being to material components and since it is impossible to believe that consciousness is but a product of matter, d'Espagnat asserts that the idea that Being is somehow prior to the mind-matter dualism is scientifically defensible. "So that, even though it is not 'reachable' the 'Being' in question appears to be an 'I don't know what' to which it is conceivable that the human mind is not altogether extraneous. A Being, in other words, that may constitute

---

[55] David Bohm, *Wholeness and the Implicate Order* (London: Ark, 1983), 209–10. David Bohm with Louis de Broglie formulated the pilot-wave theory.
[56] D'Espagnat, *On Physics and Philosophy*, 454. If Aristotle's theory of causes is incorrect, then is modern physics suggesting that there is a sole infinite Cause acting universally upon creatures according to "Its" own natural laws? Of course, the answers to such metaphysical questions would necessarily transcend the bounds of physics!

for it a horizon. What I mean is that, perhaps, the archetypes of some of our feelings, great longing, love, etc., are hidden there."[57]

Summary

In the previous chapter we followed a certain irrefutable idea, being in general, which when applied in various ways led to the proposition that: *The existence of God, in the sense of an infinite, all-powerful, eternal, and immaterial First Being, is a certain conviction of the human mind such that to doubt it is to deny the first principles of the intellect.* Indeed, that an infinite Being is possible—that is, that it can exist—has also necessitated our assertion that it must exist. For our demonstration of its possibility "results in an extraordinary conclusion: Infinite Being cannot be possible, unless it is necessary. But it is necessary that it is possible. Therefore, it is necessary that it exists."[58] Or as Theodore Sider puts it:

> But anything that is metaphysically, naturally, or technologically necessary, for example, must be true. (If something is true in all metaphysically possible worlds, or all naturally possible worlds, or all technologically possible worlds, then surely it must be true in the actual world, and so must be plain old true.)[59]

In this chapter we examined the Kantian idealist (and by extension the radical idealist[60]) objections to this—that because our ideas

---

57 D'Espagnat, *On Physics and Philosophy*, 463. See also Henry P. Stapp, *Quantum Theory and Free Will: How Mental Intentions Translate into Bodily Actions* (New York: Springer, 2017), 73.
58 Antonio Rosmini, *The Problem of Ontology: Being as One* (Durham: Rosmini House, 1998), sec. 101. This is valid according to S5 modal logic. See Sider, *Logic for Philosophy*, 170–72. Rosmini here closely follows Scotus's modality argument in *De Primo Principio*, 3.20. The distinction is that Rosmini's (and Scotus's) argument is not merely the modality of possible worlds, but of modes of Being, i.e., an ontological modality (such as: potential/actual, finite/infinite, necessary/contingent, real/ideal, substance/accident, etc.) rather than a merely logical one.
59 Sider, *Logic for Philosophy*, 167.
60 For example: Fichte, Schelling, Hegel, and Schopenhauer. These radical idealists wanted to banish any notion of substantial reality whatsoever. German philosophy has never recovered from Kantian idealism.

cannot refer to anything real but merely express the way we are designed to think, then any notion of mind-independent Reality is illusory. There were two elements to this objection: that we can know *nothing* of the substantial (noumenal) and that we impose our *a priori* ideas upon experience. We have disproved the former by providing evidence of the astonishingly precise quantities involved in physical theories and confirmed by independent observation. Also, the ability of our theories to yield ever-increasing explanations of greater elegance and predictive power, which enables us to understand principles that lie hidden behind phenomena, falsifies this idea that little if anything of reality can be known by us. In the words of Henri Poincaré:

> Equations express relationships and it is because the relationships preserve their reality that the equations remain true. They inform us... that there is a relationship between something and something else. Now, we used to call this something *motion*, and presently call it *electric current*. But these appellations were just images, substituted to the real objects that nature will hide from us forever. The true relationships between these real objects constitute the only reality that is attainable by us, and the only condition is that there should be the same relationships between the said objects as between the images that we are forced to substitute for them.[61]

We recall that existence precedes knowledge, i.e., if thought did not *exist* (in act) there could be no knowledge. But this logical requirement—that existence comes first—demands that its primacy informs experience and knowledge, not the other way around. "With the corollary that, while it is quite proper to make the idea that a particular thing exists depend upon the notion of possible knowledge of the said thing, it is inconsistent to refer the very notion of existence (in itself) to the one of possible knowledge."[62] As we said in chapter one: *the mind cannot confer on mere logical being a capacity for real existence.*

---

61 In *La Science et l'hypothèse*, quoted in d'Espagnat, *On Physics and Philosophy*, 372.
62 Ibid., 240.

Thought cannot generate reality.[63] Since predication cannot consist in abstraction alone, the Real has to be more than a mere object of thought. To affirm the Real—i.e., Being in act—is but to recognize that which interacts with us and modifies or opposes us. Thus our knowledge of relationships and principles *ultimately rests upon the Real*, which informs and sustains *them*!

The second Kantian objection—that our ideas are imposed on the world—foundered before the strangeness of quantum theory. The ideas of the latter are incongruous with Kant's Cartesian-Newtonian *a priori*s. Yet the principles of quantum mechanics (such as electron tunneling) have been employed in the design of the central processing units of the very computers utilized by postmodern idealists to write their monographs. Moreover, however consistent, powerful, or beautiful our physical propositions may seem, they can be confounded by experiment. This makes physics independent of even Gödel's theorem (that the internal consistency of the propositions of mathematics is ultimately undecidable), because even though physics relies upon mathematics, it has a higher court of appeal, namely the real, which is required in order to demonstrate that its propositions are not merely speculative. No matter how consistent the proof, something says "no." Moreover, this something cannot just be us. Finally, the fact that we are led to new concepts and insights foreign to those of our ordinary experience makes it impossible that the Kantian categories exert a formative influence on our understanding of the world. Our ideas are too rich and our theories are too heuristic to be thus attenuated.

---

63 Not even the *a priori*s of mathematics can do this. For one thing, mathematics lacks any idea of substance, potency, act, quality, motion, time, or form, having only two metaphysical categories: multiplicity (from which we derive such notions as number and sets) and extension (from which we derive space and geometry). Also, the numbers 0 and ∞ are inconsistently used in mathematics. Sometimes zero signifies nothing (zero gravity) and sometimes it represents something, such as a locus on a continuum (e.g., vector coordinates). Because mathematics is conceptually deficient, its ideas—such as point, line, ∞, 0, i, etc.—must be informed by metaphysics and demonstrated by a testable physical theory before they can be accepted as real. For other aporias, such as the theorems of Cohen, Church, and Löwenheim-Skolem, see Morris Kline, *Mathematics: The Loss of Certainty* (Oxford: Oxford University Press, 1980).

Conclusion

We may safely conclude that not only is the idea of a First Being a certain *formal* conviction of the human mind, as demonstrated in our first chapter, but that this idea is supported by cosmology and underpinned by quantum physics, especially since both disciplines utilize arguments reminiscent of the five ways of St Thomas. Firstly, the facts of cosmology support the first two ways which had demonstrated the existence of a first mover and a first cause. The Big Bang Theory informs us that not only did the universe begin from nothing,[64] but that this beginning set in motion all the changes and formations of the cosmos. But from nothing at all comes nothing at all, since what does not exist cannot act. All too often the word "nothing" is reified as though it has a referent, but we have understood it to mean *not anything that can be thought*, because it is the opposite of what only *can* be thought: viz., some being. And since what has a beginning cannot precede itself, therefore, the physical universe has a non-physical, eternal cause.

Furthermore, because less can only come from more, and order (energy) cannot come from disorder (entropy), the precision and order

---

64 The Borde, Guth, Vilenkin Singularity Theorem has proven that all universes, which inflate at an amount where the average Hubble parameter $H_{av} > 0$, require a boundary to past time—i.e., must have a beginning. This applies to: all string cosmologies such as Steinhardt-Turok Ekpyrotic universes, Gasperini-Veneziano Pre-Big-Bang inflation models, the L. Susskind et al. string landscape theories, and Quantum Gravity models such as non-boundary beginnings (Hawking-Hartle) or quantum tunnelling from nothing (Vilenkin). Other theories (such as De Sitter Cosmology or the Baum-Frampton Phantom Bounce theory where $H_{av} < 0$, or M-theories) either contradict observable cosmology or result in implying an actual beginning to the universe. It should also be noted: that there are as many as 10^{500} possible string theories; that they are highly speculative with no supportive evidence; that they fail to explain large-distance physics or make definite predictions or derive general relativity; that they ignore the implications of Gödel's theorem (that mathematical models cannot be accepted solely upon the basis of consistency, but must be *shown* to refer to reality) or Church's theorem (that no mathematical algorithm exists that will determine whether or not any theory can be proved by formal arguments alone). See Bruce L. Gordon, "Inflationary Cosmology and the String Multiverse" in Robert J. Spitzer, ed., *New Proofs for the Existence of God* (Grand Rapids: Eerdmans, 2010), 75–103; Lee Smolin, *The Trouble with Physics* (London: Penguin Books, 2006), 184–99, esp. 194. Also see Luc Brisson and Walter Meyerstein, *Inventing the Universe* (Albany: State University of New York Press, 1995).

of the universe supports St Thomas's fourth way as well. The degrees of perfection within the cosmos necessitate something more perfect as their source; and its rational precision, and formal intelligibility, requires an intelligent source. Also, the interconnectedness and interdependence of everything in the cosmos upon these precise quantities, which have led many to advance the anthropic principles, confirm the fifth way. The universe seems to have a purpose which includes us.

Lastly, when we examined the quantum world, it was discovered that it is but a distribution of potentials so that it is utterly contingent upon some formative principle — whose existence *cannot* come from us. This confirms St Thomas's third way: the way of contingency. A thing in potency must be actualized by some other thing already in act. Yet the elements of the brain are thought ultimately to be quantum states; and these latter, being potentials, must in turn be contingent on something actual.[65] If, therefore, the underlying reality in quantum mechanics has the ontological semblance of unextended thought rather than the character of localized particles, then it is feasible that Reality is fundamentally singular, so that there is no logical aporia of the mind-body sort that plagues classical physicalism or Kantian idealism. The brain (indeed any organ or computer consisting ultimately of quantum states) being contingent must rest upon a necessary cause — a Cause, moreover, which also sustains even our own (autonomous) minds.

Philosophers have disputed whether a physical organ can generate mind. The *idea* of being in general is simple (atomic) as we noted in the first chapter. Therefore the mind — an intellective principle capable of intuiting being — is also simple, since what is compounded of parts cannot generate that simple idea (i.e., being in general) because each part will contribute diverse effects. And, therefore, since the mind, or soul, is a simple ontologically aware principle, then no complex organ could generate (or evolve) the mind either, because each substructure (whether the brain acts as a whole or in part) would *ipso facto* produce some part of the mind. But the mind — like being itself — has no parts,

---

65 See Roger Penrose, *The Emperor's New Mind* (London: Vintage, 1990); H. P. Stapp, *Mind, Matter, and Quantum Mechanics* (New York: Springer-Verlag, 1993).

i.e., is unextended, and therefore immaterial or spiritual. Therefore, the mystery of human consciousness cannot be resolved by reductionism.

Indeed, we have already observed that there exists a bond between the mind's ontological awareness of itself and the body's own fundamental feeling (*coenaesthesia*). This union entails our body's having already become subjectively felt as extended in that corporeal feeling — as our biologically inherited, characteristic, homeostatic state — and then intellectually expressed as *myself*, as an *ens*. Because the idea of being in general is the (supreme) formative principle of the intellect, the single, simple, human subject unites what is felt (the extended element) with what is understood (ideal being), thus comprehending it as a homogeneous and ever-present sense of self. Thus the substance of the human soul is a fundamental (animal) feeling found in the depth of *myself*, but made intelligible through the self-concept — its form. A single human individual *is formed* from the union of these two natures (animal and spiritual) by means of that supreme principle which virtually cognizes in itself all its subordinate activities *as they are felt*. This supreme principle is first intuited at the highest point of the human soul and is communicated to it by an infinitely perfect and all-embracing Reality.[66]

* * *

Whether gazing horizontally into the past or peering vertically into the depths, we are compelled to acknowledge the presence of something, whose essence we cannot fathom, yet is the Substantial Cause of all that is, discerned only through the traces of its effects upon creatures, and understood according to their likeness to it. All perfection, order, beauty, and intelligence come from this Reality and are sustained by "it" and allude wonderfully to "it" so that we have no hesitancy in calling this eternal, infinite, immaterial, all-powerful Being, God. But without presumption, since talk about God is primarily analogical. Yet though he remains unknown in his Substance, nevertheless we may affirm:

---

66 See Rosmini, *Essence of the Human Soul*, nos. 61–81, 200–209, 641–42, 652; Malebranche, *Dialogues on Metaphysics*, II, vi; V, xiii; and XII, v, ix–x. Also see the empirically rigorous and philosophically informed critique of contemporary cognition by Edward F. Kelly and Emily Williams Kelly, et al., *Irreducible Mind* (Lanham: Rowman & Littlefield, 2010).

> The heavens declare the glory of God,
> the vault of heaven proclaims his handiwork,
> day discourses of it to day,
> night to night hands on the knowledge.
>
> No utterance at all, no speech,
> not a sound to be heard,
> but from the entire earth the design stands out,
> this message reaches the whole world.[67]

Now if God is the Being who gives being to all that is, sustaining it according to his purpose, why is there so much evil seemingly despoiling this purpose and inflicting such pain and anguish upon his creatures? How can such a good God permit evil? Either he is not good or not all powerful: either way, he is not God. We turn in the next chapter to address this remaining objection to our initial proposition.

---

67 Ps 19:1–4.

CHAPTER 3

Good and Evil

How long are the wicked to triumph?
They bluster and boast,
they flaunt themselves, all the evil doers.

They crush your people, Lord,
they oppress your heritage,
they murder the widow and the stranger,
bring the orphan to a violent death.

They say, "The Lord is not looking,
the God of Jacob is taking no notice."
Shall he who implanted the ear not hear,
he who fashioned the eye not see?[1]

OUR NATURAL REASON CONVINCES US that this is a theistic universe, and not a godless one. Beholding the beauty, precision, and order of creation, aided solely by the light of our intellects, our contemplation of reality raises us by degrees to discern the existence of the One, True, Good, and Beautiful whose perfections are disclosed to us thereby. This is the analogy of being. "For what can be known about God is perfectly plain to them, since God has made it plain to them: ever since the creation of the world, the invisible existence of God, and his everlasting power have been clearly seen by the mind's understanding of created things."[2] The universe is truly extraordinary, yet it is contingent: the universe does not have to exist. Not only its absolute beginning, but its continuance is contingent upon a necessary Being. The denial of this leads to absurdity, for being cannot be dependent upon nothing.

Nevertheless, within the harmony there exists discord; within being, non-being. Although elegant, creation is seemingly marred.

---

1 Ps 94:3–7, 9.
2 Rom 1:19–20.

The formation of galaxies, solar systems, and even our own world has been accompanied by violent collisions and explosions. Across the vista of natural history disturbing flaws are apparent: pestilence, famine, and decay have sporadically scourged life long before the advent of man. On many occasions life on this planet has come to the brink of extinction (the Permian Extinction, for example); entire species (like the dinosaurs) have perished through violent cataclysms; and the grotesque life cycle of parasites and the instances of cannibalism among animals seem to deform the image of a benevolent Creator.

Yet, this is nothing compared to the cruelty and depravity perpetrated by human beings. The history of the human species has been a litany of lies, dissipation, theft, torture, murder, oppression, enslavement, and war. Nor have these been inflicted only by evil persons upon other evil persons, but against the dependent and vulnerable — upon the elderly and especially children. Since before Job, the innocent have cried out to God in the midst of suffering: "Why do you hide your face and look on me as your enemy?"[3] "My God, my God, why have you forsaken me?"[4] There is a discomfiting antithesis, it would appear, between the beauty of creation when seen from afar and its gross imperfections when inspected more closely, such that many have come to doubt there is a wise and good God behind it all.

However, there have been many others who have attempted to defend God's justice in the face of these adversities, even to the extent of finding wisdom in the midst of suffering. It seems preposterous that the senselessness of suffering should conceal wisdom. Yet that is just what has been argued by those who have worked in the field of theodicy (from Greek: *theos* — God, *dike* — justice). First coined by Leibniz, theodicy is a specialist field within natural theology which attempts to "justify God's ways to man." To some such an attempt seems blasphemous, since they feel God needs no justification — His ways are mysterious, they argue, and we must submit to them unquestioningly — while others would consider it crass and insensitive to launch into a theological justification in the face of human misery and pain.

---

3 Job 13:24.
4 Ps 22:1.

Yet there are reasons why theodicy ought to be attempted. For one thing, part of what constitutes personal suffering is the question: Why? "Why this innocent person?" "Why the little children?" Also, as we have seen, the pervasiveness of evil predisposes many to refuse to believe in the existence of God, whereas some, overwhelmed by personal suffering, abandon their faith. Nonetheless, not a few, even in the midst of intense suffering, have come to believe in God, while many others have found their faith deepened. What do the latter understand that the former do not? Certainly, the pursuit of these questions is not without merit. Shining some dim light on the problem of evil could, at least, fortify faith if not also foster some reconciliation between God and man — not just for the faithful, but for the perplexed. However, no complete answer will be given here — assuming that such were possible given the limits of human reason — since our main purpose is to answer the objection (raised at the end of Chapter One) that the prevalence of suffering necessarily negates the existence of a good and all-powerful God. For this reason, therefore, we shall offer only general answers to this perennial question, sensitive to the genuine anguish of those who ask it, while at the same time robbing that objection of its force.

SEEKING AN ANSWER

We have noted that the universe is not absolutely perfect. The operative term here is "absolutely" — for only God is an absolutely perfect Being, perfect Form. It follows that God cannot create an *absolutely* perfect universe. The reason for this does not reflect negatively upon God, but upon the creature, which is necessarily limited. The limit is in the creature, not in God. Since God is infinite perfection, any created thing insofar as it differs from him must lack some perfection or other, or *it* would be God. This follows from the principle of identity and from the unity of God. Therefore, it is unreasonable to demand from God absolute perfection (i.e., without limit) for his creation. This is precisely what it means to be a creature: finitude and imperfection. "No one is good but God alone."[5]

---

[5] Mt 19:17 = Lk 18:19.

Part One: Reality

However, creatures can have relative goodness insofar as they act according to their nature. For example, the weak anthropic principle whereby the forces and properties of the universe are such as to bring forth life illustrates one form of goodness. The existence of volcanoes and plate tectonics play their role in this and, along with the climatic changes they produce, together drive the phylogenesis[6] of plants and animals. Indeed, we have seen that the entire cosmos is needed simply to keep the forces and processes of the earth itself in balance. Moreover, every animal and plant is good according to its kind. Each does that which it is designed to do, playing its part in maintaining the ecology of the entire planet. A thing is what it is. An animal, for example, is a sensual, instinctively-ordered creature designed to forage or kill in order to live. Perhaps God should not have created animals? Or perhaps not even volcanoes, storms, or neutron stars? It is presumptuous to demand that the natural world should be other than the limited imperfect being it is; or to require that God not create at all.

There is a metaphysical truth here: every being acts according to its nature, simply because its nature is its form in act. Recall that there can only be one principle in act in a given being—otherwise there would be two conflicting intrinsic principles and two identities or natures. Were a being to have more than one principle, only one of these would be in act, since a being cannot at a given moment be in potency (passive) and in act (active) in the same way in violation of the postulates of identity and contradiction. This is but the intrinsic reason of being that we encountered earlier: a thing is its own essential nature (its intrinsic formal principle) from which it derives its properties. Therefore, things are intelligible insofar as we are able to discern this principle or form within a thing. And insofar as a thing acts according to its nature, it is well-ordered and, therefore, good. This is the essential meaning of

---

6   By the term phylogenesis is meant the natural history or descent of classes of organisms (plant or animal phyla), which exhibit a pattern of increasing complexity from simple forms leading eventually to the human species. We will not use the term "evolution" since its equivocal application—to the *theory* of natural selection, to phylogenesis proper, or to change in general—has generated much confusion and debate. This is done to avoid commitment to any existing theoretical account of what appears to be a general principle of life.

those verses in the first chapter of Genesis where God reflects upon his creation and at each stage pronounces it good.

Each level of creation has its formative principle. Hydrogen and oxygen are combustible gases. But when organized in the proper proportions (H_2O), water comes into being with its own intrinsic properties explicable according to its emergent form. This principle of formal emergence is observable at other levels as well. Consider what happens when life comes into being. At this level inanimate structures become organized to serve the living form. In the case of plants there is a vegetative principle which we understand to be encoded in the plant cell, contained holistically within its genome, and informing the whole. Then with the emergence of the animal form, the vegetative principle becomes subsumed to the new sentient principle which holistically informs its genome. With human beings, the mind or soul[7] is the formal principle and the animal and vegetative principles are to be subordinated to it. We say "are to be" because humans have the freedom to abandon reason and live sensual animalistic lives should they so choose. We do not have to live like the beasts, although at times we do descend to this level and even lower, because we are not impeded by instincts. We also observe that humans are able, through substance abuse, for example, to descend even below the bestial state to a vegetative level—a life of mere existence. And of course should death then ensue, the body through corruption will ultimately revert to the inorganic state so that the entire process is reversed and the lower material principles regain their various operations. If this course is deliberately pursued, our behavior is intentionally diverted from its proper rational end. And because the will is engaged it is moral evil.

We will investigate moral evil shortly, but first we must comprehend the nature of evil in general. Just as being in general is understood to mean existence, and non-being is therefore non-existence, so evil is simply something acting contrary to its nature or concrete existence, being other than what it is supposed to be. As such, evil is simply a lack of proper proportion and is, therefore, a privation, although of a specific kind. Evil cannot be privation in general, in which case

---

7 The soul cannot be generated by the organism, as we saw in the last chapter.

every limited creature would be evil — God, the only uncreated being, excepted from that. Each being is good proportionate to its form. Therefore, the privation which is evil is formal disorder, as we have seen. Evil occurs when some being is directed away from its proper end, i.e., against its nature, acting contrary to form. 'Something is wrong with such a being. Indeed, this notion of *wrong* is what characterizes evil in general. It is a distortion of reality, discordance in the harmony of the economy of creation, and a deviation from its purpose contrary to natural law. It is in this sense that evil is a lack. It becomes a moral issue only when the free will is involved.

With all that has been said it should be apparent that for God to create he must bring into existence beings relatively imperfect. This is amplified infinitely more when God elects to create creatures with free will. For it is proper to free will to have the potential to choose against the will of God. In other words, in creating free human beings God has bestowed upon them the radical possibility of their choosing to reject him. *To deny this possibility is to refuse to us our human nature.*

Therefore, since God is the Being who gives being — the defining quality of (*agapic*) love — he creates persons who are able freely to receive from him. Indeed, it is necessary that we know and revere him as the provider of all that is good for us, for all good comes from him. This is needful for our own sakes so that we may have confidence in him. God desires us to have this assurance precisely because of his infinite love towards us. So God created us free so that we might find our fulfillment in him: we who are designed to delight in him because he loves us who are also self-aware and self-directing — autonomous, free persons, made in his image. We are made that we might know God, and we are naked and weak without him. This was our original innocence.

Fundamental to this freedom is that faculty of forming a judgment about the goodness of a thing and in so doing discerning whether it is the proper thing to be desired and to what degree. "The will must tend towards being according to the order found in being."[8] Thus the essence of free will lies in this intellectual capacity of forming a well-ordered judgment based upon its own ultimate criterion: the idea

---

8 Antonio Rosmini, *Principles of Ethics* (Durham: Rosmini House, 1989), 62.

of being, which itself is the light of the intellect, given to us by God. Thus, things are to be regarded as means; persons are to be loved as ends for their own sake, for they are like us; and God, as the Supreme Being, is to be loved absolutely, simply for the sublime beauty of his Form.

> This natural movement of the soul towards the good in general is invincible, for it does not depend on us to will to be happy. We love necessarily that which we know clearly and which we feel vividly to be the true good. All minds love God *by the necessity of their nature,* and if they love something other than God *by the free choice of their will,* it is not that they fail to seek after God, or the cause of their happiness; rather they deceive themselves. It is that, feeling confusedly that bodies which surround them make them happy, they view them as goods, and by an ordinary and natural sequence they love them and unite with them.[9]

Therefore, the negative side of free will is the possibility that we deliberately refuse to exercise proper judgment. Coiled within our primordial autonomy is the moral freedom to exploit that liberty for ourselves and choose just what *we* decide is valuable and desirable. Our desire is then turned away from God's "tree of life" to the sundry, yet limited, delights of this world (symbolized by the tree of knowledge of good and evil). This predilection, of directing our estimation to worldly things in order to embrace them as more desirable than God, leads to beguilement and enslavement. Allured by these, we assimilate and identify with them, so that we resent having to relinquish our proclivity to do with them as we please. And since that for which we were originally created has been abrogated—because we have ordered our actuality to those limited perfections belonging to creatures rather than to that noble estate for which we were initially formed—disharmony now reigns within. Boethius recognized this as early as the sixth century:[10]

---

9 Nicolas Malebranche, *Treatise on Nature and Grace* (Oxford: Clarendon Press, 1992), Discourse III, 2. Italics added.
10 *Consolation of Philosophy* (London: Folio Society, 1998), Bk. 3, IX, pp. 99 & 100.

> The reason is very clear. That which is one and undivided is mistakenly subdivided and removed by men from the state of truth and perfection to a state of falseness and imperfection.... Human perversity then makes divisions of that which by nature is one and simple, and in attempting to obtain part of something which has no parts, succeeds in getting neither the part — which is nothing — nor the whole, in which they are not interested.

The result of this flight from being, from truth, is the abandonment of our inherent dignity, the disruption of the proper order of things, and the perversion of the natural law. Having forgotten (*amnestos*) that primordial innocence bestowed upon us by our Creator, we descend even beneath the level of beasts. The outcome is this fallen world.

Humanity, having alienated itself from God, now protests its rights against God, refusing to recognize that all things belong to God and must be ordered to his glory.[11] Denying that God alone is God, we turn to false gods to appease our deficiencies and anxieties. To the extent to which we revere *our* ideologies and values, our causes, status, and possessions, we are owned by them and oppressed by them. In attempting to actualize ourselves, our egos harden, generating a war of each against each.[12] Spiritually dead, we become materialistic. Mutual advantage necessitates political alignments spinning out a tangled web of conspiracy, tragedy, and pain. The struggle to extricate ourselves from these problems injects ever more complexity into the system. Every attempt to overcome adversity only compounds the difficulties, calling for more intervention, generating ever greater complexity and alienation.

And "as we sow, so do we reap":

> Like good and evil, reward and punishment are opposites. The reward we see due to the good must be balanced by a corresponding punishment of the wicked. Therefore, just as goodness is its own reward, so the punishment of the wicked is their very wickedness. Now, no one who suffers

---

11 1 Cor 6:19–20, 10:31.
12 Rom 1:24–32; Jas 4:1–5.

punishment doubts that he suffers something evil. So, if they are willing to examine themselves, I do not think men can consider themselves immune from punishment when they suffer the worst evil of all: evil is not so much an infliction as a deep-set infection.[13]

With this we have arrived at consummate moral evil, for the object desired is now truly opposed to that ultimate end for which we were created: our love for God. The heart has come to despise God and his law. It is self-love that has forced this rupture with God which is the condition of mortal sin.

> The evil of wrongdoing is the result of a divergence between the will of a rational created being and the will of God. It is a revolt against the absolute sovereignty of the Creator. It is the act of rashness, if the sinner imagines he will escape from God's justice or the justice that is immanent in God's ordering of the world. It is a disorder knowingly introduced into the harmony of the universe.[14]

These are the implications of creating creatures with the capacity of freely choosing to reject the love of God. Even so, God has permitted this fall in order to bring about an even greater good. In this both his majesty and love are displayed. For, rather than avoid moral evil by curtailing human freedom (and thereby denying their human natures), God has willed through that freedom to offer to humanity a far greater good than would otherwise be obtained if humanity were prevented from falling. In fact, if God having created Homo sapiens had simply left them to forage, age, and die, then God would still have been just. Having given them life and everything necessary to life as well as the natural virtue to cultivate that life rationally and justly, he would have given them their due. Since justice is giving to one what is one's due, no breech of justice has occurred. The

---

13 *Consolation of Philosophy*, Bk. 4, III, p. 130. Thus, the sentiment of resentment, which one may feel for those who seek wealth, status, power, fame, or pleasure, betrays within oneself a secret covetousness for the same things. Rather, charity insists we pray for such souls as these.
14 François Petit, *The Problem of Evil* (New York: Hawthorn Books, 1959), 88.

suffering that we bring upon ourselves and upon our own kind does not reflect negatively upon God's justice. He owes us nothing; we owe him everything.

One might object that even if humanity had never fallen out of communion with Divine Truth, the prevalence of disease, pestilence, and predation would be a sufficient indictment against God. This would be true if we were helpless in the face of these things. But we have been given the endowment to overcome these if, through exercising proper judgment, we would choose to concentrate our efforts and resources in that direction.

Let us go even further and imagine what the world would have been like if every individual upon the face of the earth *without exception* loved one another and cherished one another as one's own self. There would be no war, crime, cruelty, violence, or oppression. There would be no selfishness, indifference, sarcasm, duplicity, or manipulation of others; no need for armies, navies, bombs, guns, prisons, lawyers, police, national defense, or fear. Greed would be non-existent: banks would vanish, and locks and safes would be superfluous. Being responsible for each other we would not require insurance or accumulation of savings. Should the humble dwellings in which we would be content to live ever burn down, the community would simply muster and erect another just as the Amish do today. The main streets of our cities would be unrecognizable. Indeed, there would be no necessity for these financial conurbations—monuments to avaricious and questionable conceits. There would be no depression, drunkenness, loneliness or despair. Neither mendacious nor cynical, we would trust one another and grow close to one another. Our lives would be simpler, more secure, and uneventful. But would all possible good be maximized?

These imaginings may be but an impossible dream or an idle thought experiment, for it is irrelevant for our purposes whether such a world could ever have been realized. The point we wish to make is that good unmixed with any evil is either impossible for us or, if possible, would prevent our attaining maximum good. We are not automatons. We do choose evil, which is the price of free will, the price of a human nature. Nevertheless, it is evident that those who live a just and prudent life do generally thrive, all things being equal, while the profligate languish, falling prey to many of the evils we have mentioned. We cannot disobey God's law with impunity: something will always go wrong. Even so, God has not left the incorrigible to their just deserts, nor, as we shall see below, has he forgotten the innocent victims.

In this scheme of things where humans have refused to submit to the will of God, moral evil is the inevitable result. But for those who pursue the good the reward is even greater than if they dwelt in a state of innocence. Nobility and dignity are attained through the effort and sacrifice it takes in preferring a moral good to a material one. The beauty of the person who lives a just and benevolent life contrasts markedly with the ugliness of the selfish and materialistic person. Moreover, a needy person in receipt of a tangible act of goodness is also enhanced spiritually especially given the prevailing context of evil against which the deed is contrasted, while others of good will are inspired to even greater works of goodness. Because that which is of more perfect form is of more worth than that which is of less, the spiritual life is far more worthy than a merely sensual existence. The accomplishments of a St Francis of Assisi, for example, outshine by far the frivolous, self-centered lives of most of those popularized in the media today and all the more against the flamboyance, dissipation, and absurdity of their milieu.

Thus, evil, being an unavoidable factor of life, continuously motivates one to rise above oneself in pursuit of the good. This occurs even if evil is merely shunned. Either way one grows in self-control, wisdom, and virtue. Humanity as a whole is spurred to greater and greater achievements. They have no choice, else they go under. This follows naturally from the Law of Requisite Variety.[15] Every system, in order to sustain itself, must have a minimum repertoire of responses sufficient to meet the vicissitudes of the environment or it will perish. Whether the system is a galaxy, a brain, an organism, a tribe, factory, or society, if it cannot respond to the disturbances that threaten its equilibrium it will become unstable and eventually

---

15 For a mathematical proof, see Arvid Aulin, *The Cybernetic Laws of Social Progress* (Oxford: Pergamon Press, 1982), 104–7.

succumb. Moreover, this variety of behaviors must not include disordered responses. In order to ameliorate the disturbing evil, the actions must be well ordered or they will exacerbate the situation and lead to even more problems requiring more intervention. The result is an inevitable increase in complexity.

The latter increase illustrates another law, the Law of Requisite Hierarchy: "The weaker the average regulatory ability and the larger the average uncertainty of available regulators, the more *requisite hierarchy* is needed in the organization of regulation and control for the same result of organization."[16] In any self-governing system there has to be a minimum hierarchy of control systems to regulate the variety of possible responses of that system. Without regulation a complex system will be disjointed and its responses misdirected and inconsequential.

Furthermore, these laws are compensatory. If the system is too rigid it will lack the requisite variety to respond to disturbances from without and will collapse. Totalitarian systems inevitably fall. Contrariwise, if a system has too much variety and too little control, it will weaken and be rendered vulnerable both to internal and external disruption. A decadent culture will either wither away or be taken over. Such laws apply to any system including psychological systems such as persons. The greater the evil, the greater is the requisite virtue to offset it.

This is not the only way that Divine Wisdom has ordered things to bring about maximum good. Not only does evil chastise the wicked and sanctify the virtuous, but in the case of the former it can act to convict them of their wrongdoing and convert them to follow virtue. With regard to the latter, suffering can bring them into a deeper, even mystical communion with God. This is so universal an observation as to need little demonstration: every major religion has commended the ascetical or eremitical life as a path to deeper union with God. In the third part of this book we will see the reasons for this. But here we wish simply to address the fact that fortuitous suffering can have unexpected spiritual benefits for those who know how to embrace it.

---

16 Ibid., 115. For proof, see also ibid., 124–25.

THE LAW OF LEAST MEANS

The renowned Jesuit priest, philosopher, and founder of the Institute of Charity, Bl. Antonio Rosmini, has identified yet another law by which God's providence works: the Law of Least Means.[17] The eternal wisdom of God is such that he will bring about the maximum distribution of good relative to the means employed in producing it.

In cosmology, we delighted in the exquisite economy by which creation is ordered with precision and elegance. Even in nature nothing is wasted, for what is considered waste at one level, for example an overproduction of offspring, at another level is supremely beneficial, for example in maintaining the food chain. There are a balance and ecology in nature which serve the whole which, in turn, sustains the individuals. Recognized also as the law of least action, it regulates the composition of the animal, its preservation, reproduction, and operations. It has been applied by Euler to central forces, by Lagrange to the time integral of motion, by Hamilton to the energy conserved in a system, and by Koenig to beehives. As the law of least time it governs optics. It has been a guiding principle in Einstein's Special Theory of Relativity. It is a factor within the ψ function in quantum mechanics and manifests itself in chaos theory as the butterfly effect, whereby tiny effects are amplified by non-linear equations. Known as the law of parsimony it limits theoretical speculations. It regulates logic, mathematics, and, because the deep structure of languages is susceptible of logico-mathematical modeling, it is a factor in the construction of artificial languages.

The actions of God will always be proportional to the end pursued. Redundant or superfluous acts are not fitting to Divine Wisdom:

> For within her is a spirit intelligent, holy, unique, manifold, subtle, mobile, incisive, unsullied, lucid, invulnerable, benevolent, shrewd, irresistible, dependable, unperturbed, almighty, all-surveying, penetrating all intelligent, pure and most subtle spirits. For Wisdom is

---

17 Antonio Rosmini, *Theodicy* (London: Longmans, Green, 1912), vol. 1, chap. viii.

quicker to move than any motion; she is so pure; she pervades and permeates all things. She is the breath of the power of God.[18]

By the "end pursued" we mean the ultimate end which consists of the greatest moral perfection of intelligent creatures, and that which is consequent upon it, their greatest eudaemonological good, i.e., the greatest happiness. The Supreme Good has for its end the maximum good which, when applied to moral-intelligent (i.e., spiritual) creatures, entails their spiritual perfection. This good forms the absolute and universal end. All other ends are a means to this one.

With regards to our consideration of the general economy of good and evil, this law ensures that good is maximized in the presence of privation (or disorder) through utilization of the least means, so that even the privation (or disorder) belonging to moral evil has been accommodated within the scheme of things. Not willing to leave creation in a limited state, Divine Wisdom has ordained things such that the moral-eudaemonological good distributed throughout creation is maximized proportionally to the means required to produce it. In order to achieve this, God utilizes the principle of least means whereby "created beings are so governed that not one of their activities remains idle, that is to say, fails to bear the fruit it could bear by being properly employed."[19] This is the essential meaning of Christ's parable of the talents where "to everyone who has [spiritual virtue] will be given more, and he *will have more than enough*; but anyone who has not, will be deprived even of what he has [viz., material possessions, life]."[20] Similarly, in the parable of the sower, the parables of the mustard seed and leaven, the miracle of the loaves, the cursing of the fig tree, and the parable of the wedding feast,[21] it is clear that God so arranges things as to bring about all the good which they can yield. From this follow a number of consequences.[22]

---

18 Wis 7:22–25.
19 Rosmini, *Theodicy*, vol. 2, 10.
20 Mt 25:29–30.
21 Mt 13:3–23, 31–33; 14:13–21; 21:18–22; 22:1–14.
22 See Rosmini, *Theodicy*, vol. 2.

First consequence: *When a specific measure of good can be achieved through the actions of created beings, it is not proper that God should accomplish it by some extraordinary and immediate intervention.*

This is why it is churlish to blame God, when human intervention could have alleviated or prevented some evil. Even in so-called acts of God, which are simply natural events, one has to question the extent to which human indifference or negligence has played its part in exacerbating the disaster. For example, an earthquake, regarded solely as such, is relatively harmless — it causes a split or shift in the earth's crust and some trembling. In a natural state — or if we were in that state of innocence where we *all* loved one another — it would cause little damage. It is we who build huge metropolises in earthquake zones, often of substandard construction and materials, and then rescind all responsibility for our part in the suffering caused. It is we who pollute the environment and undermine the ecology; or skew the economy to favor a few while shouldering the poor into perilous ghettos. We do not need to build cities at the foot of volcanoes, especially when history has repeatedly warned us of the danger. Constantly to require God miraculously to intervene in the course of affairs, when we have the foresight, ingenuity and resources to mitigate or avoid these occurrences, and thereby remove the danger to others, stunts our personal development, condemning us to moral infancy. For these reasons, God works through secondary causes which include us and call us to greater and more heroic acts of virtue in order to elevate our moral stature. Therefore, rather than asking why does God permit the innocent to suffer, we should be asking why do we do so?

Second consequence: *It is fitting to God's Wisdom that the beings he willed to create were placed in connection with one another so as to form of them a single harmonious whole.*

Since individuals are interdependent upon one another, their good and evil actions impinge upon one another throughout the nexus of human interaction. Because of this there is something in the system of things that reacts and does not let evil go too far. Moral evil rests ultimately upon selfishness and is therefore self-negating. No murderer can continue to murder for very long, because the very self-interest which motivated one to claim the life of another will also motivate others to restrain further evil acts. Eventually a thief will be stopped. Liars will no longer be heeded. Even promiscuity radiates an ecological niche which harbors the proliferation of organisms some of which become deadly. Moreover, the promiscuous communicate their inability or refusal to form permanent relationships, not to mention the psychological and spiritual debility that ensues.

Take the act of adultery. A single act of betrayal can lead to the destruction of an integrity that was once sacred. It leads to animosity and pain for the adults and heartache and confusion for the children. Professionals and others outside the relationship are drawn in to sort out the mess. And the adulterous partners? The third party in the relationship has now inherited someone who is capable of committing adultery and deceit; while the adulterer, in turn, has formed a liaison with someone who scorns the sanctity of marriage and whose selfishness is indifferent to the pain and disruption one's actions cause others. How can they trust one another? Upon what foundation can they build a solid and vital relationship?

Thus evil contains within itself its own limits which work throughout the human system in a self-negating way. This principle of negative feedback in general occurs when functional elements in a system loop back upon themselves so that part of the information serves to dampen or impede the functioning elements. This occurs in neurophysiology, computer circuits, ecology, and society. Because it comprises the possibility of being able to adjust future conduct by past performance, it can lead to social policy reform; while throughout the system negative feedback can promote stability by dampening undesirable variety.[23]

In contrast, goodness, because it is mutually benevolent, provides an example of positive feedback. Rather than impeding itself, it serves reciprocally to enhance the relationships. Each act of goodness tends to elicit similar acts promoting benevolence throughout the system. Whereas a society of utterly selfish, self-serving individuals ends up

---

23 See Norbert Wiener, *The Human Use of Human Beings* (New York: Avon Books, 1967); W. Ross Ashby, *An Introduction to Cybernetics* (London: Methuen, 1956), 80, 91.

frustrating itself through internal contradictions, a society of completely unselfish and loving people would simply thrive upon the inherent generosity of each towards each. Such caring would only serve to elicit more acts of love binding one another together ever more intimately. A loving world would expand infinitely under its own *élan vital*. It would continue to flourish until such time as it would be confronted by some evil.

While it was possible for us to imagine a totally benevolent society, it is impossible to imagine a totally evil one. For an evil system *to persist* it must limit the destructiveness of its members if only so that they can continue to indulge their evil appetites. The evil society must maintain a minimal degree of organization and control simply to perdure. Such a system would fight to defend its population, while striving to furnish the basic requisites for survival. It would even struggle to defend the predominant hierarchy. An evil society, precisely because it is essentially self-inhibiting, would smolder in incessant internal conflict and oppression. Should God finally separate good from evil, pure good would eternally flourish from its own benevolent bounty; whereas a *thoroughly evil* system would be impossible because it would immediately destroy itself. Absolute evil is inconceivable simply because it is utter *non*-being. Therefore, the mere continuance of a predominantly evil regime necessitates, in spite of itself, a measured order.

Third consequence: *It was fitting that the universe be ordered according to the principles of gradation and variety.*

Because all creatures are necessarily limited, the Creator, in order to produce the greatest good, has brought into being an enormous variety and gradation of creatures from quarks to quasars, from amoebae to angels, with humanity occupying the middle sphere. We have already marveled at the fact that the entire cosmos, with all its various forces and properties, ordered with exquisite precision and perfect balance, is necessary to generate and sustain our world and ultimately us. It is as though God wanted to manifest his glory through the sheer grandeur and variety of perfections displayed. So among us humans, a great diversity and gradation of individuals are observed. The Law of Least Means requires that God should draw the maximum good by distributing the maximum variety of skills, abilities, propensities, and knowledge among us so that each of us can fulfill ourselves by contributing variously to the whole. There is enough opportunity for each one of us uniquely to give of oneself at each person's own level and sphere, with every part forming its necessary link and every evil or privation providing its opportunity for good.

These opportunities for good also serve to sanctify those who are of good will. Not only does patience in the face of suffering sanctify, but our good works increase virtue in our souls. This flowering of virtue leads to further acts of goodness and to a consequent expansion in character. Virtue then becomes an habitual quality attaching to our souls, and the strength of character which it engenders renders our souls pleasing to God and predisposes us towards him. We grow closer to him, loving him more and becoming more beautiful thereby. Growing in virtue we become happier even in the midst of suffering, which in turn renders us more meritorious in God's eyes from whom we receive even more grace. This is the secret understood by all the saints.[24]

Fourth consequence: *The delight that God takes in the variety and gradation of creatures leads to a fourth consequence: the Law of Formal Inclusion. Wisdom has for her end the complete realization of the formal species, not the mere multiplication of individuals.*

St. Thomas teaches that insofar as God creates us for the end of participating in his goodness (for God is the Supreme Good), then a spiritual or formal good is far more excellent than a material one. In Thomas's words: "In substances the matter exists for the form; *since it is by the form that they partake of the divine goodness,* for the sake of which all things have been made."[25] Every being acts in accordance with its nature, including God. For God, who acts with supreme wisdom, must act for his own glory since his Wisdom is identical to his Substance. By this Wisdom God has allotted to creatures their several forms through which they partake of the Divine

---

24 Mt 5:11; Rom 5:3–5; 1 Pet 2:19, 3:14, 4:12–14, 5:10; Jas 1:12, 5:7–11.
25 *Contra Gentiles*, III.75, n. 6.

Goodness. All things are created with God as their end, and insofar as they realize their ends in their variety of forms, they are good and God's wisdom is manifested. All creation is a symphony to God. All nature bows in adoration of the Creator.

We too have been given the opportunity of harmonizing our voices with this universal chorus. We do this by directing our moral appreciation and affection not just to the concrete thing known, but to the Eternal Essence which is exemplified in the several perfections manifested throughout creation. Thus the finitude and privation of every creature become the occasion for worship and adoration. The negative through lack reveals the positive. This is another example of the analogy of being.

Furthermore, through esteeming in each creature that quality or excellence of the species which is realized in that concrete individual, we honor the Exemplary Cause. To treat each creature in relation to its proper end, and not abuse it, is a manifestation of respect for the Creator. For by loving one of them we love them all, honoring the Divine idea embodied in each. Human beings have been given the free choice to use or abuse the animate and inanimate creatures placed in their stewardship. If they are used properly we benefit, natural law is realized in its purpose, and God's benevolence is affirmed. If they are abused, the complexus is interrupted, we suffer, and God's justice is served. Either way the wisdom of the natural law is manifested.

There is another advantage gained by formal inclusion or, what is entailed, the permission of variety within the formal species: the measure of God's love is gauged by the degree of being, and therefore of goodness in a thing (since goodness and being are convertible), not by any disorder which actually or possibly accrues to a creature. This means that God's love for us is not diminished by any accidental privation or perversion of our nature. Nor is his love for us increased by our accomplishments. In short, God loves us for what we are *essentially*—for the *universal* idea or *form* we embody: for we are made in his image as beings who are intellectually aware. God loves truth, goodness, and beauty, for all these participate in him. Therefore, evil cannot destroy God's love for those of good will who faithfully trust in him and seek to conform to him. On the contrary, "God works everything for good for those who love him and are called according to his purpose."[26]

But the real benefit is mystical. By having excluded parity from all created things, the good is maximized because each concrete entity exists for the whole nature so that each creature is but a reflection of some aspect of the Divine Goodness. Since everything is the embodiment of form and each form is a perfection reflective of Divine Wisdom, then anything utilized or accomplished in a spirit of adoration or love for goodness as its end is done for the glory of God and brings us into the life of God. Because of the analogy of being and because all creation is contingent upon God's sustaining activity, when any thing or action is ordered to God, used or performed in the appropriate manner, reverencing his will for each thing, in a spirit of devotion, and we also submitting to his will in this, then our life as a whole becomes infused with grace. We become gracious and our lives become works of art.

Thus, in the notable words of Malebranche:

> God can only act for himself, only through the love that he bears for himself, only from his will, which is not as in us an impression which comes to him from somewhere else and leads him elsewhere. In a word, he acts only for his glory, only to express the Divine perfections which he invincibly loves, which he glories in possessing, and in which he delights by the necessity of his Being. He wants that, in its beauty and its magnificence, his work bear the character of his excellence and his greatness and that his ways do not contradict his infinite Wisdom and his immutability.... For the beauty of the Universe and for the salvation of men, he did everything he can do — not absolutely, but acting as he must act: for his glory in accordance with his nature. He loves all things in proportion as they are lovable. He wants the beauty of his work and the salvation of all men; he desires the

---

26 Rom 8:28.

> conversion of all sinners. But he loves his Wisdom more: he loves it invincibly, follows it inviolably. The immutable order of his Divine perfections comprises his law and the rule of his conduct, a law which does not prohibit him from loving us and wanting all his creatures to be just, holy, happy, and perfect, yet a law which does not permit him to depart at every moment from the generality of his ways for the sake of sinners. His Providence bears sufficient marks of his goodness toward men.[27]

This sustaining activity is necessitated by God's eternal nature. Indeed, Boethius has bequeathed to us and for all time that profound delineation of the personal nature of the Eternal as: "the complete, simultaneous, and perfect possession of everlasting life."[28] Since this is clearly a property of the mind of God, then, it follows that:

> His knowledge, too, transcends all temporal change and abides in the immediacy of his presence. It embraces all the infinite recesses of past and future and views them in the immediacy of its knowing as though they are happening in the present. If you wish to consider, then, the foreknowledge or prevision by which he discovers all things, it will be more correct to think of it not as a kind of foreknowledge of the future, but as the knowledge of a never-ending presence. So that it is better called Providence, or "looking forth" than prevision or "seeing beforehand." For it is far removed from matters below and looks forth at things as though from a lofty peak above them.[29]

Of course, the power of this knowledge, which embraces all things in its consummate understanding, owes nothing to events which come after it, and, therefore, places no obstacle to human freedom. Rather, human freedom remains inviolate and reward and punishment (as understood in the mind of God) are not imposed unfairly, because our will is free from all necessity: "God has foreknowledge and rests a

---

27 Malebranche, *Dialogues on Metaphysics*, xii, xxi.
28 *Consolation of Philosophy*, Bk. 5, VI, p. 169.
29 Ibid., 171.

spectator from on high of all things; and as the ever-present eternity of His vision dispenses reward to the good and punishment to the bad, it adapts itself to the future quality of our actions. Hope is not placed in God in vain and prayers are not made in vain, for if they are the right kind they cannot but be efficacious."[30]

Fifth consequence: *When God by his providence has obtained all possible good from all the activities of his creatures, it accords with his goodness that God should then add his own immediate action, so as to produce in them and to derive from them that good which they could not accomplish by themselves; while universally conserving, by this supernatural action also, the law of the least means.*

The existence of God expands the horizons of our hope, for it perforce opens the possibility of the timely intervention of God in history. This intervention includes choosing a people to unite unto himself and calling forth leaders on their behalf, his transmission to them of certain prophecies through chosen individuals, the providential advancement of salvation history, and even the consummate revelation of his Wisdom in and through the Person of his Divine Son. It also includes miracles.

The possibility of revelation, prophecy, or miracles ought not to be a difficulty in a theistic universe. For God does not communicate his power to move minds randomly, but only after having foreseen all the consequences of the movements of minds, including the effects of matter. Because all causes can act only through the efficacy of Divine Will, Hume's objection, that through such prodigies the laws of the universe are violated, simply betrays the fallacy of equivocation.[31] Laws are not forces in nature: they are merely observed regularities which can permit exceptions. For example, the law of conservation of matter-energy is not violated by the spontaneous appearance of virtual particles, provided they appear and disappear within the boundaries of Planck time. Again, quantum entanglement or superposition is no exception to the law that two objects cannot

---

30 Ibid., 175. Also see *Catechism of the Catholic Church* 600 & 1037.
31 If one cannot discern the nexus between cause and effect, then how can Hume know that these laws cannot be contravened even by God?

be in the same place at the same time. The quantum field being simpler than the particles or waves it contains is more inclusive and not bounded by the restrictions upon subordinate contours within the field. The universe is rational, to be sure, and insofar as it is the reflection of Divine Reason, there is no offence committed when God by some higher law or principle intervenes in a timely fashion. The only difficulty standing in the way of belief in miracles is either prejudice or a lack of faith. God can do anything—i.e., anything possible—and who can delimit the possible, especially when considering the omnipotence and omniscience and inclusivity of the Being behind all that is?

It gives substance to prayer. For it is most seemly that God should so arrange things that we are able to intercede on behalf of others and thereby obtain help for them and at the same time provide opportunities for our own sanctification. Once again the eternal Wisdom of God is manifest through the bestowal upon us of the dignity of cooperating even in supernatural works. As we shall observe throughout the remainder of this book, people are called upon to participate in the Divine Life through works of prayer and sacrifice in intercession for others, bringing down upon themselves many gifts. The respect and reverence that God has for us, his creatures, is shown to us by his associating us with the work of grace and bestows upon us a dignity and nobility in imitation of even that of Christ.[32] This is the substance of the analogy of being.

SUMMARY AND PROSPECT

This last consequence takes us beyond the limits of natural reason to the question of faith and must bring the first part of this book to an end. Having followed the idea of being in general, we have learned that the existence of God is a certain and natural conviction of the human intellect such that to doubt it leads to our having to embrace absurdity: that existence has no ultimate explanation. Furthermore, we have found that the repeated use of the analogy of being enables us, although not without difficulty, to discern principles and marvels

---

32 1 Cor 11:1; Eph 5:1; Phil 2:3–8; 1 Jn 2:6. See also Mt 5:48; Jn 13:12–15.

beyond the mere appearance of things which establish our confidence in our affirmation of the existence of a necessary Being. For not only did we discover just how wonderful and elegant the cosmos is or how precisely ordered and balanced it is, but by peering into its nature we discovered a bizarre and fascinating world — utterly contingent — demanding the existence of a necessary, more inclusive and, therefore, simple Substance that sustains and forms it. Finally, turning to the paradox of the existence of evil, rather than finding a contradiction to our proposition, we discerned a wisdom and an economy which further confirmed our conviction. God exists, and evil, far from being a contradiction, has been subsumed within the scheme of things to maximize goodness. Evil, being a privation or distortion of the good, cannot exist except as a parasite upon the good, but goodness in order to perdure can only respond through increase. This principle is evident throughout history, natural as well as human, as we have shown.

Thus, the objection — that the existence of a benevolent and all-powerful God is somehow negated by the existence of evil — defeats itself, because it does not take its own assumptions seriously. For if, as is hypothesized, God is all powerful, then he can bring good out of evil, and if he is supremely good then he will assuredly do so. This answer is precisely the one given by God to Job's question as to why the innocent suffer. For if the book of Job is read canonically, one will readily perceive that the thrice-holy God of Israel is most certainly all powerful and pre-eminently good; but that he works unseen behind the cloud that veils his Presence. Moreover, at its conclusion the book relates those specific goods that God did bring forth by restoring to Job — *while he was interceding for his friends* — double of what he had before, including (figuratively!) an incredibly long life. Thus, although we may not fully understand why God "hides his face," nevertheless we may be certain that the Divine Wisdom cannot but act providentially. For indeed, such has been the promise given throughout the Scriptures that God will finally provide his decisive answer to the question of evil: the fruits of which are offered to us who suffer in this "vale of tears."

Then I saw a new heaven and a new earth; for the first heaven and the first earth had passed away, and the sea was no more. And I saw the holy city, new Jerusalem, coming down out of heaven from God, prepared as a bride adorned for her husband; and I heard a great voice from the throne saying, "Behold, the dwelling of God is with men. He will dwell with them, and they shall be his people, and God himself will be with them; he will wipe away every tear from their eyes, and death shall be no more, neither shall there be mourning nor crying nor pain any more, for the former things have passed away." And he who sat on the throne said, "Behold, I make all things new."[33]

This has been the hope of all the saints, as we shall see.

As far as moral evil is concerned, arising as it does from our own free natures, evil remains essentially a scandal and an affront to God, demanding our response. However, it is not the petulant response of blaming God for our sins of commission or omission, and then relishing this opportunity to deny his existence, but rather the catalyst for a change of mind and heart which becomes open to all possibilities inspiring us to ever greater goodness and virtue, even including that of offering our sufferings in intercession to God, and the transformation and mystical union which that can bring.

*   *   *

Is God then personal? Has God sought to make himself known? Is there evidence in human history of individuals who have known him in a personal way? Has he established a community under his protection and guidance? Does God's largesse embrace even the lowliest individual? Does God's love extend to providing the very means to raise us above our proud and selfish natures? To these questions of faith we now turn, where we will discover a solemn but sublime resolution to the problem of personal pain, and then we shall be able to savor just "how rich and deep are the wisdom and the knowledge of God."[34]

---

33   Rev 21:1–5. See also Rev 21:8; Rom 14:11–12; Phil 2:10–11.
34   Rom 11:33.

PART TWO

WISDOM

*I am the light of the world;
he who follows me will not walk in darkness,
but will have the light of life.*
John 8:12

CHAPTER 4

Son of God

*In all truth I tell you,
before Abraham was,
I am.*[1]

AVING APPLIED OUR NATURAL REASON by the light of the analogy of being to the understanding of reality, we have come to the formal conviction that there exists a Being who is the creator and sustainer of all that is. As such this Being is eternal, immaterial, infinite, and all powerful and has the transcendent qualities of unity, truth, and goodness as well as beauty, since all perfections are grounded therein. We have found that the evidence from cosmology and quantum physics has confirmed this and has enriched our appreciation of the powers of the human intellect to discern this reality with remarkable precision, predictive power, and heurism, albeit from a distance. So intricately and precisely structured is the universe, so rational and mathematical its design, that we can *by analogy*[2] even attribute to its Creator the quality of intelligence—since more cannot come from less. For the entire universe seems to be formed for the purpose of supporting conscious intelligences like us. Especially so, since we have intimated the marvelous economy by which every finite thing is ordained to bring about the maximum amount of good, even from privation, and in particular, our own moral and spiritual flowering. Thus, far from contradicting the existence of God, we have also discovered that the presence of evil in the world has a purpose which enables the Creator to bring about even greater good through the cooperation of human freedom than if God had refused us this faculty, leaving us in the state of animals.

---

1 Jn 8:58.
2 Analogy of proportion, not similitude.

We have called this Being "God," but we cannot yet affirm, solely on the basis of what we have discovered so far, that God is truly personal—i.e., that God is anything more than the deistic conception of some substantial, elegant, eternal Principle grounding spacetime. Three monotheistic faiths—Judaism, Christianity, and Islam—conceive of God with very similar attributes to those we have delineated above, but believe that he is also personal. However, of these only Christianity claims that the very Wisdom of God has manifested itself to us in the person of the man, Jesus of Nazareth. This extraordinary claim, if true, would establish the personhood of God immediately, since we take personhood to be a rational *suppositum*. Now human beings are clearly rational *supposita* as we have demonstrated. We have the light of being: we are ontologically self-aware, knowing ourselves as beings—a concept which is the foundation of all knowing. By establishing that Jesus Christ knows himself *as God*, we would confirm the personhood of God directly. This is the gravity of the present chapter.

SOME METHODOLOGICAL OBSERVATIONS

Before we begin, it is essential to present our methodology and the reasons for its adoption. We have demonstrated that when speaking about the nature of anything one can only take the middle way between univocity and equivocity by appealing to the principle of the analogy of being. Capable of discerning form, but not substance, the remarkable insights afforded to us through the application of this principle enabled us to trace the likenesses of Being in created things. Because the question of Jesus's self-consciousness involves the nature of his personal identity with God, we shall find it profitable to use this principle in this present investigation. Finally, since Jesus was a Jew living in a Jewish religious context, it is natural to ask if Jesus was aware of a personal identity with the God of Abraham, Isaac, and Jacob.[3]

Since the evidence for our understanding of Jesus's self-consciousness comes solely from the Gospels, it is essential that we clarify our

---

3 Ex 3:15.

position regarding them. It is our considered opinion that the Gospels can at last be treated as early, eyewitness accounts taken from the personal testimonies of named individuals, rather than layered traditions representing unknown, hypothetical communities as previously surmised by the form theorists. Before substantiating our own view of the nature of the Gospels, we must invalidate the latter theory. However, in order to pursue that adequately, we must first look at the limits of empirical methods in general.

The limits of method

During the Middle Ages theology was the queen of the sciences because its assumptions rested upon the revelation of God in Jesus Christ and because the formal conclusions derived therefrom were tautological.[4] However, ever since Francis Bacon (1521–1626) presented his inductive method as the certain way to truth and Kant produced his *Critiques,* empirical science began to supplant the formal sciences, eventually proffering itself as the sole vanguard of knowledge (*scientia*). But subsequent to these early philosophers of science, some others began to doubt empiricism's sole claims to truth. The result has been a severe restriction upon what the empirical sciences can claim to know beyond brute facts.

Now all methodologists agree that any empirical method or measurement must be valid, i.e., that it must accomplish or measure what it is designed to do. This results from the principle of identity. For example, if one is to measure the cosmic background radiation from the Big Bang, one has to ascertain that one is not measuring something else (radio transmissions, noise from nearby stars, tremors from within the earth, etc.), otherwise the results will be irrelevant. The difficulty, however, is that one cannot demonstrate validity purely on methodological grounds, i.e., inductively, because this will involve one in an infinite regress — of using a method whose validity has yet to be established in order then to determine the validity of the first method and so forth.[5] The validity of a method can only be argued

---

4 And because of the supreme excellence of its subject.
5 This is essentially the thrust of Chaitin's proof that no mechanical procedure exists that will decide in a finite number of steps if a program is likely to halt at

for formally, but formal arguments (e.g., theories) must be tested empirically.[6]

However, there is a possible way around this aporia: the principle of reliability. This principle requires that all reliable methods should produce consistent results which can be replicated by others, and, since every valid method is also reliable,[7] if the results of one's method are replicable, then, at least, validity is not confounded. Obviously, if the method is unreliable, it cannot then be valid, because if it is giving inconsistent results, it is not consistently measuring what it is supposed to. Thus, if one can argue formally that one's method is valid, then, provided it is also reliable, tentatively all is well. However, there are two difficulties with this: the problems of reference and of empirical proof.

Taking the problem of reference first: for a theory to be empirically valid, at least some of its concepts must refer to or correspond to the real world. Otherwise it remains purely formal. However, William Craig has proved,[8] propositionally, that one cannot by empirical methods replace a hypothetical construct or "auxiliary expression" with a verifiable referent, i.e., an observable entity.[9] A hypothetical construct or auxiliary expression is any idea which cannot be directly observed, such as energy, superstring, ego, or Q.[10] However, there can never be an empirical method that will replace all the purely theoretical entities in a theory with something which *is* empirically verifiable. Craig has used Gödel's theorem to prove that all theories will contain some

---

a given solution. See Gregory Chaitin, "A Random Walk in Arithmetic," *New Scientist*, 24 March 1990, 30–32.

6 For example, in chapter two we used the evidence of cosmology and quantum physics to support the proposition (formally demonstrated in chapter one) that there must be an Intelligence behind the cosmos. And in chapter three we used examples from systems theory to show that good does come out of evil.

7 This also follows from the principle of identity, since if a method measures what it is supposed to, the results will change only if the identity of the object should change. This is rare, since it is the accidents which change.

8 William Craig, "The Replacement of Auxiliary Expressions," *Philosophical Review* 65 (1956): 38–45.

9 P. W. Bridgeman had previously proposed the substitution of operational definitions for hypotheticals.

10 Q is a hypothetical source document for the material which the Gospels of Luke and Matthew have in common against Mark.

propositions whose status of being either hypothetical or observable is undecidable within the formalism of the theory. It is impossible, in other words, to judge whether or not a given theory maps reality better than another, because there will always remain in any theory expressions whose reference to the real world is undecidable. This means that one cannot design a method that will verify all the unobservable (hypothetical) concepts in a theory. The consequence is that we can never create a theory consisting *solely* of empirically observable terms or expressions until all possible *empirical* investigations are completed. Until that is done one cannot know that one's theory still retains terms which have no real referent. One cannot, therefore, compare theories to determine which is the more referential or the more applicable to reality, because one cannot determine which has the least unobservable content; and one cannot do that because one cannot know that all possible observations have been made. And if the content of a theory is unobservable, then *ipso facto* that theory is unempirical.

But why would we want to compare the real content of one theory with another? Can we not simply prove the theory true and have done with it? The answer is no because of what is known as the fallacy of affirming the consequent. In any empirical method, a testable proposition, p, is expected to yield the consequent observation, q. The logical rule of *modus ponens* requires that: if p implies q, and provided that p (the antecedent) is indeed the case, then q follows necessarily. However, an actual observation can only determine if the *consequent* (q) is confirmed. A confirmation of the predicted outcome can only *support* the conclusion, q, but does not prove that q necessarily follows from p. Logical implication in this case does not point backwards, since it could be objected that something else could also account for the observation. One also has to eliminate the objections.[11] This was the solution of F. S. C. Northrop:

> The introduction of crucial experiments in order to mitigate the danger of the fallacy of affirming the consequent in the mere experimental confirmation of a scientific theory without the consideration of other theoretical possibilities,

---

11   As we did in chapters two and three.

means that there can be no trustworthy science, even with experimental confirmation ... unless as much attention is given by scientists to the consideration of theory and of rival theoretical possibilities and to deductive logic as is given to induction, factual data, and experimentation. The point is that the mere experimental confirmation of a scientific theory through its deductive consequences is not generally regarded by competent scientists as a sufficient criterion of the scientific validity of that theory. One must go further and show as far as possible that the theory in question is the only one which is capable, through its deductive consequences, of taking care of the natural history data.[12]

Then can one simply empirically falsify the opposing theory, leaving one's own supported theory the only remaining logical choice? Again, no: theories are too complex to be falsified empirically. They consist of undefined terms, axioms, unobservable referents, and propositions derived from axioms, leading hopefully to some testable propositions, i.e., hypotheses. It is, therefore, practically impossible empirically to falsify the entire content of a theory.

In fact, one cannot even compare theories according to their truth content. Miller and Tichy[13] have proven that, for two separate theories A and B, it is impossible to determine that A has more or less verisimilitude (truth content) than B. The adequate comparison of the verisimilitude of two theories involves the ability to determine the total number of true and false propositions within these theories, including the propositions used to make that argument. But to determine that would implicate one in attempting to establish the entire truth content of one's own language in order to avoid an infinite regress. Moreover, Gödel's undecidability theorem shows that all formal theories contain propositions whose truth is undecidable.

---

12 F. S. C. Northrop, "The Method and Theories of Physical Science in their Bearing upon Biological Organization," quoted in R. W. Marks, *Great Ideas in Modern Science* (New York: Bantam, 1967), 45.
13 See W. H. Newton-Smith, *The Rationality of Science* (Boston: Routledge & Kegan Paul, 1981), 58.

Therefore, there will always be, within any well-constructed (*wff*) theory, propositions comprising statements whose truth or falsity is undeterminable, making it impossible to compare the falsity content of a given theory with another. Only hypotheses can be falsified as specified by the rule of *modus tollens*.[14]

For these reasons, reliability — the production of consistent results — remains the essential criterion in any method used to confirm a theory. A method found to be unreliable is *ipso facto* invalid and that method must be rejected in favor of one that reliably tests the theory. Without a reliable method to support it, the theory is to be regarded as mere speculation. All things being equal, therefore, theories with reliable (i.e., objective) methods to support them are to be preferred over those consisting of hypotheticals.

The resulting stipulation for modern (empirical) science is that one must construct formal theories which generate some empirically falsifiable propositions, i.e., hypotheses. Observations which test these hypotheses are performed and, if they are not falsified, but supported by replicable *objective* evidence, then the tentative theory survives until a more elegant theory comes along.[15] In the meantime such theories are to be considered as only explanatory models or analogies because of the problem of the presence of auxiliaries or unobservable referents discussed above. This is all that *any* empirical method can do, whether, for example, in physics, biology, the behavioral or social sciences, or in historical-critical methods such as form criticism.

Form criticism

In the light of what has been said above we shall briefly examine the validity of the methodology of form criticism. Form criticism (*Formgeschichte*) was first applied systematically to the Gospels just after World War I by three German scholars: K. L. Schmidt, M. Dibelius, and R. Bultmann. Working independently they sought to identify the primitive oral forms behind the various literary sources of the

---

14 Recall from chapter 1 that *modus tollens* specifies: if p then q, ~q, therefore ~p.
15 Providing, of course, that it does not multiply redundant entities as specified by Ockham's principle of parsimony. A theory which is parsimonious, comprehensive, consistent, and harmonious is described as having elegance.

Gospels in order to discover their history (*Geschichte*), i.e., to trace the development of these hypothetical units of oral tradition (*pericopae*) during what they presumed was a long period of time. These isolated units were then threaded together like beads on a string and arranged according to the purposes and needs of the communities who preserved them. Moreover, they were especially interested in uncovering the situation in the life (*Sitz im Leben*) of these communities which, it was again assumed, had collected, selected, preserved, and transmitted these traditions. This life context, comprising the existential needs, problems, and hopes of the post-Easter communities, was believed to exert a determining influence upon the shaping and retention of the oral forms as they were handed down within these communities. For Bultmann, this meant that "the forms of the literary tradition must be used to establish the influences operating in the life of the community, and the life of the community must be used to render the forms themselves intelligible."[16] The result was a demarcation and polarization between the Christ of faith and the Jesus of history. It was Bultmann who notoriously said that "we can know practically nothing about Jesus's life and personality, since the Christian sources had no interest in such matters."[17] This method, which grew up as an application of twentieth-century existentialist philosophy to a first-century Jewish milieu, has mesmerized and controlled New Testament exegesis ever since.

Yet there is not a single scrap of hard evidence to support any of the hypotheses upon which form criticism was built. They are all hypothetical constructs. There was no independent empirical evidence to support the idea that the Gospels were late, no evidence to suggest that *communities* wrote or edited the Gospels, no evidence that the existential needs of communities shaped oral tradition.[18] The entire edifice was built like a house of cards where every hypothesis or "suggestion" supported each other but rested upon no firm, independent, empirical evidence. The idea that the Gospels consisted of layers of

---

16 Rudolph Bultmann, *The History of the Synoptic Tradition* (New York: Harper & Row, 1963), 5.
17 Rudolph Bultmann, *Jesus and the Word* (New York: Scribner, 1958), 8.
18 In fact this is contradicted by Paul's letters to the Corinthians which are critical of that community.

tradition like strata in an archaeological record was simply assumed and accepted without evidence by the exegetes who spent their careers endeavoring to save the theory against mounting criticism.

And the criticisms were many:[19] many of the classifications of Dibelius and Bultmann do not depend on literary form, but on content; form tells us nothing about the historical reliability of a tradition; a reliable taxonomy of forms has failed to be accepted; the dating of the forms is inexact, confused, and inconsistent; an extended oral period of transmission has not been proved; the traditions were not always preserved because of the value to the community, but because they were held to be the sacred words and deeds of Jesus; it neglects the fact that sacred traditions become canonical, determining which traditions are to be accepted into the community; it denies the abundant emphasis upon geographical and biographical details in the Gospels; it ignores the controlling influence of contemporary eyewitnesses; it requires commitment to an unproven philosophical perspective (existentialism); and the "beads-on-a-string" hypothesis has been contradicted by the unity and overall construction of the Gospels revealed by literary analysis.

In addition to these, Richard Bauckham, professor of New Testament studies at the University of St Andrews, adds: there is no reason why traditions should not have existed originally in modified or mixed forms; there is no correlation between a given form and a *Sitz im Leben*; there are no consistent continuous laws of tradition; form criticism assumes a comparability with folklore which is not accurate;

---

19 See Robert Alter and Frank Kermode, *The Literary Guide to the Bible* (London: Fontana, 1987); Brevard S. Childs, *The New Testament as Canon* (London: SCM, 1984); John Drane, *Introducing the New Testament* (Sydney: Lion Publishing, 1986), 176–89; H. H. Hutson, "Form Criticism in the New Testament," *Journal of Bible and Religion* 19 (1951): 130–33; G. E. Ladd, *New Testament and Criticism* (Grand Rapids: William Eerdmans Publishing, 1983), 141–62; Tremper Longman III, *Literary Approaches to Biblical Interpretation* (Grand Rapids: Academie Books, 1987); Robert H. Stein, *The Synoptic Problem* (Grand Rapids: Baker Book House, 1987); Stephen H. Travis, "Form Criticism," in I. Howard Marshall, ed., *New Testament Interpretation* (Grand Rapids: William B. Eerdmans Publishing, 1985), 153–62; Bruce K. Waltke, "Oral Tradition," in Harvie M. Conn, ed., *Inerrancy and Hermeneutic* (Grand Rapids: Baker Book House, 1988), 117–35.

a distinction between Palestinian and Hellenistic communities has not been established; the implicit denial that written records were kept is no longer tenable; the anthropological evidence from oral communities shows that they exert an exacting, controlling influence upon traditions considered sacred in distinction to those recognized as merely legendary.[20]

Given what we know from philosophy of science, it is clear that form criticism has produced unreliable results, and if it is unreliable it *cannot* be a valid method. As Professor Bauckham concludes:

> Even a few of these criticisms would be sufficient to undermine the whole form-critical enterprise. There is no reason to believe that the oral transmission of Jesus traditions in the early church was at all as Bultmann envisaged it. It is remarkable that this is not more widely acknowledged explicitly, though, once one is aware of it, it is not difficult to see that many contemporary Gospels scholars acknowledge it implicitly by ignoring form criticism in its classical form. But what form criticism has bequeathed as a long enduring legacy is the largely unexamined *impression* that many scholars — and probably even more students — still entertain: the impression of a long period of creative development of the traditions before they attained written form in the Gospels. The retention of such an impression is not defensible unless it is justified afresh, for *the arguments of the form critics no longer hold water.*[21]

Given that form criticism as such must be rejected as intrinsically invalid, there is now no longer any reason merely to suppose a late date for the Gospels. Rather than simply accepting the hypothetical constructions of the form-critical method and its temporizing perspective, we are now free once again to take seriously the extant *objective* evidence for the dates of the Gospels.[22]

---

20 Richard Bauckham, *Jesus and the Eyewitnesses: The Gospels as Eyewitness Testimony* (Grand Rapids: William B. Eerdmans, 2006), 246–47.
21 Ibid., 249. Final italics added.
22 One of the regrettable outcomes of this sort of "scholarship" was the constant attack on the reputability or authenticity of any documentary evidence

The Gospels as early, eyewitness testimony

That the *Acts of the Apostles* is early can be inferred from its failure to chronicle significant events such as Nero's persecution from AD 64–68, the deaths of St James the less in 62, of St Peter c. 64, and St Paul c. 66–67, the Jewish revolt and the flight of Christians to Pella in 66, climaxing with the prophesied fall of Jerusalem in AD 70. Even so, scholars desiring a late date for Acts have objected, without evidence, that Luke "wanted" to end with Paul still alive, triumphantly preaching in Rome. But if such a flourish is needed, then why not end with the greatest sacrifice one can make for the Gospel: martyrdom? Why would Luke deprive Paul's life's testimony of this victorious crown?[23] One can only imagine how jarring this would sound to Theophilus, to whom the book is addressed, and how disparaging it is of St Luke who had written his Gospel with the intention of providing an accurate, orderly, truthful account (*diegesis*).[24] However, an alternative to this claim — that in Acts Luke intentionally modified the ending to a historical narrative directed to an eminent contemporary — is given by the Muratorian Canon.[25]

> The third book of the Gospel, that according to Luke, was compiled in his own name on Paul's authority by Luke the physician, when *after Christ's ascension Paul had taken him to be with him like a legal expert.* Yet neither did he

---

that contradicted their assumed dating of the Gospels or other Biblical books. Thus, the testimonies of Josephus, Clement, Irenaeus, Eusebius, etc. were all considered untrustworthy casting a slur on their reputations, which are only recently being repaired.

23   Given the expectation of Paul's eventual death placed in the reader by Acts 9:15–16 and 21:13, the existing ending is an anticlimax. Paul's death would be the "natural" ending. See also Acts 5:41, 14:22.

24   Lk 1:3–4. Luke was not writing a modern novel, but followed an established Greek genre.

25   It was discovered in 1740 by Ludovico Muratori (1672–1750), scholar, historian, and antiquary, who is regarded as the father of Italian history. This fragment of eighty-five lines consists of a list of those New Testament books considered canonical at the time. Composed in Rome, it can be dated to the third quarter of the second century because of its assertion that Hermas wrote *The Shepherd* "*lately in our times* while his brother Pius, the bishop, was sitting in the chair of the church of the city of Rome" (Pope Pius I: AD 140–55).

Part Two: Wisdom

see the Lord in the flesh; and he too, as he was able to ascertain events, begins his story from the birth of John.

* * *

The Acts of all the apostles, however, are written in one book. Luke, *to the most excellent Theophilus,* includes events *because they were done in his own presence,* as he also plainly shows *by leaving out* the passion of Peter, and also *the departure of Paul* from the City on his journey to Spain.

Thus, Luke included in Acts those events to which he also was a witness, not constrained to rely solely upon eyewitnesses as in his earlier Gospel. The passion of Peter was not included, even though (as is assumed) Luke knew of it, because he was not present at that time. But if that is so, why was the omission of the death of St Paul not also justified by the Canon, given the supposition that Acts was written later? If the exclusion of St Peter's martyrdom required an explanation, then all the more does that of St Paul, who is the principal character in Acts. The contention of the Muratorian document is that Luke did not have to omit the death of St Paul, but only his departure from Rome, because he *was still alive and was on his way to Spain,*[26] to which Luke (who apparently had left for Philippi c. AD 62[27]) was not a witness.

The supposition that Luke "doctored" his endings cannot be accepted without independent documentary confirmation against Luke's honesty, objectivity, and thoroughness as a historian. For these reasons we conclude that these historical markers require a date for Acts around AD 64–65. Therefore, it follows that Luke's Gospel must

---

26 "After reaching the *limits of the West* [Paul] bore witness before the rulers." Clement of Rome, *First Epistle to the Corinthians* (5:7). Paul made it to Spain comfortably after his release: cf. Joseph Holzner, *Paul of Tarsus* (London: Scepter, 2008). Paul was rearrested and sentenced to death c. AD 66–67. Nero committed suicide in the summer of AD 68.

27 Ahead of Epaphrodotus—Luke is not mentioned among those who send their greetings to the Philippians. Luke, who had accompanied Paul to Rome (Acts 27:1, 28:16) and visited him during his first imprisonment (Col 4:14; Phlm 24), later returned to visit Paul when he was reincarcerated (2 Tim 4:11). Cf. Holzner, *Paul of Tarsus*, 506, 515, 521.

be dated earlier, say AD 60–62. And, although the interrelationship between the other synoptic Gospels is extremely complex, we must place them even earlier, bearing in mind the clear presence of substantial Markan material in Matthew and Luke, and the tradition of Papias[28] that "Matthew composed his *logia* (oracles, sayings) in the Hebrew dialect." Thus there was also (presumably) a non-Greek (i.e., Aramaic) proto-Matthew.[29] Therefore, our position on the dating of the synoptics is substantially that of John A. T. Robinson who on even more cogent grounds concludes:

> The final stages of the three synoptic gospels as we have them would then have occupied the latter 50s or early 60s. In any case, whatever precise pattern of synoptic interdependence will prove to be required or suggested by the evidence, all could quite easily be fitted in to comport with the writing of Acts in 62+.[30]

But what of the fourth Gospel? Once again it is evident that John's Gospel, like Acts, does not contain any allusion to the turbulent

---

[28] Eusebius, *Ecclesiastical History*, trans. C. F. Cruse (Peabody, MA: Hendrickson, 1998), III.39.16. Irenaeus (c. AD 130–200), who was taught by Polycarp, a disciple of John the Apostle, states in *Adversus Haereses* 3.1.1: "Matthew also issued a *written* Gospel among the Hebrews in their own dialect, [then? while?] Peter and Paul were preaching in Rome, and were laying the foundations of the Church." This period can be interpreted as being either before or during AD 60–64. Irenaeus continues: "But after their departure [death], Mark, the disciple and interpreter of Peter, has handed down to us, also in writing, what had been preached by Peter. And Luke also, the companion of Paul, recorded in a book the Gospel preached by him. Afterwards, John, the disciple of the Lord, who also had leaned upon his breast, did himself publish a Gospel during his residence at Ephesus in Asia." Similar statements are to be found in Origen, Epiphanius, Cyril of Jerusalem, Jerome, Gregory of Nazianus, Chrysostom, and Augustine, as well as Syrian and Coptic authorities. See John Wenham, *Redating Matthew, Mark, and Luke: A Fresh Assault on the Synoptic Problem* (London: Hodder and Stoughton, 1991), 117–19.

[29] See Claude Tresmontant, *The Hebrew Christ: Language in the Age of the Gospels* (Chicago: Franciscan Herald Press, 1989), for the numerous "Hebraisms" which substantiate Papias and render a considerable amount of Matthean material quite early, supporting the existence of a proto-Matthew.

[30] John A. T. Robinson, *Redating the New Testament* (London: SCM, 1976), 116. See also F. F. Bruce, *Commentary on the Book of the Acts* (Grand Rapids: William B. Eerdmans, 1977), 22–24.

events that transpired between AD 64 and AD 70.³¹ Also, the Muratorian fragment presupposes that John's "fellow disciples and bishops" were still alive, exhorting him to write in his own name, and (at the instigation of Andrew³²) he (John) consented:

> The fourth of the Gospels was written by John, one of the disciples. When exhorted by his fellow-disciples and bishops, he said, "Fast with me this day for three days; and what may be revealed to any of us, let us relate it to one another." The same night it was revealed to Andrew, one of the apostles, that John was to write all things in his own name, and they were all to certify.

Furthermore, the numerous Hebraisms,³³ the many local geographical details, and the knowledge of the temple and the Sadducees, require an eyewitness proximate to and contemporary with the events. Given the failures of form-criticism, there is no longer any reason not to accept the objective, documentary evidence. We cannot with certainty, therefore, project the date of John's Gospel beyond that of the synoptics.³⁴

Because the Gospels are early they are well within the control of eyewitnesses. In fact, Richard Bauckham has recently drawn upon internal statistical evidence, the use of personal names in first-century Palestine, contemporary studies of memory, as well as recent discoveries of how oral tradition is transmitted to argue that the Gospels do rest upon trustworthy eyewitness testimony. He has shown that the named individuals in the Gospels were authentic persons who could not have been invented, but whose names were preserved so that they could be located and examined by their contemporaries. The result is that the pericopae containing named persons belong

---

31 Ibid., 254–85.
32 A third-century apocryphal *Acts of St Andrew* relates that he was crucified at Patras in Achaia in the year 60.
33 Tresmontant, *The Hebrew Christ*, shows that John contains more of these than any other Gospel.
34 See also Robinson, *Redating the New Testament*, 254–311. Irenaeus's evidence that John wrote his Gospel during his residence at Ephesus leaves the date of his stay there unspecified: it could have been either before or after his exile at Patmos.

more to the category of testimony than to the categories of the form critics. The division between the Jesus of history and the Christ of faith is a false dichotomy, therefore, and should be replaced by the Jesus of testimony.

> Reading the Gospels as eyewitness testimony differs therefore from attempts at historical reconstruction behind the texts. It takes the Gospels seriously as they are; it acknowledges the uniqueness of what we can know only in this testimonial form. It honors the form of historiography they are. From a historiographic perspective, radical suspicion of testimony is a kind of epistemological suicide. It is no more practicable in history than it is in ordinary life. Gospels scholarship must free itself from the grip of the skeptical paradigm that presumes the Gospels to be unreliable unless, in every particular case of story or saying, the historian succeeds in providing independent verification. For such a suspicious approach the Gospels are not believable until and unless the historian can verify each claim that they make to recount history. But this approach is seriously faulty precisely as a historical method. It can only result in a misleadingly minimal collection of uninteresting facts about a historical figure stripped of any real significance. Neither in this nor in countless other cases of historical testimony can the historian verify everything. Testimony asks to be trusted.[35]

This testimony involves real people reporting actual events significant to them. Such events, however exceptional, gain authenticity by the commitment and veracity of the eyewitnesses demonstrated by their willingness to suffer or even die for what they believe. People do not die for what they know to be false. The idea promulgated by the hermeneutics of suspicion, that the church freely created pericopae in order to address existential concerns so that with their faith now strengthened they could evangelize, suffer, and die confident in their own designer religion, is absurd. Moreover, the Jesus of the

---

35 Bauckham, *Jesus and the Eyewitnesses*, 506.

reconstructed history of the form critics is not worth dying for. On the contrary, the apostles and their disciples were honest witnesses to something so majestic and glorious that they endured persecution, impoverishment, ostracism, enmity, and even death for the sake of the good news that God had become man in Jesus Christ.[36]

JESUS'S SELF-AUTHENTICATION

No reputable historian doubts that Jesus was a Palestinian Jew who grew up in Nazareth in Galilee early in the first century. The Jewish scholar and historian Geza Vermes[37] declares: "No objective and enlightened student of the Gospels can help but be struck by the incomparable superiority of Jesus."[38] After referring to Jesus's "sublimity, distinctiveness and originality," his "profundity of insight and grandeur of character," and his spiritual insightfulness, Vermes states:

> The positive and constant testimony of the earliest Gospel tradition, considered against its natural background of first-century Galilean charismatic religion, leads not to a Jesus as unrecognizable within the framework of Judaism as by the standard of his own verifiable words and intentions, but to another figure: Jesus the just man, the *zaddik*, Jesus the helper and healer, Jesus the teacher and leader, venerated by his intimates and less committed admirers alike as prophet, lord and *son of God*.[39]

The impact of Jesus upon the world is incomparable. Yet he never spread his message by war, nor sent troops into battle, neither did he ever kill or order anyone's assassination; rather he forgave those who mocked and persecuted him, even to sacrificing his life for them. Jesus was aware that as a son[40] of God he was "destined for the fall and for

---

36   2 Cor 5:19; Col 1:19–20, 2:9–10; Phil 2:5–11.
37   Pronounced Ver*mesh*.
38   Geza Vermes, *Jesus the Jew: A Historian's Reading of the Gospels* (Philadelphia: Fortress Press, 1981), 224.
39   Ibid., 224–25.
40   When a Jew became *bar mitzvah*, he understood himself to be a son of the commandment and therefore a son of God through the covenant.

the rise of many in Israel,"[41] declaring: "Everyone who acknowledges me before men, I also will acknowledge before my Father who is in heaven; but whoever denies me before men, I also will deny before my Father who is in heaven."[42]

Throughout their history the Jews revered their God as the One who had formed a special relationship with them, promising to be with them until the end; who gave them the *Torah*, the prophets, a land, and a religion — for he had made a covenant with Abraham, Isaac, and Jacob, personally identifying himself with their names, requiring that he is to be known by that appellation throughout all generations.[43] This God, who directed all things according to his eternal providence, and was therefore the Lord of history, had a plan that would establish Israel as the light of the nations through his agent, the Messiah.

Jesus is the only founder of a religion who was anticipated beforehand. Indeed by Jesus's time, the Messiah had already been given the status of a pre-existent, semi-divine being in the various traditions.[44] For example, the Midrash on Proverbs declares the Messiah to be among the seven things existing before the world.[45] He is superior to the patriarchs, greater than Moses, and even loftier than the angels.[46] The pseudepigraphical Book of Enoch written between 150 and 63 BC and quoted in the Epistle of Jude,[47] declared the Messiah to be a son of God ("I and My son").[48] In the central section, known as the *Similitudes,* written between 95 and 63 BC, the Messiah's pre-existence as a Divine idea is proclaimed, evincing an elevated Christology approaching that of the prologue to John's Gospel:

---

41 Lk 2:34; Is 8:14.
42 Mt 10:32–33 = Lk 12:8–9.
43 Ex 3:15.
44 See Ps 110:1–10; Prov 8:22–31; Mic 5:2; Is 9:6; Jer 23:5–6. For other prophecies of Christ, see below, p. 127, n. 4.
45 They are: the Throne of Glory, Messiah the King, the Torah, the idea of Israel, the Temple, repentance, and Sheol.
46 *Tanch. Par. Toledoth* 14.
47 Jude 14.
48 Enoch 105:2. *Book of Enoch*, in *Apocrypha & Pseudepigrapha of Old Testament* by R. H. Charles (Oxford: Oxford Press, 1913).

Yea, *before the sun and the signs were created,*
Before the stars of the heaven were made,
His name was named before the Lord of Spirits.[49]
He shall be a staff to the righteous whereon to stay themselves and not fall,
And he *shall be the light of the Gentiles,*[50]
And the hope of those who are troubled of heart.
All who dwell on earth *shall fall down and worship him,*[51]
And will praise and bless and celebrate with song the Lord of Spirits.
And for this reason hath he been chosen and hidden before him,
Before the creation of the world and evermore.[52]
For he hath preserved the lot of the righteous,
Because they have hated and despised this world of unrighteousness...
For in his name they are saved.[53]
...
And there was great joy amongst them,
And they blessed and glorified and extolled
Because the name of that Son of man had been revealed unto them.[54]
And he sat on the *throne of glory,*[55]
And the *sum of judgment* was given unto the Son of man.[56]

After causing sinners to be destroyed from the face of the earth and be imprisoned in an "assemblage-place of destruction," the Son of man would establish peace over the earth where the righteous "shall not be separated from him for ever and ever."[57]

---

49 Jn 1:1–2.
50 Lk 2:32.
51 Jn 20:28.
52 Rev 1:8.
53 Mt 1:21; Acts 2:21, 4:12.
54 Jn 1:14.
55 Mt 19:28.
56 Enoch 48:3–7; 69:26–27. Cf. Jn 5:22, 27.
57 Cf. Rev 21:1–6.

In the Jewish third book of the *Sibylline Oracles*,[58] which dates from over a century before Christ, the Messiah is "the king sent from heaven" whom "God will send from the sun" who will establish "a kingdom for all ages over men" where "all must sacrifice to the Mighty King." The apocryphal *Psalms of Solomon*, written some 50 years before Christ, similarly depicts him as the son of David and as Christ the Lord.[59] Pure from sin, wise in counsel, and mighty in word and deed[60] he will destroy his enemies, purify Jerusalem, and will sit in judgment upon the nations.[61]

Even though Palestine was under Roman occupation, the people, already aware of Daniel's ancient[62] prophecy of the coming of a Son of Man,[63] looked for a Messiah who would soon free them from their misery. So intolerable were these times that one community, the Essenes, withdrew and dwelt in the desert at Qumran to purify themselves in preparation for his coming. The pseudo-Danielic $_4QPS\text{-}DanA^a$ summarizes the general expectations of the period:

> He shall be called *son of God*, and they shall designate him son of the Most High. Like the appearance of comets, so shall be their kingdom. For (brief) years they shall rule over the earth and shall trample on all; one people shall trample on another and one province on another until the people of God shall rise and all shall rest from the sword.[64]

---

58 *Sibylline Oracles*, Bk. 3, 652–808.
59 *Psalms of Solomon* 17:36. This is exactly as in the Septuagint of Lam 4:20 where the Hebrew, *Mashiach YHWH*, is translated by the Greek, *Christos Kyrios*.
60 *Psalms of Solomon* 17:41.
61 *Psalms of Solomon* 17:25–35. See also 1 Enoch 69:26–29, 71:14–17 and 2 Bar 25–30, where two comings of the Messiah are indicated.
62 See Flavius Josephus, *The Antiquities of the Jews*, trans. William Whiston (Peabody, MA: Hendrickson, 1993), 11.8.5. Josephus states that Alexander the Great was shown a book of Daniel while visiting the temple in Jerusalem (c. 330 BC) and that Alexander supposed himself the subject of the prophecy. Cf. Dan 7:6; 8:3–8, 20–22; 11:3. Later, coins showing Alexander wearing the ram's horns (Dan 8 passim) were minted. Such coins have been found in the treasury at Persepolis. Whatever the accuracy of this quotation, it was clear to Josephus that the Jews of the time revered Daniel's prophecies as being quite ancient.
63 Dan 7:13–14.
64 Geza Vermes, ed. and trans., *The Dead Sea Scrolls in English* (Harmondsworth: Penguin Books, 1987), 31. Italics added.

This was the real *Sitz im Leben* of Jesus. Clearly the common folk would have been predisposed to accept similar claims made by him.[65] Therefore, Jesus's rejection by the Jewish authorities required something more offensive than just making messianic claims similar to the foregoing popular sentiments. Something more must have been asserted, since Jesus was condemned for blasphemy.[66] Thus, when we consider Jesus's claims to divinity, we must keep in mind what was really being communicated to his hearers, and not read back into his claims our own modern conceptions;[67] for we shall discover from the Gospels that our (hitherto ontological) understanding of God will have become profoundly transformed.

Jesus's self-understanding in the synoptic Gospels

It is clear from the foregoing literature that during the intertestamental period the Messiah had come to be portrayed as a pre-existent, heavenly (possibly divine), being. He would receive the titles son of David, son of Man, and son of God. He was to be worshipped. This "Mighty King" would wield all power and authority over the nations and would judge mankind. Salvation would be proclaimed in his name, and he would reign in heaven forever as Christ the Lord.

It must be borne in mind that, while concepts such as substantial union (*homoousios*) were foreign to the Jewish mindset, yet on the other hand names given to individuals did serve to express the substantial identity of a person. To be someone's son was to belong to his heritage, community, authority, and lineage: entitled to be the recipient of everything that belonged to the *name* of the father.[68] So when we hear Jesus say in Q:[69] "I thank thee, Father, Lord of heaven and earth, that thou hast hidden these things from the wise and understanding and revealed them to babes; yea, Father, for such was

---

65 Mk 12:37; Lk 19:48, 21:38.
66 Mk 14:64.
67 Nor should we interpret his claims according to Egyptian or Greco-Roman ideas of their gods. The Hebrew God was nothing like these immoral, treacherous beings who were themselves created by the cosmos and spent their time visiting mischief upon mankind.
68 These ideas are obscured when the Bible is translated by inclusive language.
69 Mt 11:25–27 = Lk 10:21–22. Recall that Q is the material common only to Matthew and Luke.

thy gracious will. All things have been delivered to me by my Father; and no one knows the Son except the Father, and no one knows the Father except the Son and any one to whom the Son chooses to reveal him"; we have in these authentic words of Jesus[70] early testimony of his own consciousness of somehow being intimately related to God—even to being God's beloved Son[71]—an intimacy expressed by mutual knowing. But this was no ordinary knowing since it is an intimate, divine knowledge of the person of God which no one else possesses. Moreover, this personal knowledge was entrusted to Jesus as a revelation to humanity. This special wisdom which Jesus receives from his heavenly Father involves a very close relationship, closer than any prophetic office. For while the vocation of prophet was indeed that of a spokesman for God, here we have the consciousness, expressed in the midst of prayer, of a unique filial relationship entitling Jesus to be the authoritative voice of God's plan and will, which, *because he is God's Son,* informs Jesus's will also.

This issue of authority did not escape the scribes and Pharisees, who asked Jesus, "By what authority are you doing these things, or who gave you this authority to do them?"[72] But Jesus countered by challenging them to explain the authority whereby John baptized. When they demurred, he also refused to respond concerning John. Then he proceeded to relate a parable about a householder who entrusted his vineyard to some tenants.[73] The householder sent a series of servants to receive of the fruit of the vineyard, but their fate was to be beaten or killed. Finally the householder sent his "beloved son" thinking they would respect him. But they killed him also, intending to obtain his *inheritance* for themselves. The point was not lost on the scribes and Pharisees who understood that they were meant as the wicked tenants, for they tried to arrest Jesus, but, fearing the people, they departed.

Since this parable was given in answer to the officials' question about who gave Jesus authority, it is clear that he identifies himself

---

70 John Reumann, *Jesus in the Church's Gospels* (Philadelphia: Fortress, 1985), 292.
71 Mk 1:11 = Mt 3:17 = Lk 3:22; Mt 12:18 (cf. Is 42:1), 17:5.
72 Mk 11:28 = Mt 21:23 = Lk 20:2.
73 Mt 21:33–46 = Mk 12:1–12 = Lk 20:9–19.

as the son who was sent at the end. As was customary with Jesus, he reverted the question of authority onto the interrogators. Distinguishing between the prophets of Israel (who were either dismissed or killed by those in authority) and himself who comes at the end as a son, Jesus requires them to see the hypocrisy of their question, exposing their real intentions towards him. However, the meaning should also not be lost on us that Jesus possesses his inheritance as his filial right precisely because he is the Son sent by the Father.

Another passage where Jesus is described as Son of God occurs after Peter's confession "You are the Christ, the Son of the living God."[74] In all three passages of the synoptics Jesus does not deny the assertion, but only admonishes them not to tell anyone else.[75] In Matthew, however, we have Jesus going on to quote Isaiah 22:22 as he gives the keys of the kingdom to Peter. In Isaiah the passage shows God giving the keys of the House of David to Eliakim *and his posterity*.[76] That Jesus, himself, should exercise this same Divine Authority to dispose of the keys of the House of David is remarkable in the context of Peter's confession.

One might cite in objection to this claim that "all things have been delivered to the Son" the passage in Mark 13:32 (Mt 24:36), where Jesus, when asked the time of his coming again, replies: "But of that day or that hour no one knows, not even the angels in heaven, nor the Son, but only the Father." Jesus uses the title of Son, but to express his ignorance of certain things. That this passage is authentic is supported by the principle of negative attribution,[77] since the implicit imputation of ignorance to the Son of God is not something the evangelists would be desirous of making. Rather, this is evidence of honest reporting of an authentic saying of Jesus. Nevertheless, this passage does not support the above objection, since it does not contradict the notion of inheritance from the Father, but only that the Son respected the Father's wish that this not be revealed.

---

74 Mt 16:16 = Mk 8:29 = Lk 9:20.
75 This is not to be construed as a denial, but simply one of those things not to be revealed until the appropriate time.
76 Is 22:24.
77 Also known as the criterion of embarrassment: a source is more likely to be authentic if, even when quoted, it causes embarrassment to the early church.

The relationship of Jesus with his Father illustrated in the previous passage is not unlike that of the agony in the garden of Gethsemane where Jesus fell on the ground and prayed: "Abba, Father, all things are possible to thee; remove this cup from me; yet not what I will, but what thou wilt."[78] In this passage, Mark has Jesus use the intimate term "Abba"—although Matthew does use the Greek *pater mou*, my Father. In this passage as in the previous one, Jesus is shown as humbly submitting to the will of the Father concerning what he is to know and to suffer on earth. This requires we consider the relationship of the Son to the Father as not simply one of status—where one has a right to a certain inheritance—but the profounder and more intimate desire even to suffer for the Father's sake. The closeness which Jesus consciously felt towards his heavenly Father could not be more poignantly expressed than in this passage.

However, the most dramatic of these passages, illustrating Jesus's understanding of himself as Son of God, occurs when he is brought before the Sanhedrin. Jesus is pointedly asked by the high priest, Caiaphas: "Are you the Christ, the Son of the Blessed?"[79] Jesus answers "I am" in Mark and Luke, while in Matthew he says something like "as you have said." In any case, the reaction of the high priest shows that he thought that Jesus had blasphemously condemned himself from his own lips. No further witnesses were needed and the chief priests and the elders took counsel to have Jesus put to death.

What was there in the words of Jesus that brought down upon him such a sentence? It was the blasphemy that Jesus "though only a human being, is making himself God."[80] The authorities had understood that Jesus was claiming a divine status for himself as Mark, himself, had already related when Jesus had forgiven the sins of the paralytic: "It is blasphemy! Who can forgive sins but God alone?"[81] Given the background of the entire sacrificial cult upon which the priesthood rested, this alone would have been a tremendous affront

---

78 Mk 14:36 = Mt 26:39 = Lk 22:42.
79 Mk 14:61 = Mt 26:63 = Lk 22:67. While Matthew has "Son of God," Mark seems to be sensitive to the tradition of not pronouncing the sacred name.
80 Jn 10:33.
81 Mk 2:7.

to God. But with regards to Jesus's answer before the Sanhedrin, it is clear that Jesus's words were taken by the chief priests and elders as once again claiming equality with God.

The reason for this judgment is contained in Jesus's full statement: "I am; and you will see the Son of man seated at the right hand of Power, and coming with the clouds of heaven." Contained in these words are two Old Testament texts which Jesus links and applies to himself. The first is Daniel 7:13–14 which identifies the Son of Man as coming on the clouds of heaven, upon whom the Ancient of Days bestows dominion and glory and kingdom which shall neither pass away nor be destroyed. The second is Psalm 110:1: "The LORD says to my lord: 'Sit at my right hand, till I make your enemies your footstool.'" But it is also possible that the council were reminded of a verse from Isaiah 14:12–15, where a similar claim was made by the pagan King of Babylon: "I will ascend above the heights of the clouds; I will make myself like the Most High." After that it is not surprising that the high priest tore his garments and said: "You have heard his blasphemy." And just as God had pronounced the judgment upon the pagan king ("You are brought down to Sheol, to the depths of the pit") so the council condemned Jesus as also deserving death.[82]

The previous examples illustrate how Jesus understood his filial relationship to the Father based upon those passages in the synoptics where Jesus speaks of himself as Son. However, there are many other passages where Jesus is aware of his exalted status. Firstly, Jesus is conscious of possessing a dignity above that of men and angels. He is aware of exceeding the prophets and kings of Israel, Jonah and Solomon, Moses and Elijah.[83] Jesus maintains that it was he, himself, whom David was referring to as lord.[84] He claims authority over the angels who are his ministers and who will accompany him at his second coming.[85]

---

82 This makes clear the sort of testimonies the council sought from witnesses to bring against Jesus; the authorities clearly were looking for a charge of blasphemy of some kind so that they may kill him (Mk 14:55).
83 Mt 12:41–42; 17:3; Mk 9:4; Lk 9:30.
84 Mt 22:43ff.; Mk 12:36ff.; Lk 20:42ff.
85 Mt 4:11, 13:41, 16:27, 24:31, 26:53; Mk 1:12, 8:38, 13:27; Lk 4:13.

Secondly, like God, he sends out prophets, seers, and teachers of the law, giving them "a mouth and wisdom, which no adversary can withstand."[86] He exercises the authority of altering or even nullifying the precepts of the law given by God to Moses.[87] He proclaims himself Lord of the Sabbath[88] and establishes a new covenant with his community.[89]

Thirdly, Jesus imposes upon his disciples obligations which only God can demand, namely absolute love for him even to the extent of demanding good works (Hebrew: *mitzvot*) on his behalf and of dying for him.[90]

Finally, Jesus is conscious of possessing supreme authority: "All authority (Greek: *exousia*) in heaven and on earth has been given to me," commissioning his apostles to make disciples of all nations, baptizing them in the name of the Son (which he associates with the names of God the Father and his Holy Spirit), and teaching them to observe his commandments.[91] This authority is further manifested through his ability to bestow upon others the power to heal and cast out demons in his name.[92] Yet more wonderful is his consciousness that his personal sacrifice will serve to atone for the sins of others.[93] He is even able to promise that he would be with his disciples to the end of the age.[94]

There can be no doubt about the Divine Consciousness of Jesus in the synoptics. When one also considers the holiness of his life, his exalted teaching, the profundity of his wisdom, and the sublime poignancy of his passion through which he gave his ultimate personal testimony, it should be clear that we are beholding someone of an extraordinary and unique majesty. To say that Jesus, with all his self-possession and wisdom, was unmindful of his claims of being the Son of God strains credulity.

---

86   Mt 23:34; Lk 21:15.
87   Mt 5:21ff.
88   Mt 12:8; Mk 2:28; Lk 6:5.
89   Mt 26:28 = Mk 14:24 = Lk 22:20.
90   Mt 10:37–39, 25:31–46.
91   Mt 28:18.
92   Mt 10:1, 8; Mk 6:7; Lk 9:1, 10:17.
93   Mt 20:28, 26:28.
94   Mt 28:20.

Part Two: Wisdom

Jesus in John's Gospel

That the fourth Gospel may be early, we have argued above. That it is an eyewitness account written by a disciple of that name is well-attested in the tradition.[95] There is a problem, however, of just who this John is, which arises when one considers that, as Papias implies,[96] there were two Johns, one John the Apostle, son of Zebedee; the other, John the Elder (presbyter), although there is no evidence that the latter ever wrote anything.[97] This controversy need not detain us, nor should it detract from the authenticity of the accounts, since as Professor Bauckham argues[98] the fourth Gospel is evidently the account of an eyewitness, the Beloved Disciple intimately associated with Jesus, whose protected anonymity argues against forming any conclusions that it is pseudepigraphical:

> ...why not claim for the Gospel a more explicit and convincing authorization from Jesus than the ingenious but obscure interpretation of a saying of Jesus that ostensibly means nothing of the kind (21:22–24)? For a disciple who could make his audacious claim to testimony more significant than Peter's only by some such means, the combination of modesty and audacity in the Gospel's portrayal of the Beloved Disciple is a brilliant strategy. But it is hard to believe that a pseudepigraphical writer would have invented a character who required such a brilliant strategy to establish his claim to witness.[99]

It is generally acknowledged that the Christology of John's Gospel is elevated. Yet it does contain ideas that we have encountered before. That Jesus is the pre-existent Word,[100] that he is glorious, that he is son of man, son of David, and Son of God, and that he is to be worshipped, were already present in those passages quoted

---

95 By Clement, Papias, Irenaeus, Polycrates.
96 Eusebius, *Ecclesiastical History*, III.39.3–4.
97 Robinson, *Redating the New Testament*, 310.
98 Bauckham, *Jesus and the Eyewitnesses*, 358–411.
99 Bauckham, *Jesus and the Eyewitnesses*, 409.
100 Philo of Alexandria (c. 20 BC–AD 45) was the main Jewish thinker to utilize the Stoic concept of an eternal logos.

from Proverbs, Isaiah, Daniel, and the Similitudes of Enoch as well as in John's Gospel. When everything is considered, the Christ of the fourth Gospel does not appear that much more exalted than in the synoptics.[101]

In fact, the essential Christological difference between the synoptic Gospels and that of the Beloved Disciple is the latter's emphasis upon the closeness of the Father-Son relationship. This is reflected most clearly and tenderly in Jesus's *high priestly prayer* to God:[102]

> Father, the hour has come; glorify thy Son that the Son may glorify thee.... I glorified thee on earth, having accomplished the work which thou gavest me to do; and now, Father, glorify thou me in thy own presence with the glory which I had with thee before the world was made.
>
> I have manifested thy name to the men whom thou gavest me out of the world.... Now they know that everything that thou hast given me is from thee; for I have given them the words which thou gavest me, and they have received them and know in truth that I came from thee; and they have believed that thou didst send me.
>
> The glory which thou hast given to me I have given to them, that they may be one even as we are one, I in them and thou in me, that they may become perfectly one, so that the world may know that thou hast sent me and hast loved them even as thou hast loved me....
>
> O righteous Father, the world has not known thee, but I have known thee; and these know that thou hast sent me. I made known to them thy name, and I will make it known, that the love with which thou hast loved me may be in them, and I in them.

Jesus is claiming an intimacy with God which is not known by the world and an authority to unite his community to him and to God

---

101 This supposed elevated Christology has been used as the main reason for dating John's Gospel late. But Christologies of various forms and levels have existed side by side throughout the Church's history, and still do. See Jaroslav Pelikan, *Jesus through the Centuries* (New York: Harper & Row, 1985).
102 Jn 17:1–26.

Part Two: Wisdom

based precisely upon that loving relationship that he has with his heavenly Father. He is conscious of possessing a glorified, pre-existent relationship with God that he wants to manifest to those whom God has entrusted to him. He attests that in his person he has revealed to his flock the very name of God.

This name of God, the Tetragrammaton (YHWH), was so sacred that Jews would not pronounce it, substituting instead such circumlocutions as "Lord" or the "Blessed One." This name was revealed to Moses at the burning bush after he had protested that, unless he knew God's name, the people would not receive his witness. God says to Moses: "I AM THAT I AM.... Say to the people of Israel, 'I AM has sent me to you.'"[103] Similar "I AM" (Hebrew: *ani hu*; Greek: *ego eimi*) statements occur in John's Gospel on the very lips of Jesus in contexts where he also is challenged about his witness. Many scholars take these as Jesus deliberately identifying himself with the Divine Name. For example, Dodd[104] connects *ani hu* with Rabbinic usage of the Divine Name in the Feast of Tabernacles and in passages such as Isaiah 43:10: "My servant whom I have chosen, that you may know and ... understand that *I am he*"; as also being reflected in John 8:28: "When you have lifted up the Son of man, then you will know that *I AM*, and that I do nothing on my own authority but speak thus as the Father taught me." Canon Redford takes up this point, building upon the work of others,[105] also to argue that Jesus applied this term consciously to claim of himself "I AM."[106]

Three of these claims are made as the Jewish authorities deny the testimony Jesus was making in the temple, because he was bearing witness to himself. Jesus replies: "Even if I do bear witness to myself, my testimony is true, for I know whence I have come and whither I am going."[107] He then goes on to say: "You know neither me nor

---

103 Ex 3:14.
104 C. H. Dodd, *The Interpretation of the Fourth Gospel* (Cambridge: Cambridge University Press, 1953), 94–96. See also Joseph Ratzinger [Benedict XVI], *Jesus of Nazareth* (London: Bloomsbury, 2007), 347.
105 Such as Ball, Brown, Daube, and Schnackenburg. See Joseph Redford, *Bad, Mad or God?* (London: St. Paul's, 2005), 243–49.
106 Redford, *Bad, Mad or God?*, 243.
107 Jn 8:13–14.

my Father.... You are from below, I am from above; you are of this world, I am not of this world.... You will die in your sins unless you believe that I AM (*ego eimi*)."[108] But because they did not understand, it was then that he added: "When you have lifted up the Son of man, then you will know that I AM (*ego eimi*)."[109]

The point that Jesus keeps making here is that his personal testimony is true, not because he is testifying to himself but because his witness is grounded in his intimate relationship with the Father: that it arises out of the personal unity he has with the Father. Jesus is conscious that truth exists in him as a living Word from the Father forming the substance of his Person. He *is* the way the truth and the life.[110] Every action and word of his manifests the truth of his Father's self-expression speaking and acting in him. Jesus is the Father's Word in act. He can bear witness to the Father, because the Father bears witness to him by this gift of communion between them,[111] since everything that Jesus wills and does comes from the Father, grounded in the Truth expressed by the Father, which is in Jesus. The Son submits to the will of the Father and glorifies the Father in his surrender to the Father, just because he loves the Father. "And this is eternal life, that they know thee the only true God, and Jesus Christ, whom thou hast sent. I glorified thee on earth, having accomplished the work which thou gavest me to do; and now, Father, glorify thou me in thy own presence with the glory which I had with thee before the world was made."[112] The Father glorifies his name for the sake of the Son who loves Him; and the Son glorifies the Father for the sake of the Father whom he loves: "Glorify thy Son that the Son may glorify thee."[113] Everything Jesus does manifests this mutual communion of Persons—a communion of mutual self-giving love. That is what Jesus meant when he said that it is only when he is lifted up on the cross that "you will know that I AM."

---

108 Jn 8:19, 23–24. The word "he" is added in the RSV, but it does not occur in the original Greek text.
109 Jn 8:28.
110 Jn 14:6.
111 Jn 8:18.
112 Jn 17:4–5
113 Jn 17:2.

Part Two: Wisdom

However, the Jewish officials just could not get it, because as Jesus said they were judging according to the flesh. They could not or would not see that Jesus's authority comes from his relationship with God: "He who is of God hears the words of God; the reason you do not hear them is that you are not of God."[114] This led the Pharisees to inquire pointedly: "Who do you claim to be?"[115] After reiterating the formula that the Father who glorifies Jesus is the one whom Jesus knows and whom the Pharisees do not know, Jesus then declares that he is the one whose day Abraham rejoiced over and was glad to have seen.[116] "The Jews then said to him, 'You are not yet fifty years old, and have you seen Abraham?' Jesus said to them, 'Truly, truly, I say to you, before Abraham was, I AM (*ego eimi*).'[117] With this they took up stones to throw, but Jesus hid and then left the temple."

Once again we see the reaction of the authorities to the blasphemy they understood Jesus to have made. They correctly perceived the implications of Jesus's claim, a claim which not only placed Jesus outside the category of physical nature, but claimed for himself an eternal existence not bound by birth and death. However, Jesus's third repetition of the "I AM" phrase together with his claim of possessing an exclusive knowledge and communion with God, constituted a claim to Divine Authority, which the authorities had clearly perceived.

The final use of the "I AM" occurs at the Last Supper. After Jesus washes the disciples' feet he alludes to his betrayal and then says: "I tell you now, before it takes place, that when it does take place you may believe that I AM."[118] This phrase echoes that "lifting up" of the Son of man when the "I AM" would be revealed as the sacrificial victim lovingly offered to the Father.

But he instructs the disciples not to be troubled at his departure, since after he had gone he would prepare a place for them. This prompts Thomas to inquire of the way whereby Jesus was going. Jesus answers "I am the way, the truth and the life; no one comes to the Father but by me." Then Philip asks to be shown the Father, to which

---

114 Jn 8:47.
115 Jn 8:53.
116 Jn 8:56.
117 Jn 8:57–58.
118 Jn 13:19.

Son of God

Jesus replies: "He who has seen me has seen the Father, how can you say, 'Show us the Father?' Do you not believe that I am in the Father and the Father in me? The words that I say to you I do not speak on my own authority; but the Father who dwells in me does his works. Believe me that I am in the Father and the Father in me; or else believe me for the sake of the works themselves."[119] Jesus not only reiterates the theme of mutual communion but makes it clear that the Father dwells in him, giving him authority. With this authority Jesus then promises to send the Holy Spirit, who would keep his apostles in the truth, and who would comfort them after he had gone. Yet the disciples still do not understand the meaning of his departure, so Jesus says: "I came from the Father and have come into the world; again, I am leaving the world and going to the Father."[120] Then the disciples finally realize that Jesus came forth (Greek: *exelthon* — aorist) from God; and Jesus encourages their belief. It is then that Jesus offers that high priestly prayer, from which we quoted earlier, entrusting to the Father his apostles and those others who also at last understand and believe.[121]

The question of Jesus's authority runs throughout the entire Gospel of John. We have seen that Jesus grounds his authority upon the unique and formative indwelling of the Father within him. Jesus is conscious of being loved by God and loving him in return. He is also aware that everything he says, thinks, and accomplishes comes from this union. Jesus is conscious of his pre-existence — not merely the pre-existence of his name as one of the seven things first created by God — but of his personal coming forth from the Father before Abraham, even before the world was made. Therefore, when Jesus declares that he is one with the Father, and that the Father is one with him, he is expressing much more than a mere moral union, or even a mystical one, but one that pre-exists this time frame, that pre-exists even his manhood.

One is either willing to see this or one is not. And that is precisely the point of John's Gospel: for one to see the reality of Jesus one must somehow be open to his light, to that glory of the only Son

---

119 Jn 14:9–11.
120 Jn 16:28.
121 Jn 17:7–8, 20–21.

from the Father; a glory full of grace and truth.[122] To see the truth one must be in the truth, otherwise one will not recognize it when it manifests itself. "No one has seen God," says John in his prologue. "The only Son, who is in the bosom of the Father, he has made him known."[123] But the Son has made God known precisely because God's glory shone forth from within him. Jesus knew this and knew that his Father knew it and willed it. That was his authority.

We have not considered — either in John or in the synoptics — the miracles of Jesus. For if one accepts the authority of Jesus, then miracles can only stand to confirm one's faith in him, but if one does not believe that God was in Christ Jesus, then miracles can add little.[124] But we have previously demonstrated that an eternal Principle — one, good, true, and beautiful — exists in which all things are grounded and whose Wisdom permeates and orders all things. To then *see* that this Wisdom is a real, formative Principle in Jesus; that Jesus is conscious of this and is aware of a profound relationship with his Father even from before the foundation of the world; that Jesus bases the authority for all he says and does on this awareness; and that he even goes to his death to confirm and exemplify this relationship, wonderfully transforms our conception of God and serves as solid foundation for our faith.

We have come to conclude that God is truly mysterious and is somehow self-aware. Out of this awareness comes the Word, the eternal utterance of the Father which proceeds immediately from his substance, having the same form: a real, complete, natural, and well-defined image of God, fully and perfectly expressing his Reality, nature, excellence, majesty, perfection, and divinity.[125] This Word is properly and rightly called and *is* the beloved Son of the Father, his eternally generated self-expression. "And the Word became flesh and dwelt among us, full of grace and truth; we have beheld his glory, glory as of the only Son from the Father."[126]

---

122 Jn 1:14.
123 Jn 1:18.
124 Even Moses, the prophets, and other holy persons have worked miracles.
125 Jean-Michel de Coutances, *Carthusian Spiritual Exercises* (London: Burns and Oates, 1913), 384.
126 Jn 1:14.

CHAPTER 5
Lamb of God

> *He was oppressed, and he was afflicted,*
>   *yet he opened not his mouth;*
> *like a lamb that is lead to the slaughter,*
>   *and a sheep that before its shearers is dumb,*
>   *so he opened not his mouth.*
> *By oppression and judgment he was taken away;*
>   *and as for his generation,*
> *who considered that he was cut off*
>   *out of the land of the living,*
>   *stricken for the transgression of my people?*
> *And they made his grave with the wicked*
>   *and with a rich man in his death,*
> *although he had done no violence,*
>   *and there was no deceit in his mouth.*[1]

JESUS HAD REPLIED TO THOSE WHO DOUBTED his authority: "When you have lifted up the Son of man, then you will know that I am."[2] And at the Last Supper Jesus, mindful of his impending passion, repeated this: "I tell you this now, before it takes place, that when it does take place you may believe that I am."[3] What then is the significance of the cross to which Jesus is referring when he says "then you will know, you will believe, that I am"? Why is this gruesome means of execution taken as *the* sign which will reveal to us the reality of who Jesus is?

Of all the prophecies in the Hebrew Scriptures which spoke of the Christ,[4] Jesus clearly identifies himself most supremely with those

---

1 Is 53:7–9.
2 Jn 8:28. Note it is the officials who are lifting him up, so the "lifting up" cannot refer to the resurrection.
3 Jn 13:19.
4 Gen 3:15; Gen 49:10; Num 24:17; Deut 18:15; Job 19:25; Ps 2:1–2, 7–9; Ps 16:10; Ps 22:1, 6–8, 10–11, 24, 27–31; Ps 72; Ps 89:19–29; Ps 110:1–4; Is 7:14; Is

concerning the suffering servant, the sacrificial Lamb of God who was to take away the sins of the world.[5] "For the Son of man also came not to be served but to serve, and to give his life as a ransom for many."[6] The reason for this identification is simply that "it was the will of the LORD (YHWH) to bruise him; to put him to grief... to make his soul (Hebrew: *nephesh*) an offering in restitution."[7] That Jesus understood God's will in this way is clear from the way he behaved at the Last Supper where, after having washed his disciple's feet as an example of service to them, he offered the bread as his body and the wine as his blood which would be poured out for many for the forgiveness of sins. That, for Jesus, was the meaning of his passion, and why it was to be the supreme moment of his self-revelation. Therefore, to plumb the depths of the mystery of Jesus's self-consciousness, it is necessary to understand what Jesus was communicating to his disciples in this last moment of communion with them before his passion and death.

JESUS AS REDACTOR OF THE PASSOVER

That the Last Supper was celebrated on the Passover (Greek: *Pascha*; Hebrew: *Pesach*) is asserted by all four Gospels. As described in Exodus 12, the traditional elements of this feast were: the slaughter of a lamb without blemish, the sprinkling of its blood on the lintels and doorposts of each family's home, the consumption of the lamb in haste, the eating of unleavened bread for the seven preceding days, and an assembly of all the people which was to precede and follow those seven days. The feast itself was to be performed in the private homes of families led by the father of the household. "And when your children say to you, 'What do you mean by this service?' you shall say, 'It is the sacrifice of the Passover of the LORD (YHWH),

---

9:2–7; Is 11; Is 24:16, 23; Is 40:3–5; Is 42:1–9; Is 53; Jer 23:5–6; Jer 30:21–22; Ez 17:22–24; Dan 7:13; Dan 9:24, 27; Joel 3:16; Mic 2:13; Mic 4:3–4; Mic 5:2–4; Zeph 3:14–18; Zech 3:8; Zech 6:12–13; Zech 9:9–10; Zech 11:12; Zech 12:10; Zech 14:4–5; Mal 3:1–4.
5   Jn 1:29.
6   Mk 9:12, 31; Mk 10:45; Mt 17:12, 22–23; Mt 20:28; Lk 17:25; Lk 18:32–33; Jn 12:24.
7   Is 53:10.

Lamb of God

for he passed over the houses of the people of Israel in Egypt, when he slew the Egyptians but spared our houses.'"[8]

The original Passover protected the first-born sons of the Israelites from the final plague that would strike down the first-born sons of Pharaoh and his people. The Israelites were commanded to offer up a lamb which would be taken instead of their first born, recalling the time when God himself had provided the lamb to substitute for the sacrifice of Abraham's first born, Isaac. Furthermore, they were commanded by God to keep it as a memorial for ever on the anniversary date.[9]

Nevertheless, Jesus made two significant changes which were intended to convey a new meaning, indeed, a new covenant. Firstly, no lamb was provided; instead Jesus offered his body to be eaten and his blood to be drunk rather than sprinkled on the lintels and doorposts. Secondly, this was not performed in their several homes by the father of the house, but with the twelve apostles led by Jesus.

This feast was traditionally a celebration and re-enactment of the deliverance of the children of Israel from slavery in Egypt by God through Moses, in order to bring them to the promised land of Canaan, where various sets of sacrifices were to be perpetually offered up in the tabernacle eventually situated in the temple at Jerusalem. Although the words of Jesus also parallel these events, his meaning is more universal. The Last Supper was to signify not merely a deliverance from physical bondage but was to be perpetually offered in memorial of Jesus's death for the forgiveness of sins in expectation of the coming kingdom of God.[10] That Jesus took it upon himself to alter this sacred tradition is certain testimony to his perceived Divine Authority, but it is only when the meaning of the elements used in the feast itself are considered that Jesus's self-understanding is more fully disclosed.

Jesus intentionally proffered himself as the substitute lamb to be sacrificed and consumed. This intent is made explicit in the dialogue he had with the multitude who, after being miraculously fed by Jesus, had followed him across the Sea of Galilee to Capernaum.[11] They

---

8   Ex 12:27.
9   Ex 12:14.
10 Mt 26:26–29; Mk 14:22–25; Lk 22:15–20.
11 Jn 6:22–69.

had believed him to be the "prophet (i.e., Messiah) who is to come into the world." Perceiving that they were but seeking signs, Jesus recalled to them the perishable food he had miraculously provided for them earlier on the mountain and enjoined them to work, rather, for food that is imperishable. They then inquired whether Jesus would perform further signs. Apparently they were hungry again. After all, Moses had given them bread from heaven to eat, yet that heavenly manna had been perishable also — the daily amount to which they were restricted had to be eaten straightaway lest it corrupt and become infested with worms.[12] Was the bread Jesus was providing somehow superior to that of Moses?

Jesus then explains to them that *he* is the bread of life, that whoever comes to him will not hunger, because, having been brought to him by God's providential will, Jesus will not cast them out, since he has come down from heaven to do the will of the Father. "And this is the will of him who sent me, that I should lose nothing of all that he has given me, but raise it up at the last day. For this is the will of my Father, that everyone who sees the Son and believes in him should have eternal life; and I will raise him up at the last day."[13]

When the people murmured (as did the children of Israel in the wilderness) wondering how he could be the bread come down from heaven, Jesus repeated similar sentiments and then added more emphatically: "I am the bread of life. Your fathers ate manna in the wilderness, and they died. This is the bread which comes down from heaven, that a man may eat of it and not die. I am the living bread which came down from heaven; if anyone eats of this bread, he will live forever; and the bread which I shall give for the life of the world is my flesh."[14]

When the people continued to dispute among themselves wondering how Jesus could give them his flesh to eat, Jesus then replied with a solemn oath: "Amen, amen, I say to you, unless you eat the flesh of the Son of man and drink his blood, you have no life in you; he who eats my flesh and drinks my blood has eternal life, and I will raise him up at the last day. For my flesh is true (*alethes*) food and

---

12 Ex 16:14–24.
13 Jn 6:39–40.
14 Jn 6:50–51.

my blood is true drink."[15] Many of the disciples found Jesus's saying so hard they could barely listen to it. Again they murmured.

But it is here that Jesus, perceiving they were taking offence, gives the answer we seek: "What if you were to see the Son of man ascending where he was before? It is the spirit that gives life, the flesh is of no avail; the words that I have spoken to you are spirit and life. But there are some of you that do not believe."[16] This latter is distinct from the previous discourse about consuming his flesh, since his reply is an answer to the offence to belief that Jesus's words had caused the disciples. Where previously he used the term "my flesh" now he is using the term "the flesh." His rejoinder is that if they saw Jesus ascend from the dead would they still believe? No, because it is the Spirit who gives life; no one can come to Jesus unless God draws them: "This is why I told you that no one can come to me unless it is granted him by the Father."[17] Jesus words were uttered in the Spirit and were meant to give life to those who would hear, those drawn to Jesus by the same Spirit of the Father.

Indeed, at that point many of the disciples withdrew and ceased to follow him. Letting them depart, Jesus then asked the twelve: "Do you also wish to go away?" And Simon Peter, spokesman for the twelve, declared: "Lord, to whom shall we go? You have the words of eternal life; and we have believed, and have come to know, that you are the Holy One of God."[18] It is precisely because Jesus is the Holy One of God, having come down from heaven, that he, upon ascending to where he was before, could confer upon his apostles the authority to offer his body and blood in the unbloody offering (Hebrew: *minha*)[19] of bread and wine as a perpetual memorial of Jesus's once-and-for-all sacrifice given for the remission of sins.

This is no mere metaphor but a reality that the risen and glorified Jesus would make available perpetually. To see that this is indeed the case we must turn to another aspect of the Last Supper: the tradition

---

15 Jn 6:53–55.
16 Jn 6:62–64.
17 Jn 6:65. See also Jn 6:44.
18 Jn 6:66–69.
19 Mal 1:11.

of the bread of the Presence (Hebrew: *panah*—literally: face, countenance). Of the various offerings made by the priests (burnt, cereal, peace, sin, and trespass offerings) the only one not involving animal sacrifice was the cereal offering (*minha*). This offering was burnt as thanks for the first fruits of the harvest. However, part of the cereal offering consisted of twelve cakes, unleavened with no additives except salt, which were to be incensed and burnt every Sabbath perpetually in memorial of the covenant.[20] This was the bread of the Presence which was to be reserved solely for the priests in the temple and was to be offered every Sabbath without profaning the priests even though they were performing a work on that obligatory day of rest. This bread was the same bread which David ate when he was hungry after having fled King Saul.[21]

Similarly, when the disciples were hungry, they plucked from the standing grain reserved for the poor.[22] It was the Sabbath. When some Pharisees complained that they were doing what was unlawful on the Sabbath,[23] Jesus pointed out that, although David had eaten the bread of the Presence reserved only for priests, and though the priests were offering the bread of the Presence on the Sabbath, when it was unlawful to work, both were without guilt. He then admonished: "Something greater than the temple is here. And if you had known what this means, 'I desire mercy, and not sacrifice,' you would not have condemned the guiltless. For the Son of man is lord of the Sabbath."[24] In other words, like David and the priests, the disciples were guiltless, since there is a higher law: the law of mercy. The Pharisees were exhorted to show mercy to the disciples rather than demand the sacrifice of hunger even though it was a holy day: the day set aside to honor God. Moreover, Jesus was lord of the Sabbath: the disciples were doing what he had permitted. That much is obvious. However, Jesus had also asserted that "something greater than the temple is here." Once again he raises the issue of authority.

---

20 Ex 25:30, 39:36, 40:23; Lev 24:5–9; Num 4:7–8.
21 1 Sam 21:6.
22 Deut 23:25.
23 According to the Mishna one is guilty of desecrating the Sabbath if one "takes ears of grain equal to a lamb's mouthful." *Shabbath* 7:4, cf. 7:2.
24 Mt 12:1–8 = Mk 2:23–28 = Lk 6:1–5.

For the children of Israel, the Sabbath was what distinguished them, what constituted them as a people before God. More especially, the Sabbath day of rest was what characterized Israel as that people who, like God, rested on the seventh day. The Sabbath observance was the means whereby each Jew, as it were, entered into the Holy of Holies, dwelt there, and rested before the Presence. That was why the bread of the Presence, which symbolized God's nurturing of the children of Israel with heavenly manna for forty years in the wilderness, was a memorial offered perpetually in the temple on the Sabbath. It commemorated God's eternal presence with his people.

Now Jesus had already declared himself the source and object of Sabbath rest in the verses immediately preceding this Sabbath narrative: "Come to me, all who labor and are heavy laden, and I will give you rest. Take my yoke upon you, and learn from me; for I am gentle and lowly in heart, and you will find rest for your souls. For my yoke is easy, and my burden is light."[25] A contemporary Jewish Rabbi, Jacob Neusner, has also followed this question of authority through the Sermon on the Mount, but when he came to this passage he is recorded as remarking: "No wonder, then, that the son of man is lord of the Sabbath! The reason is not that he interprets the Sabbath restrictions in a liberal manner.... Jesus was not just another reforming rabbi, out to make life 'easier' for people.... No, the issue is not that the burden is light.... Jesus's claim to authority is at issue. Christ now stands on the mountain; he now takes the place of the Torah.... Is it really so that your master, the son of man, is lord of the Sabbath? ... I ask again — is your master God?"[26]

To answer the rabbi's question, it is necessary to consider the symbolism of bread, which is too strong here to be ignored, especially since it was Jesus himself who made this connection. The disciples were consuming *wheat* (*stachuas*) on the Sabbath; and Jesus linked (Hebrew: *kesher*) that with the bread of the Presence with regard to both David and the Sabbath offering. This bread was kept in the tabernacle, in the Holy Place, to the north of the Ark of the Covenant, opposite the menorah (the seven-branched golden candelabrum)

---

25 Mt 11:28–30.
26 Quoted in Ratzinger, *Jesus of Nazareth*, 110.

which was on the south.²⁷ The Golden Altar of Incense was between them. A heavy double veil separated the Holy Place from the Holy of Holies, which originally contained the ark of the covenant but in the second temple period was empty, except for the foundation stone. It was here that the holy Presence (*Shechinah*) filled the tabernacle.²⁸ Only the high priest could enter the Holy of Holies on one day in the year: the Day of Atonement. On that day the mercy seat (which supported the two cherubim), the veil of the sanctuary, and the horns of the altar were sprinkled with the blood from the sin offerings. Only on one day of the year, therefore, was blood sprinkled on the altar near where the bread of the Presence was kept in the Holy Place. Only then were these two elements brought together. Similarly, at the Last Supper Jesus also brought together his atoning sacrifice and the perpetual offering of the bread of the Presence. When Jesus, mindful of the death he was about to suffer, declared the bread to be his body and the wine his blood as a memorial, the traditions of the perpetually offered bread of the Presence and the singular offering of blood on the Day of Atonement in the temple were merged in his Person. Jesus made his body the temple of sacrifice.²⁹

On one other occasion Jesus declared himself to be the locus where an atoning sacrifice would be made: at the first cleansing of the temple. When asked for a sign of his authority Jesus declared, "Destroy this temple, and in three days I will raise it up." As St John adds: "He spoke of the temple of his body."³⁰ Jesus not only takes the place of the Torah, but of the temple as well. That which is prefigured is always greater than the figure, because it is the fulfillment of that to which the analogue is proportionate. Greater even than the temple, Jesus is lord of the Sabbath — a point which did not escape Rabbi Neusner.

To summarize, at the Last Supper Jesus (who was clearly aware of the inherent symbolism of what he was doing) established himself as the new deliverer, prefigured by Moses, who would lead the reconstituted twelve into a more glorious land of promise, the Heavenly Kingdom where he would remain with them as the new Temple.

---

27 Ex 25.
28 Num 9:15–16.
29 See Heb 9:1–28.
30 Jn 2:19, 21.

Meanwhile, in anticipation and as a memorial, his apostles were to consume his body and blood as a perpetual unbloody offering (*minha*) in his name. No gentile at the time would have been so familiar with the priestly traditions as to unify all these elements and themes together in this manner. And neither would Paul[31] or any of the Jewish disciples[32] ever have dared to: the consumption of human flesh or blood was proscribed in Jewish law.[33] Only if Jesus were the Son of God could he have had the authority to transform the Passover in such a radical way. Only if his disciples had revered him as such would they have followed him in this. For his sacrifice was intended to end and replace all the others, completely demolishing the entire temple cult. That it did so is a matter of historical fact.

Jesus was arrested, tried by the Sanhedrin for blasphemy, and crucified under Pontius Pilate. He died between two thieves, forgiving his persecutors. Jesus — who had made the deaf to hear, the lame to walk, and the blind to see; who had spoken sublime words of hope and encouragement which the common people had gladly received; and who had promised eternal life in his name — was killed because "he had made himself equal to God."[34] The last good work before his death was to grant the request of one of the thieves: admission into paradise — something only God could bestow.

His work perfected, Jesus dropped his head and gave up his spirit having consciously offered himself for our sake, so that we might become worthy to enter the Kingdom of Heaven. "For our sake he made him to be sin who knew no sin, so that in him we might become the righteousness of God."[35] There can be no doubt that Jesus was fully aware that he had come from God for just this: "that the Son of man must suffer many things and be rejected by the elders and the chief priests and the scribes, and be killed, and after three days rise again. And he said this plainly."[36]

---

31 1 Cor 10:16, 11:23–26; 2 Cor 3:6.
32 Heb 7:26–28. This is the historical-critical principle of double discontinuity.
33 Lev 17:12–13, 26:27–30; Num. 5:2, 6:6, 19:11–13.
34 Jn 5:18, 10:33; Mt 26:65; Mk 14:64.
35 2 Cor 5:21.
36 Mk 8:31–32 = Mt 16:21–28 = Lk 9:22–27.

Part Two: Wisdom

THE RESURRECTION

This new covenant could have ended with a dead Galilean hanging on the cross. However holy his person, however glorious his teaching, however loving his companionship, it could have ended there in futility with his disciples confused and disarrayed, cowering fearfully, hiding from the authorities. That it did not end there is the only reason why the Gospels were ever written. Their intended purpose was to proclaim the resurrection of the one who had shown himself to be the Christ — not the triumphant world-conquering Messiah but the sacrificial lamb, offered for our sins and risen in triumph. The whole of history was consummated in this pre-eminent act. The entire saga of their sacred scriptures was fulfilled in this event: Christ is risen. It was then that the disciples at last realized who Jesus is.

Without the resurrection the disciples would have simply returned to their several trades — in fact, that is precisely what they did do for a while.[37] But then something happened to change them. Suddenly they became courageous, enthusiastic witnesses giving their very lives fearlessly for the Gospel truth that Jesus is the lamb of God who gave his life as a ransom for many and who was exalted into heaven by his heavenly Father.

Since Schleiermacher, the liberal construction upon this has been that the disciples' religious response was generated by those painful and disorienting feelings which followed the death of their beloved master. Remembering that Jesus had promised to be with them always, the disciples' unconceptualized feelings of dependency expressed themselves in the idea of resurrection. Jesus had not abandoned them, nor was he defeated, but he was risen, and as a somewhat divine being was still with them through his spirit and would soon return to fulfill his promises to them. The following passage from Edward Schillebeeckx is typical of this interpretation:

> At first those Christians did not know what to make of Jesus's suffering and death; so great however was their faith in God that they had more confidence in him than in all that the concrete and painful facts of history so manifestly

---

[37] Jn 21:1–3.

shouted aloud. The insight provided by their faith may have needed time; in the end they knew: through their official authorities men might give judgment against this righteous one; but he cannot be forsaken by God.[38]

Underlying these ideas is the Kantian presupposition that one cannot distinguish objective reality, that one is forced to project one's *a priori* upon events. But we have seen that this aspect of Kantianism is false. In any case there is no evidence of this sort of thing taking place among the Hebrew-speaking peoples. For them the fundamental distinguishing characteristic of a prophet was that his prophecies must come to pass: "When a prophet speaks in the name of the LORD (YHWH) and the thing does not happen and the word is not fulfilled, then it has not been said by the LORD (YHWH). The prophet has spoken presumptuously. You have nothing to fear from him."[39] In fact the penalty for false prophecy was death.[40] The only reason the prophets such as Isaiah, Jeremiah, Ezekiel, and Daniel, etc. were accepted as sacred scripture is that they were revered because their prophecies had been fulfilled. The Jews did not receive their prophets as easily as the followers of Schleiermacher presume. It was incumbent upon them to discern and to denounce false prophets.

Secondly, if the Jews were predisposed to confer bodily resurrection upon holy men after their demise, then we would have expected to find some evidence for this. But there is none. To be sure, Enoch and Elijah had been taken straight to heaven according to the scriptures, but there was no tradition of *bodily* appearances to their followers. In any case, the Sadducees continued to reject any notion of bodily resurrection, which would have been difficult to maintain if these prophets were understood to have been resurrected bodily. Even if resurrection was a post-exilic idea, then we would have expected resurrection to have been attributed to one of the holy men such as Honi the Circle Drawer or Hanina ben Dosa, or to messianic figures such as one of the Maccabee brothers, or Simeon bar Kosiba (bar Kochba).

---

38 Edward Schillebeeckx, *Jesus: An Experiment in Christology* (London: Collins, 1974), 526.
39 Deut 28:22.
40 Deut 28:20. Cf. Deut 13:1–5.

It was never done. The Jewish people knew better, they were more sophisticated than that, and they revered their traditions too much to abandon them so easily. The latter, in fact, was part of the problem the authorities had in accepting Jesus. It was part of the reason for the disciples' confusion. It even continued to be a difficulty among those early Jewish Christians who wanted to require gentile converts to be circumcised and to observe the laws of Moses.[41]

However, what the evidence does show is that those Jews, who did believe in resurrection, never believed it would occur until the end of the world, when all would be consummated. The universal belief among the Jews at that time, indeed all over the pagan world, was that after death the soul went to dwell with their ancestors in a shadowy spirit-world called Sheol (Greek: *Hades*; Latin: *Tartarus*). In a painstaking and exhaustive study of ancient pagan beliefs about the afterlife, N. T. Wright has concluded:

> Who were the dead thought to be, in the ancient world? They were beings that had once been embodied human beings, but were now souls, shades, or *eidola*. Where were they? Most likely in Hades; possibly in the Isles of the Blessed, or Tartarus; just conceivably, reincarnated into a different body altogether. They might occasionally appear to living mortals; they might still be located somewhere in the vicinity of their tombs; but they were basically in a different world. What was wrong? Nothing... the soul was well rid of its body.[42]

For the ancient world death was all-powerful and inescapable. "There was no resurrection in the Christian sense of a new embodied life which would *follow* whatever 'life after death' there might be. 'Resurrection' was, by definition, not the existence into which someone might (or might not) go immediately upon death; it was not a disembodied 'heavenly' life; it was a further stage, out beyond all that."[43] As such it was the very reversal of death.

---

41 Acts 15:1–30; Gal 2:1–10.
42 N. T. Wright, *The Resurrection of the Son of God* (London: SPCK, 2003), 82.
43 Ibid., 83.

According to Wright, three considerations arise from these facts:[44]

1. When the early Christians had claimed that Jesus had risen from the dead, the natural assumption of the time was that something unprecedented had happened. The Jews, if they were Sadducees, did not believe in it at all; or if they were Pharisees, they knew it could not have happened yet; and the pagans assumed it was impossible. When the Christians continued to proclaim Christ's bodily resurrection, both Jew and pagan would have understood that they were declaring it had happened uniquely to Jesus.

2. The Christians' belief in the divinity of Jesus could not in itself have been the cause of their belief in the resurrection. For pagans, divinization happened regularly to their emperors; and their graves were generally known. For the Jews, as we have seen, there was no such precedent.

3. Later non-Christian usage adopted the term resurrection, but applied it to denote that state of blissful, but disembodied, immortality in which they had already believed. Thus a term which denoted something which hardly anyone believed in before Christ, was much later altered into something a great number of them had already accepted. Nevertheless, it was still not the bodily resurrection which the Christians were proclaiming for Jesus Christ.

The basic belief among the Jews then was that the resurrection would not occur until the consummation of all things at the end of the world. This is reflected in the pericope where Jesus, about to restore Lazarus to life, says to Martha: "Your brother will rise again." To which she replies: "I know he will rise again in the resurrection *at the last day*."[45] The resurrection of any individual, whoever he might be, was not expected by Jews—those who accepted the concept at all—until the end of the world. Furthermore, there are several factors, in the way the Gospels narrate the event, that indicate that Jesus himself could be the only source of the belief in the resurrection:[46]

---

44 Ibid.
45 Jn 11:23–24.
46 Wright, *Resurrection*, 599–615. See also R. A. Kereszty, *Jesus Christ* (Staten Island, NY: Alba House, 2002); G. E. Ladd, *I Believe in the Resurrection of Jesus* (London: Hodder & Stoughton, 1975); F. Morrison, *Who Moved the Stone?* (Bromley: STL, 1983); G. R. Osborne, *The Resurrection Narratives* (Grand

Firstly, the habit the evangelists displayed of constantly quoting Biblical sources to validate Jesus's words and actions is missing from the resurrection narratives. This is remarkable because not only does it demonstrate that no scriptural basis could be found to validate the resurrection, but that the story was not invented solely to show Jesus as having fulfilled some prophecy. This notion, that the evangelists freely invented stories about Jesus to fulfill some Biblical prefiguring, is often given as the reason for their being specious. This is not the case with the resurrection narratives.

Secondly, it has often been noted that it is not in the interests of the evangelists to present women as the first witnesses of the resurrection or as the recipients of the first appearance of Jesus, given the prejudicial attitude against women's testimony in those days. Surely Peter, James, or John would have been the more convincing persons to validate these stories. Yet it is the women who are the original witnesses and the initial transmitters of the good news that he is risen from the dead.

Thirdly, the epistles of St Paul (as do other early Christian documents of the first and second centuries) use the resurrection as a basis for hope in a *future* world, whereas in the Gospels it is used as a basis for vindicating the Son of God so as to validate his authority as the Christ, as the justification for the apostolic commission to go out into *this* world. Also, Jesus appears (after his ascension) to Paul as a being of shining light, but in the Gospels he appears (before the ascension) as an ordinary person who can eat fish and be touched by the apostles.[47] These differences between the Gospel narratives and the Pauline paraenesis imply that these narratives are independent of Pauline influence.

Finally, if the Gospels were the result of later redactions, then why do differences between the narratives remain? One would have thought that these discrepancies[48] in the story would have even-

---

Rapids: Baker, 1984); J. Wenham, *The Easter Enigma* (Exeter: The Paternoster Press, 1984).

47 *Nowhere* in the Gospels does it say, as do some exegetes, that Jesus could "enter through locked doors": he just appears in a particular place (in spacetime?).
48 In the number and identities of women present, their reasons for visiting the tomb, the number of angels present, and exactly which of the disciples were informed by the women.

tually been removed to provide a consolidated, more convincing history, particularly if they are late. For by then they would have been known among the various communities and would have shown evidence of having been altered according to their needs. The fact that these discrepancies do remain is further evidence of the independence of these narratives. Rather they appear very much like the sort of eyewitness accounts normally found in legal testimonies. They overlap and agree on substantial points although there are surface and somewhat trivial inconsistencies. They look like natural human testimonies.

Those who deny the resurrection have invented ingenious, but disputed and unprovable,[49] hypotheses concerning layers of tradition, various postulated redactors with their several theological purposes, political or factional justifications for the presence of the individual characters and their contexts, etc., in order to explain the continuities and discontinuities in the accounts so as to save their theory of late invention or to avoid the challenge of faith.

The simpler, more parsimonious explanation is that each evangelist put the evidence together as best he could from the eyewitness accounts available, selecting and arranging them according to his own purpose. Indeed, "the very strong historical probability is that, when Matthew, Luke and John describe the risen Jesus, they are writing down very early oral tradition, representing three different ways in which the original astonished participants told the stories."[50] The latter sounds like what one normally encounters in historical investigations of any transcriptions of events.

It is St Paul who presents the state of belief of the early Christians towards Jesus's resurrection. Writing about twenty years later, Paul relates how he had received the tradition, most likely from Peter and James when he met with them in Jerusalem *not more than ten years* after Jesus's resurrection and appearances to the apostles.

---

49 Because of the fallacy of affirming the consequent, Craig's theorem, Miller and Tichy's proof, etc. See last chapter. One need only compare Perrin's liberal conclusion about the resurrection with Osborne's conservative one to see how unreliable redaction criticism is; and if the method is unreliable, it cannot be valid.
50 Wright, *Resurrection*, 611.

> For I delivered to you as of first importance what I also received, that Christ died for our sins in accordance with the scriptures, that he was buried, that he was raised on the third day in accordance with the scriptures, and that he appeared to Cephas,[51] then to the twelve. Then he appeared to more than five hundred brethren at one time, most of whom are still alive, though some have fallen asleep. Then he appeared to James, then to all the apostles. Last of all, as to one untimely born, he appeared to me.[52]

Clearly, Paul's witness is strong evidence for the empty tomb: for if, as Saul — the Pharisee, student of Gamaliel, and persecutor of Christians — he knew that the body was still in its tomb, then no apparition would ever have convinced him of a *bodily* resurrection. That the appearance to Paul on the road to Damascus was different from the appearances recorded in the Gospels does not affect the issue, since Paul clearly believed that these post-resurrection appearances were bodily:

> For someone will ask, "How are the dead raised? With what kind of *body* do they come?" ... What you sow does not come to life unless it dies. And what you sow is not *the body which is to be*, but a bare kernel, perhaps of wheat or of some other grain. But God gives it a *body* as he has chosen, and to each kind of seed its own *body*.... There are celestial bodies and there are terrestrial bodies; but the glory of the celestial is one [thing], and the glory of the terrestrial is another.... So it is with the resurrection of the dead. What is sown is perishable, what is raised is imperishable.... It is sown a physical body, it is raised a spiritual *body*.... Lo! I tell you a mystery. We shall not all sleep, but we shall all be *changed*, in a moment, in the twinkling of an eye, at the last trumpet. For the trumpet will sound, and the dead will be raised imperishable, and *we shall be changed. For this perishable nature must put on the imperishable, and this mortal nature must put on immortality.*[53]

---

51   I.e., Peter.
52   1 Cor 15:3–8.
53   1 Cor 15:35–53.

In other words, Paul, writing some twenty years after the event, concludes that resurrection involves the transformation of the body from perishable to imperishable, from mortal to immortal, from terrestrial to celestial. At the consummation of all things, the body raised up will have been changed "in the twinkling of an eye, at the last trumpet," so that it is no longer of a physically contingent nature. Yet, although this is a mystery, it *is* a body, but glorified and immortal.

It is clear from these passages that Paul believed in the bodily resurrection of Jesus which he had received as an early tradition from the apostles. But his own later experience was of Jesus's resurrection in a glorified form: the first fruits of what is to occur generally at the consummation when all would be similarly transformed. This does not substantially differ from the evangelists' accounts where Jesus's body is described as similar to ours yet possessing radically altered properties.

Apropos, if Luke is indeed the trustworthy, eminent historian many believe him to be, then within two months of Jesus's resurrection we also have this testimony from St Peter himself:

> Brethren, I may say to you confidently of the patriarch David that he both died and was buried, and his tomb is with us to this day. Being therefore a prophet... he foresaw and spoke of the resurrection of the Christ, that he was not abandoned to Hades, *nor did his flesh see corruption.* This Jesus God raised up, and *of that we all are witnesses....* Let all the house of Israel therefore know assuredly that God has made him both Lord and Christ, this Jesus whom you crucified.[54]

From what we have said so far there can be no doubt that the early Christians believed that Jesus had risen from the dead in a form that accorded with their concept of bodily resurrection, but before the "proper" time, i.e., before the consummation when it was supposed to happen. Moreover, the evidence shows clearly that while the pagans never contemplated a resurrection of the body, the Jewish traditions never attributed a resurrection to anyone else in the past or to the

---

54 Acts 2:29–32, 36. See also Ps 16:8–11, 110:1.

Messiah. Therefore, the only possible source for the idea of Jesus's resurrection was Jesus himself. This in fact is the plain interpretation of the New Testament witness.

> Throughout it all we have seen the obvious but important point, that those who held the complex but remarkably consistent early Christian view gave as their reason that Jesus of Nazareth had himself been raised from the dead. And we have now seen what they meant by this: that on the third day after his execution by the Romans, the tomb was empty, and he was found to be alive, appearing on various occasions and in various places both to his followers and to some who, up to that point, had not been his followers or had not believed, convincing them that he was neither a ghost or hallucination but that he was truly and bodily raised from the dead.[55]

Of course this does not establish the historical fact that Jesus actually rose from the dead, however parsimonious, complete, or sufficient an explanation this may provide for the origins of the convictions of the early Christians. Even controversial relics such as the Shroud of Turin or the Sudarium of Oviedo, if their authenticity were established, could only serve to corroborate the Gospel witness to the crucifixion of Christ.

Nevertheless, recent forensic examination of the Turin Shroud has established it as a definitive and material archaeological relic of the crucifixion and death of Jesus as recorded in the Gospels, and could contribute substantially to our knowledge of his historicity. The radiocarbon dating of the Turin Shroud to no earlier than AD 1260 is almost certainly erroneous and somewhat suspicious according to Ian Wilson's latest work.[56] Evidence from St Catherine's Monastery in the Sinai and from the Sancta Sanctorum Chapel of the Lateran confirms the Shroud's having been known as early as the sixth

---

55 Wright, *Resurrection*, 681.
56 Ian Wilson, *The Shroud: The 2000-Year-Old Mystery Solved* (London: Bantam Press, 2010), 136, 281. Radiocarbon dating has often been found to be unreliable particularly with organic materials such as linen. See ibid., 84–99.

century. And study of the textile weave and stitching show hidden technical features that link this expensive cloth to those produced in Palestine during the first century. Also, samples of dirt discovered on the soles of the feet of the image were analyzed to consist of rare travertine aragonite, containing trace deposits of iron and strontium, consistent with that deposited by springs in the regions of Jerusalem. Samples of pollen grains found in the Shroud also confirm this. Furthermore, forensic medical evidence has revealed that the Shroud is impossible to fake unless the patterns of blood and wounds resulted from the *actual crucifixion of a man*: who had been struck, scourged, crowned with thorns, and whose right side was pierced by a lance. Chafing marks on the shoulders are consistent with his having borne a heavy rough beam. Moreover, the same forensic evidence shows that the separation of blood cells and plasma, as well as the muscular rigidity observed over the body, indicate that the victim was dead. This refutes the assertions of those who — while accepting that the shroud was indeed that of Jesus — purport that he never really died.[57] Yet the body image shows no signs of decomposition.

However, the most compelling evidence for the Shroud's authenticity comes from the Sudarium of Oviedo: a blood-stained, coarse linen cloth believed to have been used to bind the head and to catch the life blood of the victim. The victim was clearly dead, having died from a pulmonary oedema. This blood is not smeared and has been shown to have spasmodically erupted from the lungs of a real man spreading onto the left cheek and into the beard. Further examination has shown that, consistent with his head subsequently having been in a horizontal position, the blood then flowed upwards along both cheeks. It followed the ridge of the nose to the forehead between the eyebrows, where it formed a triangle.

Research has established seventy points of agreement between the Sudarium and the Shroud including: the blood is type AB on both cloths; the nose on both the Shroud and Sudarium is eight centimeters long; it is swollen in the middle of the right side and displaced to

---

57 E.g., see Rodney Hoare, *The Turin Shroud is Genuine: The Irrefutable Evidence* (London: The Souvenir Press, 1994). This (biochemical) evidence is from one who is actually opposed to the belief of the resurrection of Christ.

the right (from a blow or a fall); the right cheek is completely bloody on both cloths; there is point-for-point correspondence between the tip of the nose, the position of the mouth and chin, and the shape of the beard; puncture wounds at the back of the neck on the Sudarium coincide with those resembling a crown of thorns on the Shroud; the hair is tied back in a ponytail on both cloths; the pre- and post-mortem blood patterns on the Shroud match their size, shape, and location on the face of the Sudarium; and the facial characteristics also correspond.[58]

Such firm links with the Turin Shroud invalidate the Shroud's radiocarbon dating. "According to the account of the bishop Pelagius (Pelayo of Oviedo), the Sudarium left Jerusalem in the Holy Ark (or chest) in the year AD 614 under the name of Sudarium Domini, the Sudarium of the Lord. According to this document, *tradition associates the cloth with the sudarium of Jesus of Nazareth and no other person.*"[59] Indeed, meticulous biochemical, physiographical, medical, and geometrical examinations yield the conclusion that both the Sudarium and the Shroud are of the same man of Middle-Eastern physiognomy. Moreover, botanical study of the pollen residue (including aloe and myrrh) supports the tradition that the Sudarium was in the Jerusalem environs before coming to Spain. It has been kept among other relics in a chest in the cathedral of San Salvador, Oviedo, since the eighth century.

Furthermore, analysis of very rare coins minted during the Byzantine reign of Justinian II (AD 692), which portray the face of Christ, has revealed over 12 points of agreement between them and the Turin Shroud.[60] The probability that the artist would have obtained this result fortuitously was calculated to be 7.26×10^{-18} or seven chances

---

58 Guillermo Heras Moreno, José-Delfín Villalaín Blanco, and Jorge-Manuel Rodríguez Almenar, "III Congresso Internazionale di Studi Sulla Sindone Turin," trans. Mark Guscin, *The Shroud of Turin* (website), June 5–7, 1998, www.shroud.com/heraseng.pdf. See also Janice Bennett, *Sacred Blood, Sacred Image: New Evidence for the Authenticity of the Shroud of Turin* (San Francisco: Ignatius Press, 2005), 69–74, 84–89.
59 Moreno, Blanco, and Almenar, "III Congresso." Italics added.
60 Giulio Fanti and Pierandrea Malfi, *The Shroud of Turin: First Century After Christ!* (Singapore: Pan Stanford Publishing, 2015), 108–25 and appendix A3.

in a billion billion. This and other findings, such as the chemical and mechanical (stress) analysis of the cloth's fibers, led to the conclusion:

> According to the authors, the two chemical dating tests associated to the mechanical test confirm that the Shroud is coeval to the age in which Christ lived. In addition, the numismatic evidence corroborates the Shroud's existence before the period between 1260 and 1390 [AD] established by the wrongly performed ^{14}C testing, because it shows that in 692 [AD] the Shroud was taken as a model for the coins depicting the face of Christ.... In fact, also the hypothesis, even if extremely improbable, that a more recent artist would have reproduced the image of the Redeemer not on a cloth contemporary to his age but on a more than 4 m (13 ft.) long sheet *dated back to the first century* [AD] and from then still well conserved (supposing that he could have found one) *should be rejected with scientific certainty.*[61]

It is evident from these studies that the Shroud of Turin and the Sudarium of Oviedo, with their separate histories and travels, their numerous points of forensic agreement, and the scientific data they contain, are of a specific person who suffered and died in a manner consistent with the Gospels' accounts of the passion, death, and entombment of Jesus. The lack of signs of decomposition on the Shroud also affirms that the body and Shroud were separated before corruption began. It is evident, therefore, that on the third day the tomb was indeed empty, but the valuable Shroud (along with other cloths) and the Sudarium were left behind.[62]

However, in spite of all this, the image on the Turin Shroud, if it should be determined to be "non-handmade" (*acheiropoietos*) — and not formed by natural means (such as a coronal discharge caused by earthquake lightning producing a type of Tesla effect in the tomb, or perhaps bacterial or biochemical discoloration)[63] — could only

---

61 Fanti and Malfi, *The Shroud of Turin*, 336. Italics added.
62 Jn 20:3–9.
63 E.g., see Fanti and Malfi, *The Shroud of Turin*, 28–29. See also Raymond

yield the conclusion that its manner of creation is inexplicable. Since empirical evidence can only secure probable confirmation of a hypothesis and since the argument from human authority is the weakest form of argument,[64] then it would be virtually impossible to prove a miraculous origin for its image.

But that is not necessary. It has not been our purpose either in this chapter or in the previous one to prove something which we have already noted is impossible to verify, viz., that Jesus is the Son of God, the Lamb of God, or the risen Lord. However, what we have shown is that the only possible source for each of these beliefs is Jesus himself. In the last chapter we dealt with Jesus's self-awareness as the pre-existent Son of God, come into the world, who proclaimed himself to be the embodiment of Divine Authority and Wisdom. In this chapter we have seen that he understood himself to be the suffering servant, who came to give his life as a ransom for many; that he is Lord of the Sabbath, and the new Temple, wherein all can find eternal rest. For these reasons he could claim the authority to alter sacred traditions and to make himself the object of veneration and the principle of everlasting life. And we have seen that very early on, the disciples were already proclaiming Jesus as the risen Lord based upon their conviction that they had seen him alive with preternatural powers: that his sacrifice conquered death and sin, and that his bodily resurrection was the irruption into the world of a new age, where all things have been subordinated to him. Accordingly, the apostles soon dared to abandon the prescribed Sabbath day, proclaiming the Lord's Day instead; and this despite the centrality and weight placed upon the Sabbath as an obligatory holy day which had defined all Israel. Henceforth, the Sacrifice of the Mass, instituted by Jesus Christ, was to remain the central rite of the Church.[65]

N. Rogers and Anna Arnoldi, "Scientific Method Applied to the Shroud of Turin: A Review," *The Shroud of Turin* (website), 2002, http://shroud.com/pdfs/rogers2.pdf.

64 *Summa Theol.* I, q. 1, art. 8, obj. 2. Divine revelation excepted — since God's authority is sacrosanct: God neither errs nor deceives.

65 "For me, the celebration of the Lord's day, which was a characteristic part of the Christian community from the outset, is one of the most convincing proofs that something extraordinary happened that day — the discovery of the

Although it may seem paradoxical to combine images of a sacrificial lamb with that of a conquering Lord, this is precisely the imagery found in the Apocalypse: "Worthy is the Lamb who was slain, to receive power and wealth and wisdom and might and honor and glory and blessing."[66] Or again, when the beast, representing imperial worldly power, and the decadent harlot who characteristically rides upon it, together make war on the Lamb, "the Lamb will conquer them, for he is Lord of lords and King of kings."[67] The Lamb simply personifies the basic precepts of Jesus that to be last is to be first and to lose one's life is to gain it.[68] It is the spiritually poor who inherit the kingdom of heaven; those who mourn who are comforted; the meek who inherit the earth; those who hunger and thirst for righteousness who are filled; those who show mercy who will obtain mercy; and those persecuted for the sake of righteousness who possess the kingdom of heaven. Jesus himself exemplified these beatitudes in his Person: they were his defining characteristics as though the very essence of his Being is to pour himself out for others. Since God is one, true, good, and beautiful, and therefore holy, and since it is the nature of his Being to give being—the essence of Love to give love—we have in Christ Jesus the exemplar of what God would look like if he became incarnate on earth. Thus, it is not perplexing when Revelation says: "And I saw no temple in the city, for its temple is the Lord God the Almighty and the Lamb. And the city has no need of sun or moon to shine upon it, for the glory of God is its light, and its lamp is the Lamb."[69]

SUMMARY AND CONCLUSION

That God exists, rather that there is a subsistent, eternal Principle underlying all things, is a conviction which follows upon the light of reason: the principle of being, which is the source of all conceiving

---

empty tomb and the encounter with the risen Lord." Joseph Ratzinger [Benedict XVI], *Jesus of Nazareth: Holy Week* (London: Catholic Truth Society, 2011), 259.
66 Rev 5:12.
67 Rev 17:14. Cf. Rev 5:8–10, 7:17, 12:11, 15:3–4, 22:1–3.
68 Mt 20:16, 10:39.
69 Rev 21:22–23.

and which itself determines the structure of reason. We have seen that the evidence from physical science confirms this idea and contradicts the (Kantian) notion that this conclusion is merely the result of our creaturely way of thinking. Furthermore, there is nothing to contradict this conviction, for it is clearly not inherently absurd, since it follows tautologically from the certain idea of being, obeying the logically necessary principles which belong to that idea. Nor is God's existence contradicted by the existence of evil, i.e., privation of the good, for we have shown that God, who alone is good, is capable of bringing good from every evil. Furthermore, in Jesus Christ we have the realization of exactly what God can bring from evil: a uniquely beautiful and supra-ordinary Person.

We have been considering this phenomenon which is Jesus Christ and have encountered him as the Son of God, Lamb of God, and Savior. This is who Jesus proclaimed himself to be. This is why he voluntarily went to his death. It is what the disciples came to affirm after witnessing his resurrection. And in the process we have found that our concept of God has metamorphosed. We have discovered that God is indeed personal, *according to the witness of Jesus Christ*, who is conscious of a profound, mutually loving relationship with his heavenly Father. God must henceforth be understood to have the form of a Father who from all eternity brought forth the Son who became incarnate for our sake in Christ Jesus.

This much is demonstrable to one who has followed the light of reason this far. However, for one to take the next step, of confessing that Jesus is *indeed* who he claims to be, requires faith in his testimony. Actually it requires a discernment of his Person such that faith in him becomes possible. Faith adds to belief the element of trust. For those who see Truth in Jesus, who can put their trust in him, Jesus becomes a sure grounding for further belief. One who believes in Jesus can believe *on* him happily trusting in his teachings and his promises. For *if God is in Christ* then Jesus cannot err, neither would he lie, nor deceive us by compromising his truth. Upon him our faith is firmly grounded.

Reason can only prepare for faith: it cannot prove it. Because of this the Church has always been attentive to the distinction between natural and Divine theology. The conviction that some Creator exists belongs to natural theology (metaphysics). Doctrines, such as the incarnation, atonement, or the resurrection, belong to Divine or revealed theology. The former conviction only requires the exercise of the natural reason reflecting upon creation according to the inner light of the intellect: the light of being. The latter doctrines, however, require the personal assent of faith according to the light of grace.[70] God, who gave us free will, does not force salvation upon the individual: we are free to choose whom or what we will serve. We are not free to serve nothing at all: "We are [as it were] condemned to meaning."[71] For it is impossible to think or act without the implicit acknowledgment of being. Thus, the Old Testament was right: the issue has never really been between God and no god at all, but between God and idols. The belief that God exists belongs to reason; the conviction, that "God was in Christ Jesus reconciling the world to himself"[72] belongs to faith.

Those who cannot or will not take the step of trusting in Jesus's witness will be unable to follow us any further, since we have now moved beyond belief based solely on reason and evidence, into the dimension of faith based on personal trust. Those who already have made this commitment or who are prepared to do so may continue to follow us as we next inquire if Jesus really intended to establish the Church and, if so, what was its intended form and purpose.

---

70 As we shall see in chapter 7.
71 M. Merleau-Ponty, *Phenomenology of Perception* (London: Routledge & Kegan Paul, 1962), xix (in opposition to Sartre's "condemned to nothingness").
72 2 Cor 5:19.

CHAPTER 6

Christ the King

Blessed are you, Simon Bar-Jona! For flesh and blood has not revealed this to you, but my Father who is in heaven. And I tell you, you are Peter, and on this rock I will build by Church, and the powers of Hades shall not prevail against it. I will give you the keys of the Kingdom of Heaven, and whatever you bind on earth shall be bound in heaven, and whatever you loose on earth shall be loosed in heaven.

JESUS CHRIST IS THE SON OF GOD. TO UNDERstand the significance of this title better, we must inquire if he really intended to found a community in his name: one with a definite form and purpose. Yet one thing is obvious: Jesus did not come into the world in order for us only to believe in God. The people to whom he came already believed in God and had done so for over two thousand years.[1] In any case, belief in the existence of God is but a philosophical question capable of being answered by the natural light of reason. "You believe that God is one; you do well. Even the demons believe—and tremble."[2]

That Jesus was a Jew among Jews is also certain. However, this fact takes on an entirely new dimension when we confess, along with Peter, that he is "the Christ, the Son of the Living God," for then everything arcs back upon itself. No longer can we regard his epiphany as merely an accident—that would be foreign to the nature of the Hebrew God which Jesus reveals. There can be no doubt that the Jews believed that God was the sovereign Lord of history. The Hebrew Scriptures are full of this conviction that all things are in God's hands and that nothing occurs without his will. From Joseph through Moses to David and the prophets, from Pharaoh through Nebuchadnezzar to Cyrus and

---

1   David Rohl, *The Lost Testament From Eden to Exile: The Five-Thousand-Year History of the People of the Bible* (London: Century, 2002).
2   Jas 2:19.

Antiochus Epiphanes, numerous scriptures attest to the fact that all history fulfils God's providential plan. The Psalms are saturated with this belief; and the prophetic utterance is impossible without it. And, most supremely, it is the view of Christ himself who in the Sermon on the Mount teaches us that God's providence extends even to the smallest of creatures: the birds of the air and the lilies of the field, so that not even a sparrow falls without his will, who even sets the number of the hairs on our heads. Therefore, Jesus was meant to be: "'O foolish men, and slow of heart to believe all that the prophets have spoken! Was it not necessary that the Christ should suffer these things and enter into his glory?' And beginning with Moses and all the prophets, he interpreted to them in all the scriptures the things concerning himself."[3]

Since Jesus came in the name of the God of Abraham, Isaac, and Jacob, then his witness is also substantiated by his Heavenly Father. This is precisely what Jesus meant when he said: "In your law it is written that the testimony of two men is true; I bear witness to myself, and the Father who sent me bears witness to me."[4] In bearing witness to himself, Jesus bears witness to the Truth which is in him by the will of his Heavenly Father: "Light from light, true God from true God." Faith in Jesus's Person necessitates this conclusion.

Moreover, if Jesus Christ, the Son of God, is not an accident, it follows that neither were the Holy Scriptures an accident. The idea that after having brought the entire history of Israel to its consummation and fulfillment in Jesus the Messiah, who was destined before the foundation of the world to be the Lamb of God who takes away the sins of the world; the idea that after so much vigilant care and consummate wisdom, God would then have abandoned his message and witness to be blown about by the wind of circumstance only to be pieced together, radically transformed, and creatively designed to meet the needs of communities, themselves accidentally formed, is a theory so outlandish that it is just as well that we are witnessing its final demise. God is not to be reduced to being a creature of social Darwinism. That is not the God that Jesus proclaims.

---

3 Lk 24:25–27. For some of these prophecies, see p. 127, n. 4.
4 Jn 8:18, 7:16–18.

This does not mean that the New Testament documents did not have a history. We noted earlier that the relationship between the Gospels is complex. However, the context of everything is radically altered once one confesses that Jesus is "the Christ, the Son of the living God." What is incomprehensible to faith, therefore, is the supposition that Providence would have left it all to chance. This is incongruous to the reality of the God of the Hebrews whom Jesus proclaimed.

The doctrine that Scripture is divinely inspired or providentially directed is one of the earliest teachings of the Christian community: "All scripture is inspired by God and profitable for teaching, for reproof, for correction, and for training in righteousness, that the man of God may be complete, equipped for every good work."[5] However, the arbitrary, sixteenth-century presupposition of *sola scriptura* does not follow, since it is affirmed in 1 Tim 3:15 that the *church of the living God* is "the pillar and foundation of the truth." Therefore, this peremptory contention that *only* (*sola*) scripture must be sufficient for articles of faith is contradicted by scripture itself which attests that there is also another foundation, viz., the Church.[6] Scripture is assuredly profitable, but Christ is the head of the Church[7] which, as we shall see, he has promised to protect and keep in the truth.

THE FOUNDATION OF THE TRUTH

The Hebrew prophets announced the coming into being of a messianic kingdom which would be national and temporal, but at the same time would be universal and eschatological. From the very beginning of his ministry, Jesus preached this kingdom as having arrived already in his Person and while it begins as an internal spiritual dominion of Christ within the soul, it is extended through a social and visible

---

5   2 Tim 3:16. This also appears to be the meaning of the quite difficult to attach text of 1 Cor 4:6 (*mathete to me hyper a gegraptai* — lit. *that you may learn the thing not above what has been written*), which, from the context at least, clearly has to do with *moral* precepts.
6   That the Scriptures are not all-inclusive, see: Mk 4:33, 6:34; Jn 16:12, 20:30, 21:25; Acts 1:2–3; 1 Cor 11:2; 1 Thess 2:13; 2 Thess 2:15, 3:6; 2 Tim 1:13–14, 2:2.
7   Col 1:18, 24; Eph 5:23. See also Rev 1–3, where Christ's authority is exercised over the seven churches.

community which already existed at the time of Christ.[8] The parables of the kingdom given by Jesus illustrate these themes clearly. The kingdom is like a mustard seed, a pearl, or a treasure hidden in a field. Its beginnings are small and interior, but it is so precious that one relinquishes everything for its sake. Its influence spreads so that many come to dwell within its compass. However, it also suffers enemies who strive to corrupt it. Nevertheless, those who oppose the kingdom will be weeded out in the end when the kingdom stands triumphant under the dominion of Christ the King.

Thus, it is Jesus himself who both embodies and brings the kingdom, immediately and forever. The kingdom of Christ transcends and includes all time, yet at each moment is present in the community gathered in his name.[9] Christ is the center of this kingdom, its life, and its principle. He is its hidden treasure, its head, and its future. As such the kingdom is both visible and invisible, consummated and advancing, holy though imperfect.

The keys of the kingdom

Nonetheless, Jesus, not wishing to leave his apostles abandoned, did institute a visible assembly or convocation (*ecclesia*) with a definite hierarchy and purpose: to preserve and hand on his teaching, to nurture and sanctify its members, and to proclaim his message to the world.[10]

Christ called twelve apostles expressly and individually by name, whom he trained and taught, often taking them aside for private explanation. He sent them out in twos and threes to preach and to cast out demons in preparation for their future commission. He involved them intimately in the Last Supper where he instituted a new Passover in his Person, which the disciples were mandated to celebrate as a perpetual sacrifice in memory of him.

Out of these twelve Jesus chose Peter, especially, to be the shepherd of his sheep.[11] And Jesus did this precisely because his heavenly Father

---

8 Mt 6:33, 7:21, 11:12, 12:28; Lk 10:9–11, 11:20, 16:16, 17:20–21.
9 Mt 18:20, 28:20.
10 Jn 14:16–21, 25–26, 15:26–27.
11 Jn 21:15–19.

had acted thus. This is brought out explicitly in the pericope which heads this chapter.[12] While Jesus was at Caesarea Philippi, but before he was to make his way to Jerusalem to die, he pressed his disciples to inquire of them who they thought he was. It was Peter who finally spoke the words: "You are the Christ, the Son of the living God." That Peter is not the originator of this utterance is plain from the words of Jesus: "Blessed are you, Simon Bar-Jona! For flesh and blood has not revealed this to you, but my Father who is in heaven." Jesus addresses Simon formally, using his family name, thereby officially sanctioning that the latter is speaking under the inspiration of God who had singled him out from among the apostles for this revelation.

That is how God always works. It is the canonical teaching of the Scriptures that God is the one who elects and who then disposes one for a purpose. Out of the pagan world God chose Abraham from whose descendants he accepted Jacob and *renamed him* Israel. Out of Israel's twelve tribes God chose Judah from whom he then selected David as king. From the descendants of David, God took Mary of Bethlehem whom he graced to be the mother of the Son of God. Out of the Jews Jesus picked twelve apostles, and from them God elected Simon for this revelation. Jesus recognized in the conferring of that revelation that his Heavenly Father had distinguished Simon whom he then renamed Peter—the only apostle to whom Jesus gave a new proper name.

Jesus plainly points out that it is Peter who is the rock: "*You* are Peter (*Petros*), and on this rock (*petra*) I will build my church." It is impossible to derive from this the conclusion that Peter's faith is the rock. The virtue of faith is not even mentioned here but must be read into the narrative. Besides, the words of Jesus preclude this interpretation. Furthermore, faith was not Peter's strongest feature: he was more noted for his impetuosity, which was often betrayed by weakness. Indeed, in the next scene Peter is shown presuming to

---

12 This narrative occurs in every single manuscript and translation of Matthew. In fact, Bruce Metzger points out that the title Jesus Christ occurring in the Greek in verse 21 is directly dependent upon Peter's earlier confession. For that reason, the committee of the *Greek New Testament* preferred to substitute "Jesus" in that verse. See Bruce M. Metzger, *A Textual Commentary of the Greek New Testament* (Princeton: United Bible Societies, 1971), 42–43.

hinder Jesus from walking to his death, only in turn to be rebuked by him. In the end Peter denies Christ three times. Later, during Jesus's examination of Peter's conscience, it is only after Peter confesses three times that he loves him that he is restored as the shepherd of Jesus's lambs. Jesus, by repeating three times feed my lambs... my sheep, is following the rabbinic tradition for elevating a disciple to an office.

Also important of note is that it is the women who show more faith than Peter: it is they who stand by their Lord at the end while the disciples are scattered. Not even Mary, who is typified as the exemplary disciple of faith, when Elizabeth filled with the Holy Spirit declares to her "blessed are you among women... blessed is she who believed that there would be a fulfillment of what was spoken to her from the Lord"[13]—not even Mary, the Mother of Our Lord, is chosen. It is to the man, Peter, that the keys are given.

The words of Jesus also preclude the interpretation that it is Jesus who is meant as rock here. *Peter* is the rock because God had graced him for this revelation. And that is why Jesus *will* (future) build his church upon *this petra* by handing to *Peter* the keys to the kingdom. The word "you" refers throughout this passage to Peter every time. Otherwise the play on the word "rock" in Greek would lack sense or context.[14] These keys to the kingdom were given to Peter to symbolize and to establish his authority to bind and to loose in perpetuity. Placing keys upon a person's shoulder had been the traditional custom in the Ancient Near East for delegating authority to anyone taking over the jurisdiction and management of a king's household. This office carried with it the prerogative to "open and shut" entry to the rooms of the palace (treasury, storerooms, repositories, armories, granaries, etc.) as well as access to the king.[15] It derived from the Pharaonic

---

13   Lk 1:41–42, 45.
14   The difference in the endings of the Greek word for rock is simply because rock (*petra*) is feminine in Greek, while Peter (*petros*) is himself masculine. However, in the Aramaic which Jesus spoke, the word for rock was identical in both cases: "You are Cepha and upon this cepha I will build...." See entries *petra* and *petros* in William F. Arndt and F. Wilbur Gingrich, *A Greek-English Lexicon of the New Testament and Other Early Christian Literature* (Chicago: University of Chicago Press, 1979), 654.
15   Is 22:22, 24; 2 Kg 18:18, 37; 15:5. Cf. 1 Kg 4:5–6; 16:9; 18:3; Rev 3:7.

office of vizier (prime minister) who was second only to Pharaoh. Precisely the office granted to Joseph in Egypt.[16]

From here on we see Peter taking a central role among the apostles which they themselves clearly understood and to which they deferred. It is Peter who is mentioned first among the three (Peter, James, and John) and among the twelve. He is the spokesman for the group at the Transfiguration, during the Agony at Gethsemane, and to the Temple tax collectors. He is the one who asks for the explanation of a difficult parable, the meaning of a precept, or the promise of a reward.[17] We have seen in the previous chapter Peter declare for the other apostles when he said to Jesus that they have nowhere to go but must stay with Jesus because he has the words of eternal life. It is Peter whose feet are washed at the Last Supper and who alone is prayed for by Jesus that his faith will not fail so that he *might strengthen the brethren*.[18] After the resurrection the women are charged to make the announcement especially to Peter who is named in distinction from the other disciples. Mary Magdalene runs to Peter and John to tell them about the empty tomb, but when they arrive at the tomb, John defers to Peter allowing him to be the first to enter. Peter was the first among the apostles to receive an appearance of the risen Christ,[19] and we have already noted that it is to Peter alone that the risen Lord gave the authority to feed his sheep.

This pre-eminence continues in the primitive Church.[20] Peter is the first to speak for the apostles after Pentecost and he is the one who speaks on behalf of those arrested by the Sadducees. He works the first miracle in the Church by healing a lame man. Even his shadow works a miracle, and he is the first after Christ to raise the dead. Peter is the first to recognize and refute heresy. It is to Peter that an angel directs Cornelius to seek instruction in the faith and who, after having received a direct revelation from God, is the

---

16 Gen 41:40–44, 45:8. Cf. Dave Armstrong, *A Biblical Defense of Catholicism* (Manchester, NH: Sophia Institute, 2003), 222–24.
17 Mt 15:15, 18:21, 19:27.
18 Lk 22:28–31.
19 Lk 24:34; 1 Cor 15:5.
20 Acts 1:15–26; 3:6–26; 4:1–12; 5:1–11, 15, 29; 8:14–24; 10; 9:40; 10:1–6, 9–48; 11:1–18; 15:7–11.

first to receive the gentiles. When he is imprisoned the entire church offers prayers for him. While it is James who presides over the first council as bishop of Jerusalem, it is Peter who, having been expelled from Rome by Claudius,[21] gives the speech to which James defers in the end. Finally, it is to Peter that Paul gives the distinction of being a compelling example to the others when Paul singles Peter out for criticism for not acting consistently towards the gentiles. Paul, who had always acknowledged Peter's eminence among the Jewish disciples,[22] was concerned lest Peter's example cause misunderstanding among the Judaizers. Far from diminishing Peter's supremacy, Paul's rebuke actually affirms it.[23]

Binding and loosing

"Binding" and "loosing" (Hebrew: *asar v' hitir*) were technical terms among the rabbis which meant respectively to forbid and to permit whatever was judged to belong to Jewish canon law.[24] Jesus applies the terms to cover sinful behavior over which the apostles are given disciplinary authority, along with the power to exclude from the community those who will not amend their faults.[25] This is very different from that granted to St Peter individually, which involves his universal authority over the other apostles and disciples for *whatever* he would bind and loose. Whereas with the apostles in general it requires that two or three of them must agree before they can exercise this authority, this is not the case with Peter. Peter has his own special power to bind and loose which he can exercise individually, but does not exclude him from that ordinary authority which he exercises together with the other apostles.

In John 20:23, Jesus gives the apostles the authority to forgive the sins of anyone (Greek: *an tinon* — of whomever), i.e., of any particular person. Once again this is a special charism, virtue, or power received by all the apostles (Peter included) when Jesus breathed upon them

---

21 Peter was bishop of Rome; see below.
22 Gal 1:18–19; 2:7–8; 1 Cor 15:4–8.
23 Mt 18:15–16; 1 Cor 6:1–6; Gal 6:1–3; Jas 5:19–20.
24 Marvin R. Vincent, *Word Studies in the New Testament* (Grand Rapids: Eerdmans, 1946), 1:96.
25 Mt 18:15–20.

saying: "Receive the Holy Spirit." It empowers them to do whatever is required in order to fulfill that commission, e.g., hearing confession, deciding its severity, determining the penance, and giving absolution.[26] It is different from that authority bestowed upon Peter individually which was exceptional and universal in scope.

Preserving the faith

The faith which Jesus Christ handed to his beloved apostles was such a precious pearl, such a treasure to be protected, that it is not surprising that he would have given various special powers to Peter and the apostles whose foremost function was to preserve the faith[27] and morals[28] of the congregations entrusted to them. After all, it was a matter of salvation. "Enter by the narrow gate; for the gate is wide and the way is easy, that leads to destruction, and those who enter it are many. For the gate is narrow and the way is hard, that leads to life, and those who find it are few."[29] Clearly Jesus did not envisage a factious Church. "Not everyone who says to me 'Lord, Lord,' shall enter the kingdom of heaven, but he who does the will of my Father who is in heaven."[30] It was not enough merely to confess faith in Jesus and then deny his teachings or spurn his example. Nowhere did the apostles teach that Jesus's authority did not matter, or that his teachings and example were of no importance, or that he accommodated himself to the world. Thus Paul could admonish the Galatians: "I am astonished that you are so quickly deserting [God] who called you in the grace of Christ and turning to a different gospel—not that there is another gospel, but there are some who trouble you and want to pervert the gospel of Christ. But even if we, or an angel from heaven, should preach to you a gospel contrary to that which we preached to you, let him be accursed (*anathema*)."[31]

---

26 1 Jn 1:9; Mt 3:2; Mt 4:17; Mt 7:14; Mt 10:38; Lk 24:47; Acts 2:38; Acts 3:19; Acts 14:22; Rom 8:13, 17; 1 Cor 5:3–5; 2 Cor 2:5–8, 10–11; Phil 2:17; Phil 3:10; Col 1:24; 2 Thess 1:5; 1 Pet 2:1–5.
27 1 Tim 4:7; 6:20; 2 Tim 1:13–1; 2:1–2; 4:1–5; Tit 1:13–16; 2 Jn 9–10.
28 2 Thess 3:14; 1 Tim 3–5; Tit 3:10; Heb 13:9.
29 Mt 7:13–14; Lk 13:24.
30 Mt 7:21.
31 Gal 1:8–9; 1 Cor 16:22; cf. Rom 9:3; 16:17.

Part Two: Wisdom

There were to be no dissensions in the Church.[32] To prevent us from falling into error or compromise it was imperative that the successors of Peter should likewise endeavor to protect and conserve the teaching given to them by their beloved Lord.

For these reasons both Peter and Paul were zealous to preserve and guard the faith, which they did by sound teaching, sifting out error, and ensuring those who were given office in the Church should retain a moral character and maintain correct doctrine. They never contended that one could believe anything or advocate any behavior contrary to Our Lord's teaching and example — however conforming it may be to worldly philosophies, ideologies, or politics — and then complacently continue to pronounce oneself Christian. On the contrary Christ's kingdom is not *of* this world.[33] Thus in order to ensure that the Church will continue to remain in the faith which Christ founded,[34] the Holy Spirit caused a definite structure to emerge very early in the Church as Jesus had promised:[35] first Peter (Bishop of Rome) and then the apostles, who were also bishops (*episcopoi*, overseers) of several churches, presbyters (*presbuteroi*, elders) who had the function of administering the sacraments to the local church, and finally deacons (*diakanoi*, ministers) who were preachers of the word and who were to help the presbyters in their duties. While various forms, roles, and offices can be hypothesized for the Church, it is a fact, as we shall see shortly, that this definite structure emerged very early in the Church's history and remained so for some two thousand years. Unless one wants to deny the integrity of Christ or the efficacy of the Holy Spirit, one must accept that it was no accident that the early Church did, in fact, structurally cohere with those forms described in the scriptures.[36] We shall look at the early Church below, but we must next investigate its sanctifying nature.

---

32 1 Cor 1:10; 1 Tim 6:3–5, 14, 20–21; 2 Tim 1:14; 2:15–17; 4:1–5.
33 Jn 18:26; Mt 13:24–30; Rom 12:2; Gal 1:4; 1 Jn 2:15.
34 1 Cor 1:8; Phil 1:10; 1 Thess 2:19; 4:3; 5:23; Jude 24.
35 Jn 16:13; 15:26–16:1; 17:17–19; 18:37.
36 Phil 1:1; 1 Tim 3:1–2; Tit 1:7; 1 Pet 2:25; 1 Tim 5:17, 19; Tit 1:5; Heb 11:2; Jas 5:14; 1 Pet 1:5; 2 Jn 1; 3 Jn 1; 1 Tim 3:8–13.

The sanctifying Church

Christ founded a Church not only to preserve the moral and spiritual teachings of its Master, but to nurture and sanctify its members. This is such a huge topic that only a very cursory overview can be given here.[37] Although Jesus did not leave us a specific moral code, he did reaffirm the Decalogue from the Old Testament, while his replacement of the entire sacrificial cultus with himself as the Temple did away with much of the priestly canon. Like the prophets of Israel, Jesus desired mercy rather than sacrifice.[38] Of course, this did not mean that commiseration for others should outweigh obedience to the moral law,[39] since that law is written into the scheme of things. As we have seen, one cannot disobey the moral law with impunity: something will always go wrong. Love for neighbor must not implicate them in sin, or encourage them to diminish themselves spiritually, or allow them morally to degrade themselves and others. Jesus commanded perfection,[40] and it is impossible to become perfect while disobeying God's law. Although we must love our neighbors as ourselves, since they too are made in God's image, yet we must love God with all our hearts, our souls, and our minds. This is the supreme commandment. Therefore, it is impious to elevate the second tablet of the Decalogue above the first; erroneous to think we love others while denying God's will for them which he wisely established at the creation.[41] This is why Jesus could also say:

> Think not that I have come to abolish the law and the prophets; I have come not to abolish them but to fulfill them. For truly, I say to you, till heaven and earth pass away, not an iota, not a dot, will pass from the law until all is accomplished. Whoever then relaxes one of the least of these commandments and teaches men so, shall be called

---

37 For a fuller account, see Louis Bouyer, *A History of Christian Spirituality*, vol. 1, *The Spirituality of the New Testament and the Fathers* (Tunbridge Wells: Burns and Oates, 1968).
38 Mt 9:13, 5:44, 12:7, 22:37; 1 Sam 15:22; Hos 6:6; Ps 50:14; Ps 51:16–17; Prv 21:3; Is 1:11; Jer 7:22; Dan 9:27.
39 Jas 2:8–9.
40 Mt 5:48.
41 Mk 10:6–9; Gen 1:27–28.

least in the kingdom of heaven; but he who does them and teaches them shall be called great in the kingdom of heaven."[42]

For these reasons Jesus wanted to ensure that his apostles would be most careful to edify those he entrusted to them, holding them responsible for any in their care who fell into temptation: "Temptations to sin are sure to come; but woe to him by whom they come! It would be better for him if a millstone were hung round his neck and he were cast into the sea, than that he should cause one of these little ones to sin."[43] Therefore, we find the apostles Peter, Paul, James, John, and Jude also teaching in their epistles the same message, viz., "It is not the hearers of the law who are righteous before God, but the doers of the law who will be justified."[44] Faith in Christ, genuine faith that justifies, either leads to good works or it is empty.[45] Thus we expect the Church to be constantly vigilant against antinomianism or relativism.

The Church, being a voluntary institution, albeit a supernatural one, was given definite spiritual seals that signified a particular state or condition in the life of its members which bound them together and sanctified them. Commonly known as sacraments, they shared the quality of being outward signs of an inward reality vouchsafed to the recipients. They originated from Christ himself as the head of the Church. The sacraments of baptism and confirmation, of marriage and Holy Orders, of penance, Eucharist, and extreme unction are variously observed by Roman Catholics, Orthodox Catholics, and Anglo-Catholics, as well as Byzantine Rite Catholics (e.g., Albanian, Belarusian, Bulgarian, Melkite, Romanian, and Slovak), and non-Byzantine Rite Catholics (e.g., Armenian, Chaldean, Coptic, Ethiopian, Maronite, or Syrian). All seven sacraments were practiced by the early Church. Clearly, the instituting of any of these sacraments by Christ requires an established formal body to administer, manage, and conserve them. The Eucharist alone would require priests to

---

42   Mt 5:17–20.
43   Lk 17:1–2.
44   Rom 2:13; Jas 1:22–23; 1 Pet 2:11–16; 3:13–15a; 4:17–18; 5:2–11; Jn 3:7–8.
45   Jas 2:14–24.

utter the words of consecration,[46] and that in turn requires overseers (bishops) to regulate the rite and, of course, a fixed building where the faithful can gather and observe it.

Proclaiming the Gospel

The apostles were commissioned to preach the Gospel to the nations, teaching them to observe all that Christ had commanded.[47] That such a burden was not misplaced, indeed, that their teaching would remain infallibly what Christ had commanded, requires that the Holy Spirit of Truth be given as he had promised. For this to be the case, it follows that the Church must be "the pillar and foundation of the truth" as already noted above. Once again we come to the absurdity of the idea that the deposit of faith was immediately abandoned to individuals to make of it what they will. Unless the Church was guaranteed to be kept sound and blameless until the coming of Christ,[48] then, given the fallen nature of human beings with their tendency to accommodate themselves to the world, it is inevitable that all that Christ had accomplished would be lost. Otherwise we make impotent the power of the Holy Spirit and we deny the integrity of Christ and the majesty of his Person.

The early Church was zealous to protect and conserve the deposit of faith in obedience to Christ, her foundation. Moreover, the primacy bestowed upon Peter, to whom the keys were given, and the promise bequeathed to Peter and the other apostles, that they would possess the Spirit of Truth, are but the essential components of the notion of infallibility. The capacity to interpret Holy Scriptures, to determine liturgy, to decide upon the application of precepts, correctly to discern heresy, and to nurture and sanctify its members are all rendered ineffectual and irrelevant if the Church cannot do this infallibly.

Thus, it is certain that Christ intended to establish a Church. This he most assuredly did, not in a stinting or half-finished manner — such

---

46   1 Cor 10:16–17; 11:23–26.
47   Mt 28:20; 5:19; 10:5–7; Mk 6:7, 12; Lk 9:2; 10:1; Acts 5:42; 8:4, 12, 40; 15:35.
48   1 Thess 23–24; 4:3; 1 Cor 1:4–9; Phil 1:10; Jude 24.

an assertion is unthinkable—but with care and diligence, with authority and efficacy, with constancy and devotion. Christ who does all things well[49] remains faithful in safeguarding his Church, ensuring that it will continue to remain the pillar and foundation of the truth, so that even the gates of the underworld would not prevail against it.[50] The gift of infallibility is consequent upon the nature of a loving Lord and Savior. His word does not return empty.[51] Therefore, Jesus could well say that to attack his Church is also to attack him, and to reject the Church is to reject its Lord and him who sent him.[52] All this could be known merely as a necessary consequence of the authority and love of Christ were it not also taught by him:

> All authority in heaven and on earth has been given to me. Go therefore, and make disciples of all nations, baptizing them in the name of the Father and of the Son and of the Holy Spirit, teaching them to *observe all that I have commanded you*; and lo, *I am with you always*, to the consummation of the age.[53]

THE EARLY CHURCH

Having demonstrated from scripture that Christ intended to establish a Church, it is now necessary to show what the early Church actually did become under the infallible guidance of the Holy Spirit. We will first inspect the early Church, returning briefly to the themes we have just considered.

The Primacy of Peter

That Peter and Paul were in Rome, that they were martyred there, and that the early Church considered Rome to be the seat of Peter is now indisputable. The earliest possible allusion to St Peter's being in

---

49 Mk 7:37.
50 Christ never promised that the Church would never be without sin; He promised that his Holy Spirit would keep her in the truth.
51 Is 55:11; 45:23; 59:21; 53:10; Mt 24:35 = Mk 13:31 = Lk 21:33.
52 Lk 10:16; Jn 12:48–49, 13:20, 15:18–27.
53 Mt 28:18–20.

Rome is given in his own epistle which is written to the "Dispersion," which may well refer to those Christians who sought refuge in surrounding Churches in the face of Nero's persecutions, which Peter was witnessing in Rome.[54] There are many references to suffering in this epistle which encourages Christians in the face of persecution: "Beloved, do not be surprised at the fiery ordeal which comes upon you to prove you, as though something strange were happening to you. But rejoice in so far as you share Christ's sufferings, that you may also rejoice and be glad when his glory is revealed."[55] The letter ends with an exhortation to stand firm, for suffering is a true grace from God; and they are not alone since the Church which is in "Babylon" is likewise chosen.[56] Babylon is Rome the great harlot arrayed in purple and scarlet and seated upon seven hills, drunk with the blood of the martyrs.[57] The natural interpretation is that Peter was writing from Rome and was about to face his own martyrdom. In St Paul's letter to the Romans[58] we read that he refrained from going to Rome "lest he build upon another man's foundations." This must be a reference to St Peter who alone could elicit the respect which caused St Paul to demur from visiting the imperial city. There is no evidence of any other founder of the Church in Rome than St Peter.

The earliest document which does place St Peter in Rome is St Clement's *First Epistle to the Corinthians*. Clement was third bishop of Rome (after Peter) from AD 89–97. Writing from Rome c. 97, Clement mentions Peter and Paul:

> Let us take the noble examples furnished in our own generation. Through envy and jealousy the greatest and most righteous pillars [of the church] have been persecuted and put to death. Let us set before our eyes the illustrious apostles. Peter, through unrighteous envy, endured not one or two, but numerous labors; and when he had at length suffered martyrdom, departed to the place of glory due

---

54 1 Pet 1:1.
55 1 Pet 4:12–13.
56 1 Pet 5:8–11, 12–13.
57 Rev 17:5–6, 9.
58 Rev 15:20–22.

to him. Owing to jealousy, Paul also obtained the reward of patient endurance, after being seven times thrown into captivity, compelled to flee, and stoned. After preaching both in the east and west, he gained the illustrious reputation due to his faith, having taught righteousness to the whole world, and come to the extreme limit of the west, and suffered martyrdom under the prefects.[59]

Clement of Rome then refers to many others who also suffered along with these holy men, setting a noble example "in our midst."

A few years later, during the reign of Trajan (AD 98–117), Ignatius, bishop of Antioch, wrote his letter to the Romans while awaiting his own execution. He begs them not to intercede to save him, adding: "I do not command it like Peter and Paul; they were Apostles, I am but a slave."[60] The allusion to these apostles in the place where Ignatius is also to be killed is further support for the association of Peter and Paul with Rome. However, Eusebius quotes even more positive references from Caius and Dionysius:

> Thus Nero, publicly announcing himself as the chief enemy of God, was led on in his fury to slaughter the apostles. Paul is therefore said to have been beheaded at Rome and Peter to have been crucified likewise. And this account is confirmed by the fact that the names of Peter and Paul still remain in the cemeteries of that city even to this day. But likewise, a certain ecclesiastical writer, Caius by name, who was born about the time of Zephyrinus, bishop of Rome ... gave the following statement respecting the places where the sacred tabernacles of the said apostles have been laid: "I can show the trophies of the apostles. For if you will go to the Vatican, or to the Ostian road, you will find the trophies of those who have laid the foundation of this church." And that both suffered

---

59 Clement, *First Epistle to the Corinthians*, in *The Fathers of the Church*, Kevin Knight, ed., vv1–7, www.newadvent.org/fathers/1010htm.
60 Quoted in Rev. D. I. Lanslots, *The Primitive Church* (Rockford: Tan, 1980), 146.

martyrdom about the same time, Dionysius, bishop of Corinth, bears the following testimony, in his letter to the Romans. "Thus, likewise you, by means of this admonition, have mingled the flourishing seed that had been planted by Peter and Paul at Rome and Corinth. For both of these, having planted us at Corinth, likewise instructed us; and having in like manner taught in Italy, they suffered martyrdom about the same time."[61]

Towards the end of the second century (c. 180), Irenaeus, a disciple in his youth of Polycarp, bishop of Smyrna, who in turn was the disciple of St John the apostle, while visiting Rome on pressing business learned of the succession of the bishops of Rome after Peter. In his *Against Heresies* he appeals to "that tradition derived from the apostles, of the very great, the very ancient and universally known Church founded and organized at Rome by the two most glorious apostles, Peter and Paul; and also by pointing out *the faith* preached to men, *which comes down to our time by means of the successions of the bishops.* For it is necessary that every church, that is, the faithful everywhere, should agree with this Church, on account of its pre-eminent authority, in which the apostolic tradition has been preserved continuously by those who exist everywhere." Then starting with Linus, whom Paul mentioned in 2 Timothy 4:21, he goes on to list Peter's successors.

One would expect that if Rome was associated with the martyrdom of these two greatest apostles then it would have become a place of pilgrimage. That this is the case is well documented by Margherita Guarducci, former professor at La Sapienza di Roma University and Vatican researcher of the tomb of St Peter. From the end of the first century to the middle of the third century Rome held spiritual primacy among the Christian churches. Professor Guarducci provides the names of many pilgrims who visited Rome, such as Albercius, bishop of Asia Minor, Polycarp, Irenaeus, Origen, Justin Martyr, Hegesippus, even heretics like Valentinus and Marcion.[62]

---

61 *Ecclesiastical History*, II.25.5–8.
62 Margherita Guarducci, *The Primacy of the Church of Rome* (San Francisco: Ignatius Press, 2003), 11–16.

Part Two: Wisdom

One of the reasons for this pilgrimage has already been given in the quotation from Caius above, who boasted of being able to point out the trophies (relics) of Peter and Paul. That the bones of St Peter were buried in the Tomb of St Peter beneath the Vatican Basilica was believed for many centuries. Between 1940 and 1949, Pius XII requested that the tomb be excavated to confirm the tradition. Beneath the altar of the confession, the site of the ancient earthen tomb was found surmounted by a small funeral monument from the second century. This tomb came to be enclosed within a large and lavish necropolis formed in the second and third centuries. Later the Emperor Constantine had the venerable bones of Peter removed from the bare earth upon which they had lain, wrapped them in a precious cloth of purple and gold, and installed them in a niche within the monument. These bones were later discovered, subjected to various tests, and identified as authentic in 1963.[63] Moreover, graffiti on the wall above the niche containing the relics mention the name of Peter written several times. Associated with one of Peter's monograms is the *chi-rho* (χ-ρ) symbol for Christ, and the name of Mary. Between the two monograms are the words DUX LUX PAX LEX and above that chain is the word NICA (victory) addressed to Christ, Peter, and Mary.[64] Thus, Christ's promise to build his Church upon the rock of St Peter could not have had a more literal realization.

Peter was greatly esteemed in the early Church. Origen (c. AD 230), writing in his *Commentaries on John*, describes Peter as him "upon whom the Church of Christ is built, against which the gates of hell shall not prevail."[65] Cyprian, bishop of Carthage (c. AD 250) in his work *On the Unity of the Catholic Church* affirms:

> And again to the same [Peter] he says, after his resurrection "Feed my sheep." And although to all the apostles after his resurrection, he gives an equal power . . . yet, that he might set forth unity, he arranged by his authority the origin of that unity, as beginning from one. Assuredly the rest of the apostles were also the same as was Peter, endowed

---

63 Ibid., 114.
64 Ibid.
65 *Ecclesiastical History*, VI.25.8.

with a like partnership both of honor and power; but the beginning proceeds from unity.... Does he who does not hold this unity of the Church think that he holds the faith? Does he who strives against and resists the Church trust that he is in the Church, when moreover the blessed Paul teaches the same thing... saying, "There is one body and one spirit, one hope of your calling, one Lord, one faith, one Baptism, one God"?[66]

In other places the same Cyprian also proclaims similar sentiments: "There is one God and one Christ, and one Church, and one Chair founded on Peter by the word of the Lord."[67] Pope Cornelius I, in a letter back to Bishop Cyprian, agrees: "We are not ignorant that there is one God, and one Christ the Lord whom we confess, and one Holy Spirit; and that there must be one bishop in the Catholic Church."[68]

Even as far away as Nisibis in Syria, the poet and apologist of the Syriac church, Ephraim, writes (c. AD 350) lyrically of Peter: "Simon, my follower, I have made you the foundation of the holy Church. I betimes called you Peter, because you will support all its buildings. You are the inspector of those who will build on earth a Church for me. If they should wish to build what is false, you will condemn them. You are the head of the fountain from which my teaching flows, you are the chief of my disciples. Through you I will give drink to all peoples. Yours is that life-giving sweetness which I dispense. I have chosen you to be, as it were, the first-born in my institution, and so that, as the heir, you may be executor of my treasures. I have given you the keys of my kingdom. Behold, I have given you authority over all my treasures."[69] Many other similar quotes could be made from Optatus of Milevis, St Jerome, Pope St Damasus I, St Augustine, St Peter Chrysologus, and Pope St Leo I. The following Decretal of Pope St Gelasius I in the year 495 should suffice as a summation of the position of the Church since the beginning:

---

66   Knight, *Church Fathers*, http://newadvent.org/fathers/050701.htm.
67   Cyprian of Carthage, *Letter to All His People* 43 (40), no. 5. Quoted in Rod Bennett, *Four Witnesses: The Early Church in Her Own Words* (San Francisco: Ignatius Press, 2002), 311.
68   Ibid.
69   Ibid., 311–12.

After all these prophetic and evangelical and apostolic writings (which we have set forth above), on which the Catholic Church by the grace of God is founded, we have thought this (fact) also ought to be published, namely that, although the universal Catholic Church spread throughout the world has the one marriage of Christ, nevertheless the holy Roman Church has not been preferred to the other churches by reason of synodical decrees, but she has held the primacy by the evangelical voice of the Lord and Savior saying: *Thou art Peter* [etc.].... Accordingly the see of PETER the Apostle of the Church of Rome is first, *having neither spot, nor wrinkle, nor anything of this kind* [Eph. 5:27]. But the second see at Alexandria was consecrated in the name of blessed PETER by Mark his disciple and evangelist... but the third in honor is considered the see of the most blessed Apostle PETER at Antioch....[70]

The faith of the early Church

We will treat briefly of the beliefs of the early Church. From the very beginning the Church strived to defend and preserve the teachings of Christ. One of the earliest documents, if not the earliest, the *Didache* (teaching) written in the first century, shows clearly that the early Church prayed the Lord's Prayer, practiced fasting, baptism, and Eucharist, accepted the doctrine of God the Father, Son and Holy Spirit, and kept the Lord's Day.

From the very beginning the Church believed it was apostolic. St Clement, bishop of Rome, writing to the Corinthians in the year AD 96, points out that "the apostles received the gospel for our sakes from the Lord Jesus Christ; Jesus the Christ was sent from God. The Christ therefore is from God, and the apostles from the Christ." Being in accordance with the appointed order of the will of God they then "appointed their first fruits, having tested them by the Spirit, to be bishops and deacons of those who should believe. And this was no novelty, for long ago it had been written concerning bishops and

---

70 H. Denzinger, *Enchiridion Symbolorum*, 30th ed. (Fitzwilliam, NH: Loreto, 1955), 163.

deacons. For the Scripture says in one place: 'I will establish their bishops in righteousness and their deacons in faith (Is. 60:17).'"[71] St Ignatius, bishop of Antioch, also writing (c. 108) of the first century, states in his letter *To the Smyrnaeans*:

> Avoid divisions, as the beginning of evils. See that all of you follow the bishop, as Jesus Christ does the Father; and the presbytery you would as the apostles; and the deacons as being the institution of God. Let no man do anything connected with the Church without the bishop. Let that be deemed a proper Eucharist which is administered by either the bishop or him to whom he entrusts it. Wherever the bishop shall appear, there let the multitude be, even as wherever Christ Jesus is, there is the Catholic Church. It is not lawful without the bishop either to baptize, or to celebrate a love-feast. But whatsoever he shall approve of, that also is pleasing to God, so that everything that is done may be secure and valid.[72]

The Church also exercised from very early on the power to forgive sins, as Tertullian states: "I also hear that an edict is published and is indeed final. Evidently the Supreme Pontiff,[73] because he is the bishop of bishops, declares: 'I forgive the sins of adultery and fornication to those who have performed the penance.'"[74] Not only penance, but confession is also implicated here since one cannot prescribe a penance without first hearing the confession. Thus, the early Church took seriously those powers of binding and loosing, confession, and the forgiveness of sins which Christ conferred upon the apostles.

The Old Testament books which the Church held to be sacred were those from which the apostles quoted, viz., the Septuagint. The books of Tobit, Judith, 1 & 2 Maccabees, Wisdom, Sirach, and Baruch (set aside by Luther) have been in the Church's canon almost from

---

71 J. Stevenson, ed., *A New Eusebius. Documents Illustrating the History of the Church to AD 337* (London: SPCK, 1987), 8.
72 Knight, *Church Fathers*, http://www.newadvent.org/fathers/0109.htm.
73 Either Pope Zephyrinus (198–217) or Pope Callistus (217–222).
74 Denzinger, *Enchiridion Symbolorum*, 43, 145–46. Cf. 1 Cor 5:3–5 and 2 Cor 2:6–8, 10–11.

the beginning.[75] Indeed, Jesus himself quoted from or alluded to (Hebrew: *kesher*) Tobit, Maccabees, Wisdom, Sirach, and Baruch.[76] Therefore, the Church, zealous to follow her Lord in all things, continued to quote and treasure these same books. The New Testament also remained virtually from the beginning what it is now, as evidenced by the Muratorian fragment. The canon for the whole Bible was first officially listed at the Council of Rome in AD 382 and finally fixed at the Council of Carthage in AD 397 and has remained unchanged ever since.[77]

The Holy Scriptures taught that after death there was a process of cleansing through which souls would be purged and glorified in order to be presented as holy before God.[78] For this reason prayers were offered up for these souls.[79] The early Church continued to teach that "in full consciousness of this communion of the whole Mystical Body of Jesus Christ, the Church in its pilgrim members,

---

75 As evidenced in the codices *Sinaiticus, Vaticanus,* and *Alexandrinus.* F. F. Bruce, *The Canon of Scripture* (Glasgow: Charter House, 1988), 69. The Hebrew canon of the Old Testament was not established until the Masoretes compiled it in Babylonia between the 7th and 10th centuries AD. Before then it was the Greek Septuagint that was used throughout Hellenised Judaism. This Masoretic canon of 39 books was embraced by the Protestants, while the Catholic canon of the OT has 46 books, and the Orthodox Church has 49. Other churches of the Eastern Rites have varying canons of the OT. Fortunately, Protestants have, however, accepted the Church's canon of the New Testament, despite Luther's suspicions about Hebrews, James, Jude, and Revelation. Bruce, *The Canon of Scripture,* 101–2.

76 Mt 6:20 = Tob 4:9; Mt 7:12 = Tob 4:15; Mt 25:35–46 = Tob 4:16; Mt 9:4 = Wis 2:14; Mt 11:25 = Wis 10:21; Mt 19:28 = Wis 3:8; Jn 3:12 = Wis 9:16; Jn 14:26 = Wis 9:17; Mt 5:28 = Sir 41:21; Mt 6:14 = Sir 28:2; Mt 6:28 = Sir 40:22; Mt 7:20 = Sir 27:6; Mt 18:15 = Sir 19:12–15; Mt 23:12 = Sir 3:18; Mt 25:36 = 7:35; Lk 12:19 = Sir 5:1, 11:19; Jn 9:4 = Sir 51:30; Jn 4:14 = Bar 3:12. These do not include those quotes or allusions made by the NT authors themselves.

77 Denzinger, *Enchiridion Symbolorum,* 84, 92. Immediately (392–405) St Jerome, having been commissioned earlier by Pope Damasus I (d. 382), began to translate both testaments into the Latin vulgate language, so as to make the Scriptures available to the common people.

78 Ps 66:12; Eccl 12:14; Is 4:4, 6:5–7; Mic 7:8–9; Mal 3:2–4; Mt 5:22, 25–26; Mt 12:32; Lk 16:2, 9; Lk 19:31; Rom 8:21, 30; 1 Cor 2:7, 3:11–15; 2 Cor 5:10; 7:1; Eph 4:8–10; Phil 2:10–11; Heb 12:5–11, 23, 29; 1 Pet 3:19–20; Rev 5:3, 13; Rev 21:27.

79 Tob 12:12; 13:2; 2 Mac 12:39–42, 44–45; Zec 9:11; 1 Cor 15:29.

from the very earliest days of the Christian religion, has honored with great respect the memory of the dead; and 'because it is a holy and a wholesome thought to pray for the dead that they may be loosed from their sins' (2 Macc. 12:46) she offers her suffrages for them."[80] This is manifest quite early from the numerous prayers and paintings on the walls of the catacombs dating from the first and second centuries.[81] Further evidence for this practice is given by the *Martyrdom of Polycarp*, Tertullian, Cyprian, Cyril, Epiphanius, and St Jerome.[82] Thus, contrary to Luther's teaching that one can do nothing but sin and that every sin is equally offensive to God, the Church has always taught along with St John the Apostle that some sins are mortal while others are not.[83] As St Augustine writes: "But of all those who suffer temporary punishments after death, all are not doomed to those everlasting pains which are to follow that judgment; for to some, as we have already said, what is not remitted in this world is remitted in the next, that is, they are not punished with the eternal punishment of the world to come."[84] Caesarius of Arles in AD 542 summarizes the sentiment:

> There is no doubt that...[there are] lesser sins which, as I said before, can scarcely be counted, and from which not only all Christian people, but even all the saints could not and cannot be free [in this life]. We do not, of course, believe that the soul is killed by these sins; but still, they make it ugly by covering it as if with some kind of pustules and, as it were, with horrible scabs, which allow the soul to come only with difficulty to the embrace of the heavenly Spouse, of whom it is written: "He prepared for himself a Church having neither spot nor blemish" [Eph 5:27]....
> If we neither give thanks to God in tribulations nor redeem

---

80 Second Vatican Council, *Lumen Gentium*, no. 50, accessed May 7, 2021 at Vatican.va.
81 J. Stevenson, *The Catacombs: Rediscovered Monuments of Early Christianity* (London: Thames & Hudson, 1978).
82 See Bennett, *Four Witnesses*, 336–41.
83 1 Jn 5:16–17.
84 Augustine of Hippo, *The City of God*, Bk. XXI, 13, in *The Great Books* (London: Encyclopaedia Britannica), vol. 18.

our own sins by good works [cf. Jas 5:19–20], we shall have to remain in that purgatorial fire as long as it takes for those above-mentioned lesser sins to be consumed like wood and straw and hay [1 Cor 3:12–15].[85]

Another belief of the primitive Church concerned the doctrine of the communion of saints and by association the intercession of Mary. From the beginning, as she does today, the Church venerated the Virgin Mary as the Mother of God. St Ignatius (c. AD 107) writes in his *Letter to the Ephesians*: "For our God, Jesus Christ, was conceived by Mary in accord with God's plan: of the seed of David, it is true, but also of the Holy Spirit."[86] Justin Martyr writing in the middle of the second century says of Mary:

> Since it is written of him in the memoirs of the Apostles that he is the Son of God, and since we call him Son, we have understood that before all creatures he proceeded from the Father by his will and power ... and that he became man by the Virgin so that the course which was taken by disobedience in the beginning through the agency of the serpent, might be also the very course by which it would be put down. For Eve, a virgin and undefiled, conceived the word of the serpent, and bore disobedience and death. But the Virgin Mary received faith and joy when the angel Gabriel announced to her the glad tidings that the Spirit of the Lord would come upon her and the power of the Most High would overshadow her, for which reason the Holy One being born of her is the Son of God. And she replied, "Be it done unto me according to thy word" (Lk 1:38).[87]

In the second century, the Christian portion of the *Sibylline Oracles* calls Mary immaculate: "Thus spoke the archangel to the maiden: 'Receive, O Virgin, the Lord in your immaculate womb.'"[88] Irenaeus

---

85 Quoted in Bennett, *Four Witnesses*, 340.
86 Quoted in ibid., 329.
87 Quoted in ibid., 329–30.
88 Constante Berselli and Giorgio Gharib, *In Praise of Mary: Hymns from the*

of Lyons writing in AD 180 in his *Against Heresies* declares: "The Virgin Mary... being obedient to his word, received from an angel the glad tidings that she would bear God."[89] And an Egyptian papyrus from the third century names Mary as the Mother of God: "In the shadow of your mercy we shelter, O Mother of God. Do not ignore our supplications in our temptation, but deliver us from danger, O pure one, blessed one."[90] Known as the *Sub Tuum* it is the earliest recording of the word *Theotokos*. Prayers to the Virgin Mary are also recorded by St Hilary, St Athanasius, St Gregory of Nyssa, St Ephraem the Syrian, and St Jerome (all fourth cent.). Understanding that Mary was holy from the beginning, and in obeisance to her prophecy by the Holy Spirit who had come upon her, the Church continued to call her "blessed"[91] and to ask for her intercession in harmony with the Scriptural doctrine of the Communion of Saints.[92]

The catacombs contain many graffiti and paintings of Mary. One very significant mural in the catacomb of Priscilla shows a picture of Balaam pointing to the star of Numbers 24:17: "A star shall come forth out of Jacob, and a scepter shall rise out of Israel." Next to this is a picture of the Virgin and Child. (As early as the second century this text is quoted twice in Irenaeus and twice in Justin.) There also appear in the catacombs of Priscilla and the *Coemeterium Maius* murals of the Virgin and Child in an attitude of prayer known as *orans*. Stevenson comments: "The dead were ultimately connected with the living, for, when the latter passed from this world they were intensely in need of the active intercession of those who had gone before them, namely, of the Virgin, or the Apostles, of the Martyrs and saints. Conversely, the prayers of the dead were necessary for the living."[93]

First Millennium of the Eastern and Western Churches (Slough: St Paul, 1981), 14.
89 Quoted in Bennett, *Four Witnesses*, 330.
90 Berselli and Gharib, *In Praise of Mary*, 16. This fragment is in the John Rylands Library, Manchester.
91 Lk 1:41–43, 48.
92 Dead saints are aware of earthly affairs: Mt 22:30; Lk 15:10; 1 Cor 4:9; Heb 12:1. They intercede for us: Jer 15:1; 2 Macc 15:14; Rev 5:8; 6:9–10; 8:3–4. Angels also watch over us and intercede for us: Tob 12:12, 15; Ps 34:7; Ps 91:11; Mt 18:10; Lk 15:10; Acts 12:15; Heb 1:14; Rev 1:4, 7:1, 8:3–4.
93 Stevenson, *Catacombs*, 155.

Reflection upon the nature of Mary's role in the Divine Economy was nourished by theological reflection upon the nature of Christ. After battling various heresies (Arianism, Apollinarianism, Sabellianism, etc.) the Councils of Nicaea and Constantinople had defined the two (human and divine) natures of Christ encapsulated in the Nicene-Constantinopolitan Creed still recited in the Church every Sunday. However, theological reflection upon how the two natures were united in Christ led one Nestorius, bishop of Constantinople, to declare that Mary must be considered to be the mother of Christ, not of God, i.e., *Christokos* rather than *Theotokos*. Nestorius could not accept the communication of idioms by which the sufferings of Christ were attributed to the Divine Person of the Son. But his solution tended to imply a division in Christ. The Council of Ephesus (AD 431) eventually approved the solution of St Cyril of Alexandria over that of Nestorius:

> For we do not say that the nature of the Word was changed and made flesh, nor yet that it was changed into the whole man composed of soul and body, but rather we say that the Word, in an ineffable and inconceivable manner, having hypostatically united to himself flesh animated by a rational soul, became Man and was called the Son of Man, not according to the will alone or by the assumption of a person alone, and that the different natures were brought together in a real union ... through a marvelous and mystical concurrence in unity.... For it was no ordinary man who was the first born of the Holy Virgin and upon whom the Word afterwards descended; but being united from the womb itself he is said to have undergone fleshly birth, claiming as his own the birth of his own flesh. Thus the holy Fathers did not hesitate to speak of the holy Virgin as the Mother of God.[94]

Thus the pre-existent Divine Person of the Word became the formative but Divine Principle in Christ; so that, in gestating and

---

94 Denzinger, *Enchiridion Symbolorum*, 111a. (Corrigenda included.)

giving birth to Jesus, Mary was simultaneously the bearer of God.[95] Thus Theotokos became Mary's distinctive characteristic and title which was to influence all subsequent theological reflection about Mary. Every Christological reflection also continued to influence the Church's understanding of Mary's position in salvation history.

Finally, we want to point out that from the beginning the Church considered that Christ was really present in the Eucharist, and that the Mass itself was a sacrifice in which, although Christ is certainly not immolated again — for "by a single offering he has perfected for all time those who are sanctified" — yet "he holds his priesthood permanently, because he continues forever. Consequently he is able for all time to save those who draw near to God through him, since he always *lives to make intercession* for them."[96] For this reason Revelation describes an altar in Heaven where the "prayers of the saints" are continually offered at the altar before the Lamb standing as though slain before the throne of God.[97] The "once only" sacrifice of the cross is from a historical human perspective a single event, while in eternity the sacrificial Lamb is perpetually interceding for us. The sacrifice of the Mass is a recapitulation and representation of the singular sacrifice of Christ on the Cross in perfect accordance with the symbolism of the Last Supper instituted by Jesus. Through the Mass our prayers are joined with the sacrifice of Christ for the sake of the elect throughout the world which gives to our earthly crosses a transcendent, Christological meaning "provided we suffer with him."[98] Moreover, insofar as we join our own sacrifices to him, as do the saints in Revelation, then these also become "a fragrant offering and sacrifice to God."[99]

This has also been the teaching of the early Church. In the *Didache* we find: "On the Lord's own day, assemble in common to break bread and offer thanks; but first confess your sins, so that your sacrifice may be pure. However, no one quarrelling with his brother may join your

---

95 Phil 2:6–7.
96 Heb 10:10; 7:24–25. See also Heb 5:6, 10; 6:20; 7:1–3, 17, 20.
97 Rev 6:9; 8:3, 5; 9:13; 11:1; 14:18; 16:7; 8:3–4; 5:1–7; 7:17; 22:1, 3.
98 Rom 8:17.
99 Eph 5:1. See also 2 Cor 1:5–6; Phil 3:10; 2 Tim 2:10–12; 1 Pet 4:13.

meeting until they are reconciled; your sacrifice must not be defiled." Note here the allusion to Our Lord's statement in Matthew 5:23–24 that we must be first reconciled to our brother before offering our gift *at the altar*.

Clement of Alexandria was the first to use the word "Eucharist" in his *Instructor*, written at the end of the second century. That the Mass is a sacrifice was taught by Cyprian of Carthage (AD 250), Cyril of Jerusalem, Ephraim of Nisibis, Gregory Nazianzan, Ambrose of Milan, John Chrysostom (all fourth cent.), Theodore of Mopsuestia, and Augustine of Hippo (fifth cent.). Such understanding followed from the Church's belief in the Real Presence of Jesus Christ in the Eucharist. In the graphic words of Jesus: "I am the living bread which came down from heaven; if anyone eats of the bread, he will live forever; and the bread which I shall give for the life of the world is my flesh."[100] The early Church, scrupulous to revere every word from its Lord, continued to speak of the Eucharist in the same realistic form. As St Paul said, "For anyone who eats and drinks without discerning the body, eats and drinks judgment upon himself."[101] This failure to discern the Real Presence was for Ignatius too the distinguishing mark of heretics: "They abstain from the Eucharist and from prayer, because they do not confess the Eucharist to be the flesh of our Savior Jesus Christ, which suffered for our sins, and which the Father, in his goodness, raised up again."[102] Thus does Justin Martyr write (c. 147) in his *First Apology*:

> This food we call the Eucharist, and no one is allowed to partake but the man who believes that our doctrines are true, who has been washed ... for the remission of sins ... and who is living as Christ commanded. We do not receive these as common bread and common drink.

---

100 Jn 6:51.
101 1 Cor 11:29. The Greek *diakrinon* (tr. "discerning") means to *judge correctly* the appearance of a thing: hence the play on the word judgment (*krima*) in this passage (both come from *krino*, to judge).
102 Ignatius of Antioch, "Communion and Excommunication: *Smyrnaeans* 6–8," quoted in Mike Aquilina, *The Mass of the Early Christians* (Huntington: Our Sunday Visitor, 2007), 38.

> For Jesus Christ our Savior, made flesh by the word of God, had both flesh and blood for our salvation. Likewise, we have been taught that the food blessed by the word of prayer transmitted from him — from which our own blood and flesh are nourished and changed — is the flesh and blood of Jesus who was made flesh.[103]

Justin also relates (as does Tertullian) that deacons carried Communion to the sick and housebound. Hippolytus (c. 215) even urged that the host be protected from mice: "For it is the body of Christ ... and not to be treated lightly."[104] This same reverence for the Eucharist was expressed by Augustine: "We faithfully confess that before consecration it is bread and wine, the product of nature; but after consecration it is the body and blood of Christ, consecrated by the blessing."[105] This continued to remain the teaching into the Middle Ages.

Thus, it cannot be denied that Jesus intended to found a Church in his name which had a definite form and purpose. Immediately upon Christ's resurrection the Church began to take on the form we have described above with the beliefs and practices we depicted. If this had been otherwise, it would have been a colossal betrayal of the promise of Christ to lead the Church into all truth. Yet we have seen that churches in Alexandria, Carthage, Hippo, Antioch, Nisibis, Salamis, Smyrnaea, Lyons, Milan, Jerusalem, and Rome all shared similar beliefs and practices so that at the beginning of the third century Tertullian could write:

> Let us grant, then, that all have erred; that the Apostle was mistaken in bearing witness; that the Holy Spirit had no such consideration for any one Church as to lead it into truth, although he was sent for that purpose by Christ [Jn 14:26], who had asked the Father to make him the

---

103 Justin Martyr, *Apology*, 66, in Alexander Roberts, James Donaldson, and A. Cleveland Coxe, eds., *Ante-Nicene Fathers*, Vol. 1 (Buffalo, NY: Christian Literature Publishing, 1885).
104 Quoted in Aquilina, *Mass of the Early Christians*, 39.
105 Quoted in *Catechism of the Council of Trent*, trans. John McHugh and Charles Callan (Rockford, IL: TAN Books, 1982), 238.

Teacher of truth [Jn. 15:26]; that the Steward of God and Vicar of Christ [the Holy Spirit] neglected his office, and permitted the Churches for a time to understand otherwise and to believe otherwise than he himself had preached through the Apostles: now, is it likely that so many and such great Churches should have gone astray into a unity of faith?[106]

THE MEDIEVAL CHURCH

It is upon churches such as these that Western civilization was built. The development of the Church continued to maintain and deepen its teachings until the Middle Ages. During the thousand years (500 to 1500 AD) after the period we have just examined, Europe witnessed the abolition of slavery, the liberation of women, checks and balances on absolutism, artistic and architectural excellence in their cathedrals, invention of the musical scale, Gregorian chant and polyphony, the creation of the university, the advancement and consolidation of philosophy, the derivation of Western law from canon law, and numerous scientific achievements.[107] All these contributions originated from the Church itself.[108] During the Middle Ages the ordinary individual enjoyed free hospital care, anesthetics, legal recourse, security of land tenure, protection from enemies, theatrical entertainments, and over sixty Holy Days during the year (in addition to the Lord's Day) when no work was to be done. Most importantly every person knew that one belonged to a single community, derived from the Apostles under Christ, upon which the dignity of each person was founded. During the Middle Ages the average person enjoyed an existential security and dignity unequalled before or since.[109]

---

106 Quoted in Bennett, *Four Witnesses*, 305.
107 Regine Pernoud, *Those Terrible Middle Ages: Debunking the Myths* (San Francisco: Ignatius Press, 2000).
108 Thomas E. Woods, *How the Catholic Church Built Western Civilization* (Washington, DC: Regnery Publishing, 2005); Francis Oakley, *The Crucial Centuries: The Mediaeval Experience* (London: Terra Nova, 1979).
109 Christopher Dawson, *The Formation of Christendom* (San Francisco: Ignatius Press, 2008).

The Catholic Church also founded the scientific method.[110] Indeed the very essence of the understanding of the Church was that God had ordered all things by measure, number, and weight.[111] Moreover, the scientific works of Aristotle who was regarded as *the* Philosopher were extremely influential. Finally, the idea that the Logos could become incarnate in human nature also facilitated the development of the medieval insight that nature was rational.

Foremost in the advancement of science was the cathedral School of Chartres. Almost every thinker of note in the eleventh and twelfth centuries was sometime associated with or influenced by Chartres, e.g.: Fulbert in mathematics and astronomy, Thierry in architecture and cosmology, Adelard of Bath in physics, and William of Conches in cosmology. Many other monks and priests were also scientists: Roger Bacon in optics and philosophy of science; St Albert the Great in physics, biology, psychology, and mineralogy; Richard of Wallingford in chronometry; Robert Grosseteste in experimental method; John Buridan and Nicholas of Cusa in astronomy; and Nicolaus Steno in fossils, geology, comparative biology, and stratigraphy. Indeed, medieval cosmologists (e.g., John Major and Nichole Oresme) even postulated the possibility of other inhabited worlds.[112] But out of all proportion to their numbers were the contributions of the Jesuits:

> They had contributed to the development of pendulum clocks, pantographs, barometers, reflecting telescopes and microscopes, to scientific fields as various as magnetism, optics, and electricity. They observed in, in some cases before anyone else, the colored bands on Jupiter's surface, the Andromeda nebula and Saturn's rings. They theorized about the circulation of the blood (independently

---

110   James Hannom, *God's Philosophers: How the Medieval World Laid the Foundations of Modern Science* (London: Icon Books, 2009).
111   Wis 11:20, 21.
112   Pierre Duhem, *Medieval Cosmology: Theories of Infinity, Place, Time, Void, and the Plurality of Worlds* (Chicago: University of Chicago Press, 1987). Following Democritus's ideas in *De Generatione* written in the fifth century BC, these medieval thinkers referred to this idea as plurality of worlds.

of Harvey), the theoretical possibility of flight, the way the moon effected the tides, and the wave-like nature of light.[113]

Given all this, why do the media and books on popular science continue to accuse the Church of opposing science? The only case they can cite is Galileo.[114] Yet, the Church had had no quarrel with Copernicus who previously had taught exactly the same thing, viz., that the heavenly bodies orbited the sun rather than the earth as was hitherto believed. Galileo himself was welcomed and celebrated by churchmen. In 1610 Fr Christopher Clavius wrote to Galileo that his fellow Jesuit astronomers had confirmed the very discoveries he had made through his telescope and Barberini, the future Pope Urban VIII, wrote Galileo a letter of congratulation.[115] The reason the Church could not accept Galileo's proposal was that he had simply not proven his case for reasons that today belong to philosophy of science.[116] Because so much was involved, *the Church was unable to alter its views without proof.* In fact, the Church was quite prepared to accept Galileo's hypotheses if he had presented them as such, but

---

113 Ashworth, quoted in Woods, *How the Catholic Church Built Western Civilization*, 100.
114 The case of Giordano Bruno, itinerant Hermetic philosopher, magician, duellist, and millenarian reformer, is sometimes cited even though the official *processo*, giving the details of the indictment against him (drawn up by the Jesuit professor Robert Bellarmine) no longer exists! It is impossible that the charge of heresy for teaching heliocentrism was on Bellarmine's list because Copernicus's theory did not become heretical until 1616. Therefore, the reason Bruno was tragically burned alive on 17 February 1600 had nothing to do with heliocentrism. See Hannom, *God's Philosophers*, 306–9.
115 Ibid., 69–70. See also Paul Feyerabend, *Farewell to Reason* (London: Verso, 1987), ch. 9.
116 See Paul Feyerabend, *Against Method* (London: Verso, 1988), ch. 13; Arthur Koestler, *The Sleepwalkers* (Harmondsworth: Penguin Books, 1982), 431–503. It is passing strange that the Church is condemned for not abandoning the (pagan) science of its day which she had received from Anaximander, Plato, Eudoxus, Aristotle, and Ptolemy; and then is accused of opposing science! Contemporary scientists also are conservative and are known to ostracize, defund, and even hinder the careers of those who do not follow the prevailing orthodoxy. See Jim Baggott, *Farewell to Reality: How Modern Physics Has Betrayed the Search for Truth* (London: Pegasus Books, 2013); Smolin, *The Trouble with Physics.*

this he refused to do. The Church censured him because it could not abandon its cosmology unless it was demonstrated to be false which Galileo could not do. Nevertheless the Church continued to provide him with patronage, gifts, medals, and commendations, and he was left free to continue his work.[117]

It was during the Middle Ages that women attained the greatest freedom and status in history to that point. This was not only the case with queens such as Theodolinda of Lombardy, Brunhilde of Spain, Adelaide of Saxony, Margaret of Scotland, Eleanor of Aquitaine, Blanche of Castile, Margaret of Anjou, and Isabella of Spain, but also with Sts. Hildegard of Bingen, Clare of Assisi, Elizabeth of Portugal, Margaret of Cortona, Juliana Falconieri, Gertrude of Helfta, Joan of Arc, and Catherine of Genoa. Catherine of Siena, e.g., is a Doctor of the Church; she advised Popes Gregory the Great and Urban VI; she was the author of a great spiritual work (the *Dialogue*) and the leader of a group of men and women clergy and laity known as her Fellowship. She even rebuked cardinals disloyal to the Holy See. Teresa of Avila was spiritual director to John of the Cross, the founder and organizer of several convents, a Doctor of the Church, and author of several spiritual volumes. Petronilla of Chemille presided over the fortunes of the order at Fontevrault which consisted of two convents: one of men, another of women.

Women were able to vote in urban assemblies and rural parishes.[118] They were managers of shops or trades, schoolmistresses, doctors, apothecaries, plasterers, dyers, copyists, miniaturists, binders, etc.[119] Many women became the managers of vast estates while their husbands were absent for prolonged periods at war or regular courtly service. They could read, write, and own property.

The reasons for the elevated status of women in the Middle Ages were the reverence the Church held towards the Virgin Mary and female saints, the dignity attributed to them by St Paul, and the rise of chivalry. The latter owed much to female influence, particularly the aristocratic ladies who presided over and molded the courtly life

---

117 Woods, *How the Catholic Church Built Western Civilization*, 73.
118 Pernoud, *Those Terrible Middle Ages*, 110.
119 Ibid., 111.

of the eleventh and twelfth centuries.[120] Unlike today, it was love, not eroticism, which was idealized. Tristan and Iseult, Lancelot and Guinevere, Troilus and Criseyde, Dante and Beatrice were typical of the idealized nature of love between a man and a woman. As C. S. Lewis expressed it: "French poets, in the eleventh century, discovered or invented, or were the first to express, that romantic species of passion which English poets were still writing about in the nineteenth. They effected a change which has left no corner of our ethics, our imagination, or our daily life untouched, and they erected impassable barriers between us and the classical past or the Oriental present."[121] It was only after the destruction of medieval society under the Dissolution, the rise of Puritanism, and the subsequent revival of classical Roman law that women began to sink in status again.[122]

It was also during the Middle Ages that the Church deepened its understanding of the Eucharist. Just how the bread and wine were truly the body and blood of Christ became a topic of considerable debate within the later Church as it continued to deepen its understanding of Christ's words. Eventually at the end of the Middle Ages the Council of Trent adopted the term transubstantiation, a term first given meaning by Alan de Lille in the twelfth century[123] to describe the mystery by which the elements of bread and wine become the whole substance of Christ while only the appearances (accidents including quantity and quality such as color, taste, etc., also known as "species") remain. This mystery involves a metaphysical change in these elements whereby Christ in his entire Person, without descending from glory, acts in and through the creaturely realities so altering their nature. No longer does the material principle remain: Christ is actually present as their Substantial Reality. Only the appearances remain, the species having been subsumed and converted into Christ's glorified body. "Now since the Body of Christ is

---

120 Oakley, *Crucial Centuries*, 196–205.
121 Quoted in ibid., 200.
122 Pernoud, *Those Terrible Middle Ages*, 111.
123 In his *Four Books Against the Heretics* (c. 1180) he first defines the term transubstantiation as "that type of change according to which both matter and substantial form are changed, while the accidents remain." Quoted in James T. O'Connor, *The Hidden Manna* (San Francisco: Ignatius Press, 1988), 115.

not present as in place it is necessary to say that it begins to be there through the conversion of the substance of bread into itself."[124] As the *Catechism of the Council of Trent* put it:

> This conversion, then, is so effected that the whole substance of the bread is changed by the power of God into the whole substance of the body of Christ, and the whole substance of the wine into the whole substance of his blood, and this, without any change in our Lord himself. He is neither begotten, nor changed, nor increased, but remains entire in his substance....
>
> Since natural changes are rightly called *transformations*, because they involve a change of form; so likewise our predecessors in the faith wisely and appropriately introduced the term *transubstantiation,* in order to signify that in the Sacrament of the Eucharist *the whole substance of one thing passes into the whole substance of the other.*[125]

Thus, through his action, the whole Christ becomes the substantial formative principle under the appearances of bread and wine. As the elements no longer possess their former material nature, what happens to the appearances during communion affects the Lord's body and blood only *per accidens.*[126] Through the sacramental species the risen Christ truly gives sanctifying grace to the recipient, who really is in substantial communion with Him, while He continues to retain His integral unity of Person.

---

124 *Summa Theol.* III, q. 75, a. 4. St Thomas goes on to point out that this is because "God is infinite Act.... Therefore his activity extends to the nature of being." For this reason God is able "to effect a conversion of the whole being so that the whole substance of one thing is changed into that of another."
125 *Catechism of Trent*, 238–39.
126 Ibid., 240. This is not what contemporary physicists understand of matter. Being empiricists, they can only know phenomena (accidents). But Christ's activity is beyond physical propositions of space and time. The reader should recall what we have said about substantial form in chapter 1 and the potentiality of matter in chapter 2. Also see Ludwig Ott, *Fundamentals of Catholic Dogma* (Rockford, IL: TAN, 1974), 380–81, and *Catechism of the Catholic Church* 1374.

During the Middle Ages a number of heresies arose to challenge many of the Church's teachings. To deal with these the Inquisition was instituted in France originally in response to the Albigensian heresy in the thirteenth century.[127] It then became established in Spain because of the many letters from Andalusia and Seville which were sent to Rome complaining of the heresies, immorality, and subversion instigated by false believers and converts (*conversos*).[128] It had jurisdiction only over those claiming to be Christians: it had none over those who were practicing Jews or Moslems.

According to Henry Kamen, who has written the definitive work on the subject, the idea that the Inquisition was feared is unfounded: "It was the testimony of the community—that is of neighbors, relatives, enemies—that the accused most dreaded."[129] While fear of denunciation was a regular feature of the secular judicial system in many countries, under the Inquisition the accused was given the opportunity to list one's enemies. If anyone on the list testified against the accused, that person's testimony was discounted while false accusations attracted severe penalties. An extremely detailed inquiry into the veracity of the accusations was carried out with cross examination of the witnesses. The judges and their methods were subject to scrutiny and were continuously revised. The accused always had the right to appeal: many such letters of appeal written to the Popes of the time still exist.[130]

Torture was used as a last resort and administered infrequently in only a minority of cases. "Confessions under torture were never accepted as valid because they had obviously been obtained by pressure. It was therefore essential for the accused to ratify his confession the day after ordeal."[131] The rules forbade anyone to be tortured more than once so that if anyone refused to ratify one's confession under torture

---

127 Q.v. Walter Brandmüller, *Light and Shadows: Church History amid Faith, Fact and Legend* (San Francisco: Ignatius Press, 2009), 100–25.
128 Warren H. Carroll, *A History of Christendom*, vol. 3, *The Glory of Christendom* (Front Royal, VA: Christendom Press, 2000).
129 Henry Kamen, *The Spanish Inquisition* (London: Phoenix, 1998), 175.
130 Matthew Arnold, *Fire and Sword: Inquisition* (Saundersfoot: St Anthony Comm., 2002).
131 Kamen, *Spanish Inquisition*, 188.

the only recourse was the *threat* of torture. The rule was that no one because of torture should lose life or limb. Reconciliation with the Church was the primary objective. Consequently many of the accused simply embraced the opportunity to confess their sins in a public declaration called the *auto da fe* so that everyone could witness their pardon.

Under Church law, ecclesiastical tribunals had no authority to execute or to shed blood. Those who refused to repent of their heresies were referred to secular tribunals to exact the punishment. In the whole of the sixteenth century in Spain and America the Inquisition had handed over for death some forty or fifty people. During the entire 350 years of the Spanish Inquisition the state executed approximately 3500 to 5000 heretics.[132] However, these figures are overwhelmed by the 11,000,000 "enemies of the state" killed during the Stalinist purges, along with the 12,000,000 who perished in the Siberian camps; or the 65,000,000 "liquidated" by the communists in China; or the nearly 2,000,000 slaughtered by Pol Pot's Khmer Rouge in the killing fields of Cambodia.[133]

The fact of the matter is there was no "Grand Inquisitor," and no clandestine agency: only inquisitorial courts consisting of two or three monks, trained in law. These courts operated according to strict guidelines and were overseen by Inquisitors General to ensure they would protect people accused of heresy through meticulous examination of the accusations. Normally there was only a single court covering a large region. Some regions far from the cities rarely saw an inquisitor, if ever. The Holy Inquisition was so popular that many of those accused of secular offences deliberately committed heresy in order to come under the jurisdiction of the Inquisition where they would receive more justice than from the secular courts of the time. In fact, when the Holy Inquisition was first disbanded in 1808 there was such an outcry among the populace that it was restored in 1814, only to be eventually annulled in 1834 after it had become virtually ineffective.

---

132   Ibid., 59–60, 198–99; Carroll, *Glory of Christendom*, 608.
133   Frank Chalk and Kurt Jonassohn, *The History and Sociology of Genocide* (New Haven: Yale University Press, 1990); Stéphane Courtois et al., *The Black Book of Communism* (Harvard: Harvard University Press, 1999).

This misrepresentation of the Spanish Inquisition as an infamous tribunal which had a web of secret agents who spread fear and cruelty throughout Spain, was entirely fabricated in the sixteenth century by John Foxe[134] of England, and by two Protestant exiles from Spain, Casiodore de Reina and Antonio del Corro, writing in Heidelberg under the pseudonym "Montanus."[135] These accounts were the sole foundation upon which the "Black Legend" was constructed. Even today they are quoted as primary sources. However the recent publication by the Vatican of thousands of the original court transcripts has completely demolished their claims.

Finally, a few words about the Crusades are necessary. Between the seventh and the end of the eleventh centuries the Mohammedans had conquered lands that had been Christian since well before the third century: Palestine, Lebanon, Syria, Jordan, Albania, Armenia, Cyprus, Crete, Sardinia, Malta, Southern Italy, Spain, Egypt, and North Africa had all fallen to the Moslems. Under the Reconquest which followed, Spain was regained by El Cid; and the Byzantines had freed Bulgaria, Albania, Cyprus, and Sicily. However Turkey (Anatolia) was being invaded by the Seljuk Turks who had already taken Iconium and Nicaea. Antioch — the holy city where Barnabus and Paul preached, where Peter visited, and where the name Christian was first used[136] — had already fallen. The Byzantine Emperor, Alexius Comnenus I, appealed to Pope Urban II for assistance. At the Council of Clermont in 1095, the pope called for a Crusade "to liberate the Church of God at Jerusalem."[137] Under the banner of Baldwin of Boulogne the Crusaders successfully repelled the Turks, then marched on Jerusalem taking it in a six-week siege in 1099.

---

134   In his work *Book of Martyrs*, which he was forced to correct later (in his *Ecclesiastical History*) after the accuracy of the original was immediately contested by several Catholic writers. Unfortunately it was then further embellished in the nineteenth century by Rev. Ingram Cobbin.
135   Kamen, *The Spanish Inquisition*, 305–8. See also Rodney Stark, *Bearing False Witness: Debunking Centuries of Anti-Catholic History* (London: SPCK, 2017), 117–18.
136   Acts 11:25–26; 15:22; Gal 2:11.
137   Tom Holland, *Millennium* (London: Little Brown, 2008), 408. See also Nicolas Cheetham, *The Keepers of the Keys* (London: Macdonald, 1982), 102–4.

A second Crusade, during the reign of Pope Eugenius III and inspired by St Bernard of Clairvaux, attempted without success to take Damascus. And the famous third Crusade led by the French king Philip II and the English king Richard the Lionheart, after Saladin had retaken Jerusalem, ended with a treaty that lasted only five years. This latter Crusade was preached by Pope Gregory VIII. Pope Innocent III launched two more Crusades: the fourth, which recovered Constantinople, and the fifth, to gain Cairo and Damietta in Egypt in order to exchange them for Jerusalem, ended in defeat. These were the only Crusades in which the Church played an active role. Further crusades were independently embarked upon by Frederick II, Louis IX, and Lord Edward of England.

These Crusades were intended to regain the holy sites, release the native Christians from their subjugation, and open up the pilgrimage routes once again. It is regrettable that some historians, in their zeal to condemn the Church, lay at her threshold the cruelties and rapacities of the Christian princes, which, incidentally, were equally matched (at least) by the ruthless behavior of the Moslem invaders. In fact Pope Urban II officially condemned such practices.[138]

A lamentable exception to this was the Crusade against the Albigensians[139] (lit. *from Albi*, the town in Provence where the heresy began). Also known as Cathars because of their strict asceticism, they opposed marriage and childbearing, believing matter to be evil. For this reason they also rejected the humanity of Christ. They embraced Manichaean dualism and antinomianism, considering that only one thing was necessary: the *consolamentum* wherein all sins were washed away so that morality could be relinquished. The Cathars presented an alternative religion to Catholicism which they hated—they attacked the Church, alluring much of the nobility along with their fiefdoms to their cause, and in 1207 ousted the bishop from the city of Carcassonne. By 1210 forty castles in the south of France were in the hands of the Cathars. The Crusaders under Simon de Montfort

---

[138] Rodney Stark, *God's Battalions: The Case for the Crusades* (New York: Harper Collins, 2009), 29, 127.

[139] See Dawson, *Formation of Christendom*, 232–33; Carroll, *Glory of Christendom*, 164–70, 172–77; Piers Paul Read, *The Templars* (London: Phoenix, 2001), 189–95.

struck back with severe cruelty. The rebels were hanged while others were blinded. During twenty years of warfare the Cathars were hunted down, their bodies often consigned to the flames. The war crimes of Emperors Otto IV and Frederick II in this regard are notorious for their barbarity.

The Albigensian Crusade and the Inquisition, instituted by Gregory IX, which was associated with it, were extremely cruel, yet were typical of those violent times. The very fabric of Christendom was being rent — not only spiritually and doctrinally but materially and structurally — by the Catharist insurgents. Entire principalities had fallen to their armies and many people were indoctrinated with their heresies. Today we are not able to appreciate how so deeply felt was their faith that a devoted populace should be so galvanized as to engage into what amounted to a civil war. But for them it was truly a choice between personal salvation or eternal damnation . . . and the survival of Christendom.

CONCLUSION

We have asked if Jesus intended to found a Church. We undertook this inquiry having already established in the previous two chapters that Jesus is aware of himself as the incarnate, pre-existent Son of God and Lamb of God who had come to give his life as a ransom for many. It became inconceivable, therefore, that he would have abandoned us. Believing Jesus to be who he claimed to be, it is natural to trust his words.

Of the more than two billion Christians today, over three quarters of them, who belong to the catholic (universal) Church, accept this. Roman Catholics, Anglo-Catholics, Greek, Russian, and Ukrainian Orthodox Catholics, Copts (Roman and Orthodox), Catholics of Byzantine and Syriac Rites (including Armenian, Chaldean, Maronite, and Melchite) receive those teachings of the early Church that we have articulated above, including some form of Petrine primacy (of honor among equals). All share a similar organization. Only cultural and historical factors separate some of these from full communion with one another.

Christ the King

* * *

Since our initial investigations into the existence and nature of God, we have succeeded in transcending natural reason to arrive finally at faith — faith in Jesus Christ and his Church. For if we deny that the Church was founded by Jesus who had promised to protect her and keep her from error, we disavow the majesty and divinity of the Christ, thereby rendering his promises without foundation and his appearance among us as a failure. To do that would be to nullify the claims he made about himself, caricaturing Jesus as a false prophet. Or if we assert that Jesus has rescinded this promise, we then impeach his integrity and thereby render doubtful his other assurances. No one who truly believes in him would speak thus of the Christ; no one who worships his Divinity could.

Genuine faith cannot stop at mere belief. Rather, it desires union with the One upon whom it places its trust. And if the One in whom one trusts is "full of grace and truth" revealing a "glory as of the only Son from the Father," then trust becomes devotion, and devotion worship. With the awakening of devotion and worship comes the religious life. The nature of this religious life will, therefore, occupy us in part three where we shall ascend even higher.

PART THREE

SPIRIT

*When the Spirit of truth comes,
he will guide you into all the truth...
He will glorify me, for he will take what
is mine and declare it to you.*

John 16:13, 14

CHAPTER 7

Purgation

You shall love the Lord your God with all your heart, and with all your soul, and with all your mind. This is the great and first commandment. And a second is like it, you shall love your neighbor as yourself. On these two commandments depend the law and the prophets.[1]

WE ACCEPT JESUS'S WITNESS TO HIMSELF as the Son of God who willed to give his life as a ransom for many, who did not abandon us but established a universal or Catholic Church, guided by his Spirit, to be the deposit of his teaching and a dispenser of his grace. Moreover we rejoice in the beauty, the majesty, and the holiness of his Person along with the sublimity of his teaching. Proclaiming the unique glory of the Christ then, is it not natural to be drawn to him? What we value we desire; for where our treasure is, there is our heart.[2] And how much more so when Christ is the treasure! For what else could stand in equal measure before him?

Christ promised he would come into our hearts if we keep his commandments: "He who has my commandments and keeps them, he it is who loves me; and he who loves me will be loved by my Father, and I will love him and manifest myself to him."[3] Since it is inconceivable that one who truly loves Christ, calling him Lord and meaning it, could refuse to obey his teachings or follow his example, then it is necessary that good works follow faith.[4] Rather than offend the one we love, we choose to become pleasing to him in body, soul, and spirit. Practically, this means purifying ourselves of whatever

---

1 Mt 22:37–40.
2 Mt 6:21.
3 Jn 14:21, 23.
4 Mt 7:21; Lk 6:46; Rom 2:13; 1 Cor 3:8–9; Gal 2:8–10; Phil 2:12–13; Jas 2:14–17, 24, 27.

displeases him and striving for whatever is pleasing to him. If we do not conform ourselves to Christ,[5] how can we truly say we love him?[6]

And since love can never love enough, there is no end to our striving as we seek to become more pleasing to the Object of our desire. Indeed this is the nature of love itself where the One who loves us desires our perfection so that we, being more like the One we love, become more united to him, not only morally (in our wills) or intellectually (in our minds), but in the very spirit of our being, so that our lives are not our own, but his life in us.[7] Such is God's love for us that he wills our sanctification.[8] God will not rest until we are rendered consummately holy.

God is the Being who gives being—the very essence of love. Authentic love is not merely the desire of psychophysical attraction (*eros*), which wants to possess the other and, lacking original innocence, debases the other.[9] Rather, it is that self-giving love (*agape*) which desires what is good for the other, since being and the good are convertible. Since God is Being, he is one, true, and good, and therefore beautiful and desirable, radiating from his infinite abundance goodness upon all who seek him. God loves us and desires our perfection because he wants what is best for us. We, in loving God, desire also to please him and unite ourselves to him in order to become one with him so that we can please Him, for without him we cannot love as we should. "Abide in me, and I in you. As the branch cannot bear fruit by itself, unless it abides in the vine, neither can you, unless you abide in me. I am the vine, you are the branches. He who abides in me, and I in him, he it is that bears much fruit, for apart from me you can do nothing."[10] More cannot come from less. We cannot live without that love which sustains us. God is that love,

---

5 Rom 8:29; 12:2.
6 1 Jn 5:2.
7 Jn 17:23; Gal 2:20; 5:24; 6:14.
8 1 Thess 4:3; 5:23; 1 Pet 1:16.
9 Heb 13:4; see also Rom 1:26–27. *Agape, eros, sorge, philia, pietas, libido, concupiscentia* are some of the different types of love in the classical and philosophical literature. Of these "loves" only *agape* (Latin: *caritas*—charity) and *philia* (friendship) occur in the New Testament.
10 Jn 15:4–5.

for he is one simple act of Being. Indeed, God loves us into being along with each and every moment. So our task is but to seek God: to love him with all our being, opening ourselves to his love, and then we shall become that which we were meant to be.

However, our imperfections impede our union with God. The reason for this is simply that our imperfections, whether venial or grave, arise ultimately from our attachments to the things of this world. Sin is idolatry: it is giving to a creature the devotion that ought to be given to God. Sin says in effect that we value some thing, some cause, more than God, who is the only uncreated and Supreme Being. This is to make the creature greater than God, which is not just irrational, but irreverent.

It also fundamentally distorts the moral life. Properly to order all things as God their creator intended is the essence of the natural law. Everything has its nature and its proper place and purpose in God's economy. Every creature is in essence what God intended it to be;[11] otherwise it would not be any particular thing. It would not even be intelligible since if it lacked an identity — a logos or form — it could not be conceived of as this particular identifiable thing. In the state of innocence all the members of our body and all our thoughts and relationships were properly ordered according to the nature given to them *in the beginning*. When our first parents, having received the gift of reason, chose to value the creature more than God, then humanity fell. With the fall, the entire scheme of things became disturbed, bringing disorder to our appetites, intellects, relationships, and society.[12] To love money, power, rights, sexuality, country, etc., more than God is idolatrous, especially since these things already manifest in their distorted natures the consequences of this fallen world.

Moreover, because we love these things for ourselves, we love ourselves in these things. This creates division and dissension, since we become possessive of these things, identify with them, and refuse to relinquish them. With this comes division, hatred, envy, malice, war, alienation and fear — in short this whole sorry mess in which we find ourselves.

---

11 Gen 1:4, 10, 12, 18, 21, 25, 31.
12 Mt 19:4, 8; Gen 1:27–28; Rom 8:22; Jer 12:4, 11.

We recall that God's remedy for this fallen world is not to destroy human freedom, but to provide human freedom with the opportunity to pursue a more exquisite good: to become like Christ. This means that every person must change. "I appeal to you therefore, brethren, by the mercies of God, to present your bodies as a living sacrifice, holy and acceptable to God, which is your spiritual worship. Do not be conformed to this world but be transformed by the renewal of your mind, that you may prove what is the will of God, what is good, acceptable and perfect."[13] Change is invariably painful and costly and places upon each person's shoulder one's own particular cross. For whoever refuses to bear one's cross cannot be called a disciple of Christ.[14] Therefore, no one can claim a special exemption, proffering one's disordered, fallen nature as an excuse.[15] We are not mere animals driven by instincts and desires we cannot control. "No temptation has overtaken you that is not common to man. God is faithful and he will not let you be tempted beyond your strength, but with the temptation will also provide the way of escape, that you may be able to endure it."[16] We are human beings with moral integrity grounded in our free will given us by our Creator. God is not the author of evil: each person is tempted by one's own desire.[17] Therefore, we must choose whom we shall serve. "No one can serve two masters; for either he will hate the one and love the other, or he will be devoted to the one and despise the other. You cannot serve God and mammon."[18] We are all called to perfection, to become like Christ who is in the form (*morphe*) of God.[19]

Yet, we cannot become perfect unless we abide in God and we cannot become truly one with God until we are perfect. This is the dilemma of the religious life. But Christ has provided the way out of this dilemma. It is important that we take confidence in this, because Christ did not intend to make a mockery of our perseverance. The

---

13 Rom 12:1–2.
14 Lk 14:27.
15 Rom 6:1–2, 11, 15.
16 1 Cor 10:23.
17 Jas 1:13–15.
18 Mt 6:24.
19 Mt 5:48; Col 1:28–29; 1 Jn 4:17; Phil 2:5–7.

idea that we can do nothing but sin is true if it refers to us in our fallen condition apart from Christ, for without him we can do nothing[20] (i.e., nothing good). But in Christ we can do all things.[21] "For if the Son makes you free, then you are free indeed."[22] Therefore, we have no excuse but to confront our individual disordered natures, to take up our crosses, and to go on to perfection, for the sake of Christ.

The spiritual way is now clear. We must seek holiness for love's sake, and we cannot become holy without God. But we have been given access to God through our faith in Christ. This means that our faith in Christ must be the means whereby we can become holy, become pleasing to God. To believe in Christ means firstly accepting that he is the Son of God who gave himself for us so that we have forgiveness in his name. This is crucial because one cannot take the first steps towards perfection if one is not first reconciled with God. But in Christ we have been reconciled, since he has merited for us through his passion and death the forgiveness of all our sins. "So for anyone who is in Christ, there is a new creation: the old order is gone and a new being is there to see. It is all God's work; he reconciled us to himself through Christ and he gave us the ministry of reconciliation.... God was in Christ reconciling the world to himself, not holding anyone's faults against them, but entrusting to us the message of reconciliation."[23]

Having been reconciled, one can begin with confidence on the path towards holiness. This spiritual path involves three fundamental modalities or ways: purging deliberate or habitual imperfections from oneself, strengthening and informing our virtues, and perfecting and completing our love for God. These three classical ways have been called respectively purgation, illumination, and union, reflecting the traditional understanding that we are body (appetite), soul (intellect),

---

20 Jn 15:5.
21 Phil 4:13; 2 Cor 12:9.
22 Jn 8:36.
23 2 Cor 5:19. God loves unconditionally, not because he wills without conditions but because everything he does is for the glory of his Beloved Son in whom we are reconciled. Just as God cannot will anything that does not accord with Divine Wisdom, so neither does his Holy Spirit distribute graces upon us unreservedly. Rather, *we are obligated to cooperate* with God's will: Mt 7:21–23, 25:1–46; Jn 14:15; Rom 8:17, 11:21–22; 2 Cor 6:1; Phil 2:12–16. In this way his love is perfected *in us*: 1 Jn 4:16–17; 5:3.

and spirit (intuition). For "you shall love the Lord your God with all your heart (*kardia*), and with all your soul (*psyche*), and with all your mind, intuition (*dianoia*)."

These three ways must not be understood as stages, as though one can first become morally perfect without the other two ways of illumination and union. Even so, the moral life is foundational for the latter two, just as union cannot be effected without the former two. Secondly, perfect union with God cannot be achieved in this life without an extraordinary grace. Thirdly, all three ways require some measure of cooperation on our part, since grace does not destroy nature but perfects it. This is because our moral integrity as free agents is always respected by God, our Creator. However, as we grow in holiness we find that God becomes more and more the principle of our lives as we become less and less the self-willed individuals we once were. "Therefore do not throw away your confidence, which has so great a reward. For you have need of perseverance, so that you may do the will of God and obtain what is promised."[24]

Here we shall treat of the way of purgation, leaving the other two ways for the remaining chapters. Yet, in all three ways we must remember that the principle of our spiritual life is the love we have for Our Blessed Lord and Savior Jesus Christ. Everything we do is for his glory that he may live in us and we in him so that his will may be done in us and his light shine in us and his kingdom be realized in us. All grace and virtue ultimately flow from Christ who has merited all grace, who is the substance of our faith, and who dwells in us through his Holy Spirit.

THE LIFE OF FAITH

No person can approach to Christ unless drawn by God, the Father.[25] Thus, God's free act is at the very commencement of a life in Christ. This is the doctrine known as prevenient (antecedent) grace, so called because it comes before the grace of justification.[26] "For by grace

---

24 Heb 10:35–39.
25 Jn 6:44, 65.
26 Denzinger, *Enchiridion Symbolorum*, 797, 813.

you have been saved through faith: and that not of yourselves, for it is the gift of God — not of works, lest anyone should boast."[27] Prevenient grace is a supernatural quality, freely created by God, which unites with the faculties of the soul, i.e., intellect and will, and which is capable of effecting *faith* in the individual. It affects the intellect through insight, understanding, intuition, imagination, by any means internal or external (e.g., the spoken word, music, the beauty of nature, or acts of kindness) which bring the soul to belief in Christ. Prevenient grace also affects the will by the Spirit of love which makes Christ Jesus attractive and delightful to the believer. This grace raises one beyond natural reason enabling one to commit oneself to trust in the Person of Christ. While reason and evidence can prepare for faith by making belief reasonable, only God can give that transcendent quality which evokes trust, turning natural, reasoned belief into supernatural, trusting faith.

Grace is absolutely necessary before one can progress in sanctification. But when one responds to grace, then God, the Father, Son, and Holy Spirit, dwells in the soul. This doctrine, that God is three Personal Relations sharing one Substantial Being,[28] is grounded in those teachings of Jesus where he claimed divinity for himself, and also promised to send his Holy Spirit. We have already seen that all beings have a threefold modality: substance (that in which a thing subsists), form (its rational principle), and activity (its life). A little thought should convince one that to assert that there exists a Supreme Being who has neither Substance, nor Form, nor Life, is absurd. God is not nothing, but Being in act. This Reality is not without its own nature or formal principle, but rather in acting expresses its nature. And from both this Reality and its Nature proceeds Spirit or Life. Thus, God, eternally transparent to himself — to whom we may analogously attribute intelligence — acts and in so acting expresses his

---

27 Eph 2:8–9; Lam 5:21.
28 "Here however there is no diversity of being, and so these three ought to have a specific name, and yet none can be found. For person is a generic name.... What, of course, we have been saying about persons in our way of talking must be understood about substances in the Greek way of talking. They say three substances [*hypostases*], one being [*ousia*], just as we say three persons, one being or substance." Augustine, *The Trinity*, VII, 7 & 8.

nature as an eternal Form, or Logos, or Wisdom, as the self-image or Son of the Father.[29] But this self-image fully generated by the Father is the perfect image of the Father so that he — His Son — is perfectly loved by the Father, since to love (*agape*) is to give fullness of Being to another. Moreover, the Son, who is the perfect expression of the Father, fully images what the Father is, so that the Son loves, or affirms, the Father precisely in receiving (*virtute assumptio*) from the Father, by *being* his true image.[30]

Thus, in denying the analogy of Being, one must also deny the Holy Trinity; for one cannot then accept both the identity of substance and the distinction of Persons in God. It is the nature of the analogy of Being simultaneously to express sameness and distinction in God.[31] This is the triune life of the one Godhead whereby the Father is expressed in the Son, who in turn conforms as perfect image of the Father, in a mutuality of love which is the Holy Spirit of God. And it is through the indwelling of the Holy Spirit of God in us that God the Father and the Son are made present, enabling us to participate in the life of God. This is the source of sanctifying grace.

We may define sanctifying grace as: "a supernatural quality, inhering in the soul, which gives us a physical and formal *participation*, although analogous and accidental, in the very nature and the life of God."[32] It is a created supernatural gift really distinct from God, but

---

29 "And therefore the Son is not Word in the same way as he is wisdom, because he is not called Word with reference to himself, but only in relationship to him whose Word he is, just as he is Son in relationship to the Father; but he is wisdom in the same way as he is being." Augustine, *The Trinity*, VII, 3.
30 Heb 1:3. (Greek: χαρακτηρ — character); also Phil 2:6–7. "So the Father knows all things in himself, knows them in the Son; but in himself as knowing himself.... Likewise the Son too knows all things in himself, that is to say as things that are born from the things that the Father knows in himself, and he knows them in the Father as the things from which are born all the things that he knows in himself. Therefore, the Father and the Son know each other, the one by begetting, the other by being born. And all the things that are in their knowledge, in their wisdom, in their being, each of them sees all at once." Augustine, *The Trinity*, XV, 23. See also XV, 39.
31 For the relation between equality and distinction of the Persons of the Holy Trinity, see Duns Scotus, *Quodlibetal Questions*, q. 6, a. II, 6.43.
32 Jordan Aumann, *Spiritual Theology* (London: Sheed and Ward, 1984), 67. Italics added.

which elevates us and constitutes us in the spiritual life. It is infused by God into the soul, modifying it accidentally by giving the soul power or virtue and light or truth enabling the soul to act in a supranatural way. The soul, thus informed and invigorated, is capable of living a life more holy and spiritual than those in the natural state. Increasing in virtue, the soul becomes more beautiful and more pleasing to the Father, because the soul is becoming more like the Son — not substantially, of course, but analogously. Insofar as the soul conforms to the likeness of God through the virtues infused into the soul, so the soul becomes conformed to what God loves uttermost: namely, his Son.[33] Therefore, we are to have this mind among ourselves, which is ours in Christ Jesus "who, though he was in the form of God, did not count equality with God a thing to be grasped, but emptied himself, taking the form of a servant, being born in the likeness of men. And being found in human form he humbled himself and became obedient unto death, even death on a cross."[34] Hence the holy life entails our taking up our individual crosses, purging ourselves of evil, and becoming increasingly virtuous as we have repeatedly affirmed. To become holy it is necessary to persevere in carrying our crosses. To refuse to carry our crosses is to refuse to become holy, to refuse to follow Christ. One cannot serve two masters.

Thus we see the analogy of being at work in our faith. It is the nature of faith to trust in the Person of Christ, to respect and honor him by following his example and his wisdom by virtue of his grace. Faith evokes devotion or it is not faith. It is absolutely impious for one who confesses Jesus, who calls him Lord, then to refuse to acknowledge him as such by deliberately flouting his will. More profoundly, as it is the excellence of the Son to submit to the Father, so it is that the Son is the true image of the Father, since the Logos of God is God's Being in Act made manifest in him. Nature follows being. Similarly, in the very act of submitting to the action of the Holy Spirit on our souls, our faith is made evident. Faith thus unites us to Christ; for it is the nature of our faith that it fosters in us a proportionate likeness to him. This is because faith itself bears an analogous nature to that

---

33   Rom 8:29; 12:2; Eph 1:5; Eph 4:13, 24; Heb 12:10; 2 Pet 1:4; 1 Jn 3:3.
34   Phil 2:5–8.

of the Logos.³⁵ To have faith is to put on the mind of Christ in a proportionate manner: for just as the Logos out of love submits to the will of the Father in being the expression of the Father, so analogously we, in our faithful submission to the will of Christ, mirror him as we express our growing love for God and for others. In this submission we become more virtuous and more Christ-like (*analogia entis*), drawing us ever more deeply into the life of Christ which is his Spirit living in us.

We then become true partakers of the very life of the Trinity. The Father begets the Son for the sake of the love he has for the Son who in turn proceeds from the Father glorifying and honoring him as his image. Similarly, we through faith in Christ obey his Spirit receiving the graces which render us more pleasing to the Father, insofar as we mirror his image, his truth. God wants us to be the image of the Son since he is truth itself, because God, who acts for the sake of his own Wisdom, does everything for the glory of his Son who is his Wisdom.³⁶ We then love the Father *with* the very Spirit of Christ in us and glorify the Father with the glory of the life of Christ within us. "The glory which thou hast given me I have given to them, that they may be one even as we are one, I in them and thou in me, that they may be perfectly one, so that the world may know that thou hast sent me and hast loved them even as thou hast loved me."³⁷

It is quite clear from this passage that Jesus is not speaking of unity in the afterlife, but in this life, since he said "so that the world may know." Our sanctification then becomes a light for the world, helping to draw others to Christ. Moreover, our growth in holiness evokes certain actions in obedience to Christ: such as prayer, worship, the Mass, charity, penance, study of the Scriptures, self-discipline, etc. This brings Christ into our relationships with others, spreading the kingdom like yeast in dough. These are the works that faith happily accomplishes. Without such works faith is dead.³⁸

---

35 John of the Cross, *The Ascent of Mount Carmel*, in *The Collected Works of St John of the Cross*, trans. Kieran Kavanaugh and Otilio Rodriguez (Washington, DC: ICS Publications, 1991), Bk. 2, ch. 9, 1–4.
36 1 Cor 1:24, 30; Col 1:15–18; Heb 1:3.
37 Jn 17:22–23.
38 Jas 2:17, 20, 26.

This is why faith is a gift, because we cannot love what we cannot know. God is incomprehensible to the intellect and imperceptible to our senses. Thus, only through faith may we apprehend God. Indeed, faith is the communication of God himself into our soul in the manner described above.[39] Our response is that of submission and obedience to his grace. It is through such patient perseverance that faith purges us of all that would separate us from the knowledge and fullness of God.

> For this reason I bow my knees before the Father, from whom every family in heaven and on earth is named, that according to the riches of his glory he may grant you to be strengthened with might through his Spirit in the inner man, and that Christ may dwell in your hearts through faith; that you, being rooted and grounded in love, may have power to comprehend with all the saints what is the breadth and length and height and depth, and to know the love of Christ which surpasses knowledge, that you may be filled with the fullness of God.[40]

With such faith comes certainty, for "faith is the substance of things hoped for, the conviction of things not seen."[41] Faith is a grace, freely given by God, in which love is poured into our hearts through the gift of the Holy Spirit by which God the Father and Son become present within us, communicating sanctifying grace into our souls.[42] Therefore, "without faith it is impossible to please God."[43]

The faith we are discussing here is faith in Jesus Christ. To reiterate: mere belief in the existence of God is not faith. Rather, such belief is a natural conviction from the light of reason supported by evidence from creation: "For what can be known about God is plain to them, because God has shown it to them. Ever since the

---

39 Eph 3:17, 2:22; 2 Cor 13:5; Heb 3:14–15.
40 Eph 3:14–19; Heb 10: 35–39.
41 Heb 11:1.
42 Rom 5:5; 1 Cor 1:4–9; Phil 1:10; 1 Thess 5:23; 1 Pet 1:2; 2 Pet 3:14.
43 Heb 11:6. See also Deut 7:9–12, 30:15–20; Mt 5:20, 7:21, 10:37–39; Mk 8:34–38; Lk 9:23, 13:3, 17:1–3; Jn 12:25, 14:23–24, 15:9–12; Acts 3:19; 1 Jn 3:10; Jude 21–23.

creation of the world his invisible nature, namely, his eternal power and deity, has been clearly perceived in the things that have been made."[44] But faith in Christ, which is impossible for us unless first given to us by God, is of a different nature. It is a supernatural gift. And with this gift comes certainty, not the certainty of reason and evidence but an interior conviction, a personal experience of the presence of Christ in us.[45]

Now God is always in act. Therefore, the presence of the Holy Spirit is neither static nor idle but communicative of an active principle within us, namely love, which slowly and patiently works its transformation upon our souls, provided we do not frustrate his work. "And do not grieve the Holy Spirit of God, in whom you were sealed for the day of redemption. Let all bitterness and wrath and anger and clamor and slander be put away from you, with all malice, and be kind to one another, tender hearted, forgiving one another, as God in Christ forgave you. Therefore, be imitators of God, as beloved children. And walk in love, as Christ loved us and gave himself up for us, a fragrant offering and sacrifice to God."[46] It is essential, therefore, that we take care to guard against anything that impedes this action of the Holy Spirit.

---

44 Rom 1:19–20.
45 In October 1999, the Lutheran World Federation and the Catholic Church signed the *Joint Declaration on the Doctrine of Justification* (London: Catholic Truth Society, 2001). "Together we confess: By grace alone, in faith in Christ's saving work and not because of any merit on our part, we are accepted by God and receive the Holy Spirit, who renews our hearts *while equipping and calling us to good works*" (*JD* 15). "We confess together that God forgives sin by grace and at the same time frees human beings from sin's enslaving power and imparts *the gift of new life in Christ*" (*JD* 22). "We confess together that in baptism the Holy Spirit unites one with Christ, justifies, and truly renews the person. *But the justified must all through life constantly look to God's unconditional justifying grace*" (*JD* 28). "We confess together that the faithful can rely on the mercy and promises of God. In spite of their own weakness and the manifold threats to their faith, on the strength of Christ's death and resurrection they can build on the effective promise of God's grace in Word and Sacrament *and so be sure of this grace*" (*JD* 34). "No one may doubt God's mercy and Christ's merit" (*JD* 36). "The understanding of the doctrine of justification set forth in this Declaration shows that a consensus in basic truths of the doctrine of justification exists between Lutherans and Catholics" (*JD* 40). Italics added.
46 Eph 4:30–5:2.

THE SACRAMENTAL LIFE

The ordinary means of grace

Christ is the Head, Savior, and Sanctifier of the Church.[47] It is from Christ as the head that all graces come via the sacraments administered by those appointed by him (Peter and his successors). These sacraments are ordinary means of grace established by Christ which effect our sanctification, truly transmitting grace to the recipient according to one's faith. They are part of the reason necessitating the formation of the Church which Christ has established for our sanctification.

The Church has always taught that these sacraments are seven. These are the three sacraments of passage: baptism (at birth), confirmation (at the age of reason), and extreme unction (at the point of death); two sacraments of state or condition: marriage and holy orders; two sacraments of reconciliation or union: penance and Eucharist. "The seven sacraments are the signs and instruments by which the Holy Spirit spreads the grace of Christ the head throughout the Church which is his Body. The Church, then, both contains and communicates the invisible grace she signifies. It is in this analogical sense that the Church is called a sacrament."[48] Similarly, Paul uses the analogy of marriage.[49] The Church is the bride of Christ, sacramentally united to him and receiving from Christ her substance; united to his Bride, Christ brings forth spiritual life in her children, the children of the New Covenant. The Church, therefore, is a mystical body—not a political or social institution. All her members are subject to Christ as her head looking to him for every grace and truth.

In addition to these sacramental means of grace is prayer. Prayer is absolutely essential for the life of faith, for it is the means whereby each soul unites itself with God. In fact, as we shall see in the last chapter, prayer is the very breath of God in the soul.[50]

The last ordinary means of grace are good works such as almsgiving, spiritual reading, intercession, acts of loving self-sacrifice and kindness,

---

47   Eph 5:23, 26–27.
48   *Catechism of the Catholic Church* 774.
49   Eph 5:23–32. Cf. Is 62:5; Jn 3:29–30; 2 Cor 11:2; Rev 21:2, 9; 22:17.
50   Gen 2:7; Jn 20:22; Rom 8:26.

teaching, visiting, witnessing, counseling, etc. These can be means of grace when they are done for the love of God, for unless our actions are done with Divine Love they merit nothing,[51] However, if in all things we glorify God and offer all things for love of Him, then everything can become a means of union with God.[52] Indeed, if at every moment of life we live in the presence of God offering all that we do, however small, for the love of God, then our daily actions become a means of grace and every moment a window to God, transforming our entire life into a prayer and each moment into a sacrament.

Mary, Our Exemplar

If one is truly desirous of seeking God with all one's heart, soul, and mind, then it behooves one to contemplate the example of the Mother of Our Lord, whom the Sacred Scriptures present to us as the exemplary disciple of faith. When the angel Gabriel announces to Mary that she has been chosen by God to be the Mother of the Christ, the entire composition of her soul is made apparent: "Hail, O favored one (*kecharitomene*), the Lord is with you!... For you have found favor with God."[53] Here we are told in a seminal verb that she is already perfectly favored, fully graced because of the nature of her election. The Greek verb *kecharitomene* is a perfect-passive, feminine participle meaning "one having been completely (or fully) graced (or favored)" by God. We have already seen that the Church from the beginning venerated Mary as immaculate in harmony with these Scriptures. For it is also the tradition of the Scriptures that God acts from eternity,[54] and, therefore, since Christ's birth was predestined, then the woman must necessarily be part of God's plan from the beginning.[55]

Furthermore, Mary gave to the angel her consent that she would become the Mother of God by the Holy Spirit who was to overshadow her. This consent must have been a wholehearted, willing,

---

51 1 Cor 13:1–3.
52 Eph 1:15–18; Eph 4:11–16; 1 Pet 2:5; 1 Pet 4:10–11, 16; 1 Pet 5:4, 10.
53 Lk 1:28, 30.
54 Jer 1:5; cf. Ps 139:15–16; Is 49:1; Rom 9; Gal 1:15; 2 Tim 1:9.
55 Is 62:11–12; Is 66:7–8, 12; Zeph 3:14–20; cf. Lk 1:46–55; Rev 12.

and pure consecration,[56] since it is inconceivable and unseemly that God would have acted upon this maiden against her consent. If there had been the slightest impediment, resistance, or reluctance on the part of Mary, then God would not have engendered the holy miracle in her, for it is neither morally nor theologically possible that God should conjoin a sinful nature to himself with such intimacy.

It was foreordained that Mary should say yes to God, to say "Behold I am the servant (Greek: *doule*) of the Lord; let it be unto me according to your word."[57] Mary *is* the one who was so composed through grace as to freely will, out of the nature divinely bestowed upon her, that very thing that God had predestined before the foundation of the world. For this reason, Elizabeth, filled with the Holy Spirit, could exclaim: "Blessed are you among women, and blessed is the fruit of your womb! ... And blessed is she who believed."[58]

In meditating upon such passages in Luke's Gospel we see that Mary exemplifies those virtues which we may treasure in our hearts as did she: the theological virtues of faith, hope, and charity; the cardinal virtues of prudence, justice, temperance, and fortitude; and the religious virtues of poverty, chastity, and obedience. Yet all these virtues are manifested in her simply because Mary considered herself to be but a servant. As the Trappist spiritual writer Thomas Merton

---

56 It was not unusual for Jewish maidens to vow their chastity to God. See *The Temple Scroll (11QT)*, quoted in G. Vermes, *The Dead Sea Scrolls in English*, 149 and in Walter Brandmüller, *Light and Shadows*, 90; cf. Num 30:4–9.

57 Is 7:14; Lk 1:38.

58 Lk 1:41–42, 45. Lutherans today also confess "Mary, the most blessed virgin." Cf. *The Formula of Concord*, Article VIII, 9.24. This is not surprising since Luther had written in 1537 that the Son "was born of the pure, holy, and virgin Mary": q.v. *The Smalcald Articles*, I, 4. Indeed, in an earlier sermon given in 1527 for the conception of Mary, Luther had already affirmed: "But the other conception, namely the infusion of the soul, it is piously and suitably believed, was without any sin, so that while the soul was being infused, she would be at the same time cleansed from original sin and adorned with the gifts of God to receive the holy soul thus infused. And thus, in the very moment in which she began to live, she was without all sin ... " For a discussion of Luther's views on Mary, see Michael O'Carroll, *Theotokos: A Theological Encyclopedia of the Blessed Virgin Mary* (Wilmington: Michael Glazier, 1988), 227. Incidentally, the Swiss Reformer Ulrich Zwingli himself also declared: "I esteem immensely the Mother of God, the ever chaste, immaculate Virgin Mary ... for it was fitting that such a holy Son should have a holy Mother." Ibid., 378.

said of her: "The sanctity of Our Lady was great indeed, but so great that it cannot adequately be expressed in anything other than the ordinary ways of human existence."[59] It is precisely because Mary has made herself the servant of God, living a poor and hidden life, having nothing of her own but receiving everything from God, that she can be truly called full of grace: full of the grace of God. Nothing in her obstructs or hinders his Holy Spirit. Mary's sanctity is the sanctity of God since there is nothing of Mary and all of God in her life. This is the secret of Mary and the secret of her holiness — complete and utter surrender to God. The nature of Divine Love is to give being to the other, and Mary's love for God gives being to God, as it were, by saying yes to his Being through her own self-emptying. By becoming nothing she makes God the holy principle of her life. "He who is mighty has done great things in me, and holy is his name." Through her self-abandonment and self-emptying God is able to work in her in the most extraordinary way by bringing forth the gift of Christ to the world. In Mary's fiat, her "let it be," we have the hermeneutical key into Mary's sanctity, which insight we too can adopt in order that in an analogous way we may also bring forth the life of Christ in us and into our world.

Ordinary holiness

The circumstances of our lives are ultimately in the hands of God who sustains all things in being. Few of us are ever called to live lives of heroic virtue or to perform extraordinary acts of holiness. Most of us are called to live lives of ordinary virtue. And many of us, often burdened by the pressure to make a difference, feel that our small acts are of little worth because they are so ineffectual, implying that our lives also are of little consequence. This is a callous persuasion belonging to worldly, consequentialist quasi-morality. The truth of the matter is that it is not we who make the difference but God, since all things are in his hands. We have seen that the Old Testament is saturated with the idea that nothing happens outside God's will, and we have heard Christ aver that not a sparrow falls unless God wills

---

59 Quoted in E. K. Lynch, *The Scapular of Carmel* (Washington, NJ: World Apostolate of Fatima, 1955), 37.

it. Even quantum entanglement, indeterminacy, chaos theory, and human free will confound any attempt to calculate the consequences of our moral acts.

The worth of one's actions is determined by the end they serve, and the greatest end any act can serve is the will of God. There is nothing more excellent, nothing more sacred. Therefore, the disposition of any soul who seeks sanctity should be conformity to the will of God: "Let it be unto me according to thy word." Also Jesus who had already taught us to pray "Thy will be done," when he was in anguish in Gethsemane, likewise prayed: "Not my will, but thine be done." Through surrendering to God's will in the horror of that moment, a thing truly evil was transformed into immeasurable blessings for humankind.

Now God had willed that moment, just as he wills each and every moment of our lives. "God's action inundates the universe; it penetrates all creatures; it transcends them all; it is to be found wherever they are; it precedes, accompanies, and follows them; we have but to allow ourselves to be carried forward on its waves."[60] Whatever may be the duties, blessings, or crosses required of us in this moment, they conceal within their appearance God's will, either deliberate or permissive. If we wish to be holy, we only have to recognize that this moment is what God has willed it to be. Then, by conforming our wills to the will of God at this present moment, we find the surest and most direct path to holiness. The sanctity of the soul consists in this simple *fiat*.

> Since it is the most perfect act of charity and the most pleasing and acceptable sacrifice that is given to man to offer to God, there can be no doubt that whoever practices entire submission to his will lays up inestimable treasures at every moment and amasses more riches in a few days than others are able to acquire in many years and with great labor. To remain indifferent to good fortune or to adversity by accepting it all from the hand of God without

---

60 Jean Pierre de Caussade, *Self-Abandonment to Divine Providence* (London: Burns and Oates, 1948), 9.

questioning, not to ask for things to be done as we would like them but as God wishes, to make the intention of all our prayers that God's will would be perfectly accomplished in ourselves and in all creatures is to find the secret of happiness and content.[61]

"In *everything* God works for good for those who love him, who are called according to his purpose."[62] It is simply up to us to love God in each and every circumstance — however sweet, however painful — thanking him and in all things giving him the glory.[63] "For from him and through him and to him are all things. To him be glory for ever."[64]

The sacrament of the present moment

If we live according to this simple *fiat*, accepting God's will, trusting in God's will, believing that each moment is willed for our good, then every moment becomes a sacrament, a means of grace. If we will each moment as God's word spoken to us, and in obedience accept its demands or its disciplines, its chastisements or its consolations, then all our days will be a constant communion with God. If we can see the truth of God in each moment, then life itself will become illuminated, suffused with light, and we shall dwell constantly before his face. All we have to do is to believe that this moment is God's will for us and faith will discern him under all appearances. We do not have to ascend "Mount Carmel" or plumb the depths of the "Interior Castle"; nor do we need to practice austerities or seek esoteric knowledge. Faith finds, in the form of each instant and in all circumstances, the Word of God, which moment by moment sustains all things in being.

> God creates at each moment a divine thought which is signified by a created thing; thus, all those things by which he makes his Will known to us are so many names and

---

61 Jean Baptiste Saint-Jure, *The Knowledge and Love of Our Lord Jesus Christ*, in *Trustful Surrender to Divine Providence* (Rockford, IL: TAN, 1983), 39.
62 Rom 8:28.
63 1 Thess 5:18; Eph 5:20.
64 Rom 11:36.

words under cover of which he shows us his desire. In itself this Will is one, its name is unknown and ineffable, but it becomes multiplied to the infinite in its effects, which are, as it were, so many names that it takes. To sanctify the Name of God is to know, adore and love the ineffable Being which this Name expresses. It is also to know, adore and love his adorable Will at every moment and in all its effects, looking at all events as so many veils, or shadows, or names of that eternally Holy Will. For that Will is holy in all its works, in all its words, in all its appearances, in all the names it bears.[65]

Just as God came to us as an infant, poor and helpless; just as he comes hidden in the Eucharist, so also he comes disguised in each moment. It is the will of God that is the decisive element, since it is God who sustains this moment and adapts it to the soul. For it is from all eternity that the divine action effects in time and space the ideas according to which we are to be formed. All our bodily states, pious sentiments, good thoughts, holy desires come from the invisible hand of God. Our lives flow ceaselessly from this unknown fount where God unseen works his marvels. The Word is the exemplar and this moment is his canvas. As God's action pervades all things, so each moment reveals his face to those who, with the eyes of faith, are willing to see. Our response is but to say: *Dominus est* (it is the Lord); and the moment will disclose its secrets.

It is through the very obscurity of this moment that faith is able to triumph *as faith*. Faith would not be faith if the path was always clear and easy. The virtue of faith consists in the act of willing, even rejoicing in whatever occurs by God's providence. God knows better than we what is good for us and, moreover, is able to bring forth from all things what is fitting and good. Sanctity of heart resides in a simple *fiat*: a will humbly disposed to the will of God. Through this discipline the soul is perfected.[66] Herein lie the purging, the self-denial, the renunciation of the creature wherein it is stripped

---

65 De Caussade, *Self-Abandonment*, 47.
66 Heb 12:5–6.

of all that is false to make room for all that is holy. The one thing needful is for us to take up these crosses and trust in God's action which cannot of itself do anything but good. This is the secret of all the saints. "The visible events are those which happen to all men, but the invisible element underneath discovered and discerned by Faith is no less than God himself working great wonders. O Bread of Angels, Heavenly Manna... Sacrament of the present moment!"[67]

Self-abandonment to Divine Providence does not imply fatalism nor does it necessitate quiescence. Each of us has duties to perform according to one's state in life: to God, oneself, one's family, and one's community—for we are to love God above all things and our neighbor as ourselves. When one has done all that is necessary and proper according to the dictates of the present moment, then one has done one's duty. Those things beyond our control or responsibility can be tranquilly entrusted to God. Therefore, there is no need to seek for extraordinary circumstances, rather let us seek holiness in all our circumstances.[68] If we do this, God will illuminate our souls and we will grow in virtue.

---

[67] De Caussade, *Self-Abandonment*, 6.
[68] Ibid., 22.

CHAPTER 8

Illumination

Make every effort to supplement your faith with virtue, and virtue with knowledge, and knowledge with self-control, and self-control with fortitude, and fortitude with piety, and piety with brotherly affection, and brotherly affection with love.[1]

GOD IS THE ULTIMATE PRINCIPLE BEHIND every instant and those who love God above all things seek continuously to please him. Our faith in God is demonstrated in this: that in all things we place our trust in him as the beginning and end of all our acts. *Be it unto me according to Thy word.* We are made for God and we find our fulfillment when we are conformed to his Being in all things by respecting in each thing the nature which it possesses by the will of God. This applies to all creatures: objects, plants, animals, persons, institutions. To refuse to order things according to the nature, form, or idea inherent in each created thing is disrespectful of their Creator.

The fundamental light of the intellect is the concept of being, without which rational thought is impossible. The authentic use of the intellect is to consider all things according to the identity revealed in their natures, since each nature follows its substantial form. The rational use of the will—upon which use our free will is grounded—is to desire that the good in each created thing be fulfilled according to its nature and for our good or the good of others. To act otherwise is to abuse both its meaning and our own freedom, contrary to the will of the Creator. We thereby abuse ourselves, our neighbors, and God, since our actions become disordered. And since the good is a transcendental *belonging* to being, the criterion of natural law is: act according to

---

[1] 2 Pet 1:5–7.

being.[2] This is fully satisfied when one accepts the will of God in each moment and when one considers everything (including oneself) according to its intrinsic nature.

Now nature is the essence of a thing considered according to its intelligible form.[3] Accidents, on the other hand, are not the nature of a thing; rather they modify its nature. Recall that a book is what it is according to its formal (organizing) principle which determines its nature. However, whether the book is red or green is accidental to its nature, modifying it but not changing what it is in essence. Its nature is determined by its intrinsic form, not by its accidents. The same applies to persons. The nature of personhood is given by its substantial form; and the *substantial nature of the human person* is the intellect whose formal principle—its *sine qua non*—is the light of being. There is an intrinsic dignity belonging to every person by virtue of the idea of being, which principle forms the nature of one's personhood, irrespective of any property accidental to the person (such as race, culture, sex, age, status, intelligence, etc.). Therefore, *it is the integral human person—a body informed and animated by an intellective and incommunicable principle or soul—who attracts rights irrespective of the accidental modifications of one's individual nature.* These rights are inalienable. This is the ontological basis for the moral dignity of each and every human being at every stage of life.

Therefore, it is an ontological error to identify any disordered inclination of the individual with the essence of one's person. This confusion between accident and nature occurs, for example, when selected individual differences are assumed to be intrinsic to the substantial nature of one's person. These differences then become constitutive of the essence of personhood, even though they are only accidental modifications or tendencies of the individual. Our moral duty is toward the intrinsic nature of the *person*, not toward one's accidental variations. Otherwise, such differences, were they essential

---

[2] Acting according to Being is also the substance of the spiritual life. (See the next chapter.)
[3] Essence considered according to its reality (that by which a thing subsists in itself) is called substance.

to a person's nature, would have to be regarded as specifying a distinct kind of individual and axiologically deserving of *different*, not equal, rights. Such arbitrary redefining of one's personhood is clearly neither morally nor politically justifiable. This is a major category error: a confusion of substance and accident.

The principle of moral *behavior*, however, is to pursue the good and to avoid evil. This is the duty of a rational person, otherwise one betrays both the nature of reason, which is to consider being, and the nature of the will, which, in following reason, is to desire that being as one's good. Moreover, one has the intrinsic right to pursue this good since it is the duty of the moral individual to pursue the good: to act according to being. It is the nature of intelligence to seek truth. To regard things truly is to consider their being and to act accordingly. This is intellectual honesty and moral integrity; the ground of our free will. Since to behave morally belongs to human dignity, to pursue the good is one's intrinsic duty and, therefore, one's right. And since it is absurd to claim one has *any* right to do what is morally wrong, all rights must defer to the moral order — to God, not to Caesar.[4]

Social rights (besides those inalienable rights intrinsically belonging to the rational person) also come from one's duty and likewise must conform to the moral order.[5] Rights proceed from duties as an effect from a cause. All social rights belong to us by virtue of our shared (interdependent) humanity and because of the duties owed by human beings to one another on account of this common dignity. Given that distributive justice is to grant to others what is their due, it follows that a just society must grant rights to individuals because of what belongs to them according to their essential nature as persons — not according to their accidental modifications or tendencies. Thus rights justly belong to one by virtue of the principle of ownership because of one's essential — not accidental — nature *as a human being*. Similarly,

---

[4] The material order — what taxes can purchase, i.e., health, education, welfare, defense, infrastructure, etc. — belongs to Caesar. See Mt 22:21; Rom 13:6–7. The moral and spiritual orders belong to God *alone*.

[5] For an expanded and detailed proof of this paragraph, see Antonio Rosmini, *The Essence of Right* (Durham: Rosmini House, 1993).

with regards to professions or institutions, rights are granted according to their essential (formal) purpose — their *raison d'être* — or intrinsic reason for being.

For example, physicians have a duty to care, heal, diagnose, counsel, etc. since each is a formal good *belonging to* that profession (they possess *no right* to kill any human being). Since physicians have a duty to care, they have the right to care, so that in pursuit of that duty physicians should enjoy whatever is necessary for its accomplishment: such as training, remuneration, resources, facilities, etc. No institution or state may legitimately override that right or curtail it in any way.

Similarly, marriage is that union which the Creator intended *from the beginning* where "a man shall leave his father and his mother and be joined to his wife, and the two shall become one flesh. So they are no longer two but one flesh."[6] "And God blessed them, and God said to them, 'Be fruitful and multiply, and fill the earth. . .'"[7] Marriage is that estate formed by a man and a woman who publicly avow to share their whole lives, in a permanent union intrinsically oriented towards the begetting, nurturing, and educating of children. Marriage is a biological, ontological, moral, and theological entity. This mutual substantial union of persons is the formal good of marriage, which attracts those rights which are in accordance with its nature.[8] This belies the absurdity of any attempt imperiously to fabricate rights

---

6 Mt 19:4–6; Gen 2:24.
7 Gen 1:28.
8 That some couples are unable to have children is no objection, since what is accidental only modifies a nature: it does not change it substantially. An appliance does not cease to be such because it has a faulty component; a cow does not lose its identity because it cannot give milk; logic itself does not cease to be valid through mistakes in one's reasoning, and marriage does not cease to be marriage simply because the couple *through no fault of their own* cannot conceive. Furthermore, equals must always be compared with equals. Thus, if one holds fertility constant for any union between couples, then only the marriage of a man's and a woman's gametes and DNA is of such a nature as to make procreation *possible*. Any other unnatural union, *all things being equal*, makes procreation *impossible*. These are contraries; and, therefore, there can be no material relation of equality here. For marriage to be natural, innocent, and chaste, it must be open to the *possibility* of bringing forth life. This self-giving union in cooperation with God's will is precisely what gives marriage its sacramental nature.

where none can exist, when, for example, political correctness arbitrarily arrogates for itself, against the Creator, the determination of what ought or ought not to *be the nature* of marriage or the family.

Finally, everyone has the duty to serve God, since God is the Supreme Good. This means that everyone has the right to religion with all that it genuinely enjoins, particularly the virtues. To live the life of perfection to which Christ has called us[9] requires not only the observance of private rituals and practices, but public virtue as well. Indeed, such a duty to pursue holiness will at times necessitate virtues and sacrifices of a heroic degree especially in this decadent postmodern culture.

The West is in a state of decadence,[10] initiated when the (so-called) Enlightenment ironically extinguished the light of reason. Its founders, the *philosophes*, all abandoned the classic concept of being in its formal or substantial sense. This has resulted in a deepening and widening chasm between thought and virtue. Indeed, in our own secular postmodern society individuals are finding their moral consciences impugned by a pervasive political ideology which has trespassed upon the moral domain.[11] In denying any foundation for moral truth, the only option for a godless society is to persuade by intimidation or indoctrination: for power, not truth, has become the only authority. We have already witnessed the extremes of political correctness in Stalinist Russia, Maoist China, and Pol Pot's Cambodia. In the

---

9 Mt 5:48.

10 Digby Anderson, ed., *Decadence: The Passing of Personal Virtue and Its Replacement by Political and Psychological Slogans* (London: Social Affairs Unit, 2005). See also Matthew Fforde, *Desocialisation: The Crisis of Post-Modernity* (Cheadle Hume: Gabriel, 2009); Robert Nisbet, *Twilight of Authority* (London: Heinemann, 1976).

11 This sort of political *praxis* has its origins in Marxism. See Karl Marx and Frederick Engels, *The German Ideology*, Vol. I: *Critique of Modern German Philosophy According to Its Representatives Feuerbach, B. Bauer, and Stirner* (Moscow: Progress Publishers, 1976), chs. II.3 (11); IV.6 (59) & IV.11 (70). See also Michael William, *The Genesis of Political Correctness: The Basis of a False Morality* (n.p.: Michael William, 2016). This form of neo-Marxism was contrived by the critical theorists of the Frankfurt School (Reich, Benjamin, Marcuse, Adorno, Horkheimer, Habermas, et al.). These "cultural Marxists" exploited Freud's idea of the id in order to promote the liberation of libidinal appetites for the expressed purpose of the revolutionary subversion of Western civilization.

face of the ominous spread of secularism and relativism, and their intrinsic denial of the moral object, as well as the state's collusion in this, the call to virtue is becoming even more pressing, especially if one is to pursue a holy life.

If it is thus with natural virtue, it is all the more vital when one accedes to Christ's call to supernatural perfection. For this requires we live beyond what is merely natural to us, even if our natures had not been weakened by the fall. Because one cannot do that which is not in one's nature to do, it is impossible for us to practice perfect charity without the help of Divine Grace. Christ's call to supernatural virtue would be not only unreasonable, but a cruel mockery, if he did not also provide, through his Holy Spirit, the graces which we so desperately lack. But since it is Christ who has called us to this state, we are confident that he will "give what he commands." For these reasons it is imperative that one consider the virtuous life.

VIRTUE

In the previous chapter we looked at the first way, purgation, which follows upon the gift of faith. We saw that purgation has as its principle complete abandonment to the will of God in all things: *fiat mihi* or "Thy will be done." And we have just seen that this gives rise to the moral life, insofar as the true believer wishes to love God above all things and one's neighbor like unto oneself. In order to live this moral life in the face of all that tends to destroy it,[12] one requires supernatural virtue. We shall define supernatural virtue as: *principles of action which God engrafts in our souls, which enable us to perform meritorious acts.*[13] These principles act upon the two faculties of the soul: enlightening the intellect and strengthening and forming the will. Thus virtue forms our character.[14] This second way of the spiritual life involves the flowering of all the virtues: the cardinal virtues of prudence, justice, temperance, and fortitude; the theological

---

12 Traditionally these are the world, the flesh, and the devil.
13 Adolphe Tanquerey, *The Spiritual Life: A Treatise on Ascetical and Mystical Theology* (Rockford: TAN, 2000), 473.
14 Rom 5:4–5.

virtues of faith, hope, and charity; and the religious virtues of poverty, chastity, and obedience.

This flowering emerges from the first way because the devoted soul, having abandoned itself to the will of God, has now begun, according to its faith and capacity, to be infused with the gifts of the Holy Spirit: "The spirit of wisdom and understanding, the spirit of counsel and strength, the spirit of knowledge and piety, and... fear of the Lord."[15] The four gifts of wisdom, understanding, counsel, and knowledge all serve to inform the intellect. The three remaining gifts of the Spirit — piety, strength and holy fear (awe) — serve to fortify the will. Four of the seven gifts of the Holy Spirit have been traditionally associated with each one of the cardinal virtues: the gift of counsel with prudence, the gift of wisdom with justice, holy fear with temperance, and strength with fortitude. The remaining three gifts have been associated with the theological virtues: the gift of knowledge with faith, the gift of piety with hope, and the gift of understanding with charity.[16] These gifts in turn propagate the fruits of the Holy Spirit: love, joy, peace, patience, kindness, goodness, faithfulness, gentleness, self-control.[17]

However, the agent in all this is the Holy Spirit of Christ who is the sanctifier of our souls.[18] Since the seven gifts belong to the operation and dispensation of the Holy Spirit, and since the fruits proliferate from these gifts, we shall confine ourselves solely to the virtues, because these are the substance of our spiritual life.

The cardinal virtues

Upon the cardinal virtues our moral life hinges (Latin: *cardo*, hinge). As the Holy Scriptures attest: "If anyone loves righteousness, [Wisdom's] labors are virtues; for she teaches temperance and prudence, justice, and fortitude; nothing in life is more useful for humankind."[19] Also, they emanate directly from the faculties of the

---

15 Is 11:2–3. See Rev 1:4; 3:1; 5:6.
16 E.g., Jordan Aumann, *Spiritual Theology*; Adolphe Tanquerey, *The Spiritual Life*.
17 Gal 5:22–23; Phil 1:9–11.
18 1 Cor 1:4–8; Eph 5:26–27.
19 Wis 8:7.

soul. However, because we are no longer in the state of innocence, these virtues are weakened and not properly ordered and require the supernatural gifts to vivify and elevate them. Therefore, we are not considering these virtues in their natural state, whether of innocence or of the fall, but in their submission to the activity of Christ's Spirit through whom they are properly formed.

We have said that the soul is a simple reality which thinks being. It has two faculties of operation: intellect by which one reasons and judges; and the will which desires the ends proposed by the intellect and directs action towards those ends. Memory and imagery (which we possess in common with the higher animals) belong to our sensory (bodily) apparatus and are not included as a faculty belonging distinctively to the soul's intellect.[20] Many of our feelings are also shared with animals so they likewise do not distinguish the soul's will. However, because the human person is a union of body and soul, the lower (sensual) animal nature is subordinated or assumed by the higher (intellective) human nature. For this reason, human emotions are generally considered to be conceptually ordered feelings.[21] (E.g., we feel pride in common with higher animals, but we alone can experience the emotion of patriotism, i.e., pride in one's country — animals, of course, being incapable of the *concept* of country. Or contrast our human emotions of ennui, angst, acedia, or despair respectively with the animal feelings of boredom, nervousness, torpor, or submission.)

---

20 St Augustine in *The Trinity* and the scholastic philosophers who followed him considered the memory along with intellect and will to be the three faculties of the human soul made in the image and likeness of the Holy Trinity. For them memory included all that today's social psychologists would include under the self-concept, i.e., everything that is an object of self-reflection. This, of course, differs from the sensory data stored in the brain belonging to our animal nature. For Duns Scotus the memory comprised the possible intellect; the agent intellect was the intellect proper; with the will completing soul's trinity. See *Quodlibetal Questions*, q. 15, a. 1, 15.52–53.

21 Emotions are sometimes regarded as those feelings which excite actions. However, since anything we do — including feeling — is an act in our meaning, the qualification we have used is more consistent. For the scholastics, the "passions" are the acts of the sensitive appetite, either in its concupiscible part or its irascible part. Cf. *Summa Theol.* I-II, qq. 22–23.

Illumination

We have also seen that the intellect formally seeks truth, or being as known; and the will, following the intellect, morally seeks the good, or being judged as desirable. When one combines with these the fact that our persons are compounded of a soul (intellect and will) incarnating a body which is in relation to others, then the derivation of the four cardinal virtues obtains: Prudence is the supernatural virtue which counsels the intellect to judge which ends are proper to us.[22] Justice is the supernatural virtue which informs the intellect to judge what is properly due to others.[23] Temperance is the supernatural virtue which restrains the will in order to moderate our attraction to pleasure (concupiscence).[24] Fortitude is the supernatural virtue which fortifies the will to control our reaction to external disturbances (irascibility).[25]

Thus the virtues can be organized according to those which belong to the intellect (prudence and justice) and those which come under the will (temperance and fortitude). Also they can be arranged as to whether whatever summons the virtue arises from within the individual (prudence and temperance) or exterior to the individual (justice and fortitude). In this latter case we are presupposing the truly detached (sanctified) individual who is not conformed to this world.[26]

Therefore, the cardinal virtues proceed ontologically from the faculties of the soul, i.e., they are not arbitrarily derived. Also they are susceptible of growth nourished by our participation in the life of God. God ordinarily causes this increase through the sacraments (primarily the Eucharist), by virtue of good works, and by means of prayer as we saw in the last chapter.

However, because these virtues facilitate the exercise of our religious and moral duties, they thereby place us in a condition where we are predisposed to receive, or made worthy to receive, an increase in habitual grace. These habitual graces actually become part of one's character and, therefore, are more integral to one's dignity—unlike the actual graces which are transient and intended as an aid in a particular action.

---

22 Prov 14:15.
23 Lev 19:15.
24 Sir 18:30; Tit 2:12.
25 Ps 31:24; 2 Cor 5:5–6.
26 Rom 12:2; Mt 5:4; 6:25–34; Gal 6:14; Col 3:2; Jas 1:27; 1 Jn 2:15–16.

Because they perfect the individual, these habitual graces slowly transform the person, making one more beautiful and meritorious before God. In short, they make the soul more compliant and receptive to the actions of the Spirit. Through prudence and justice we commune respectively in the counsel and wisdom of God receiving insight and understanding, tranquility and assurance. Through temperance we increase our modesty, chastity, humility, and gentleness. Through fortitude we attain to magnanimity, generosity, patience, and constancy. Such is the normal experience of devout Christians who commonly give anecdotal evidence of having been graced or blessed with understanding, encouragement, or consolation. Thus, the cardinal virtues supernaturally discipline, inform, and perfect our intellects and wills, adding a sublime quality to all our actions and making our moral life easier and lighter as Jesus promised: "Come to me, all who labor and are heavy laden, and I will give you rest. Take my yoke upon you and learn from me; for I am gentle and lowly in heart, and you will find rest for your souls. For my yoke is easy, and my burden is light."[27] It is solely through the grace of Christ that we have the virtues which enable us to overcome the world and to obey his commandments.[28]

The theological virtues

Unlike the cardinal virtues, which have our human relationships (with ourselves and others) as their object, the theological virtues have God directly as their ultimate end.[29] Their role is to unite us to God through Christ so that we may become sharers in the Divine Life. Unlike the cardinal (moral) virtues which facilitate our good works, the theological virtues have a unifying and transforming power which prepares us for union with God. The three theological virtues of faith, hope, and love are mentioned by St Paul: "So faith, hope, love, abide, these three; but the greatest of these is love."[30]

Faith. In the previous chapter we examined the life of faith exemplified by abandonment to the will of God, profoundly and

---

27 Mt 11:28–30.
28 1 Jn 5:2–5.
29 Gal 5:6; 1 Thess 1:3; 1 Jn 4:16–17.
30 1 Cor 13:13; 1 Thess 5:8.

Illumination

genuinely trusting in him who neither errs nor lies. This is a supernatural gift which precedes all the other graces and predisposes us for their reception. It initiates the moral life since it is the very nature of faith to seek to do the will of God, believing in Christ and the Church which he established. We may define faith as a theological virtue which inclines the soul by grace to yield a firm assent to those truths revealed by God in the Holy Scriptures and the teachings of Holy Church, because he is truth substantially.[31] Thus, faith is simply declaring that God truly is God, and not we ourselves. Therefore, it is both ontologically and theologically impossible for reason to be elevated above revelation. The intellect receives information either through the senses or via revelation; and reason, by the light of being, simply deduces and judges. But reason cannot create truth, especially the truth of the Creator, who alone is uncreated Truth. The proper function of reason is to understand the revelation of God in Christ and the Church founded by him: *Credo ut intelligam*. Authentic, humble faith is predisposed to obey God's word: *fiat mihi secundum verbum tuum*.

This predisposition of faith to obey God's word gives faith that purgative function that we saw in the last chapter, because it is faith that enables us to say, "Thy will, not my will." However, we have also observed that faith has a unitive function insofar as it unites us to the mind and will of God. As a supernatural gift, faith makes us participants (*consortes divinae naturae*) in the Divine Life and thought. Through faith, God's wisdom becomes our wisdom, his knowledge our knowledge, and his Spirit our spirit. It does this because we, having been created in the image of God, are, like him, ontologically aware: we know ourselves as beings by the light of being, just as God knows himself in the act of being—"I am who am." And because faith is obedient to the will and knowledge of God's revelation in Christ, it bears a proportionate likeness (analogy of being) to the Divine Logos who expresses the essence of the Father. The Logos obediently, as it were, proceeds as Form from Substance[32] from the Being of the Father in Act: lovingly proclaiming and expressing the

---

31 Tanquerey, *The Spiritual Life*, 1170.
32 Phil 2:6; 2 Cor 4:4.

truth about the Father,³³ for there is no discordance within the Godhead. In the loving fecundity of the Spirit the Father generates the Son, so that the Son proceeds from the Father, and in the Spirit of love the Son glorifies his Father. Thus the Holy Spirit of love which proceeds from the Father and the Son is the very life of God.³⁴ Similarly we, in obediently receiving the gift of faith along with sanctifying grace — provided we do not quench the Spirit in us — find our souls transformed,³⁵ drawing us ever more deeply into the life of the Holy Trinity, purifying us, maturing us unto salvation, and making us holy.³⁶

Because this faith is a supernatural gift, it establishes the believer in certain conviction, simply because — as it is a theological virtue having God for its object — *it places its trust in the One revealing*. One is able then to confess with certainty that one truly, profoundly, absolutely, and steadfastly believes that Jesus is the Christ, the Son of the living God: not by one's own "flesh and blood," but by the grace of Our Heavenly Father who revealed it.³⁷

This virtue comes to us ordinarily by means of the sacraments. Firstly through baptism, which initiates one into the life of grace conferring upon the baptized the several virtues and the gifts of the Holy Spirit. Through baptism one is justified, having received forgiveness of sins. God the Father, Son and Holy Spirit come to dwell within the baptized whereby one becomes an adopted child of God. One is also admitted into the community of God's people and entitled to receive everlasting life.³⁸ All this is confirmed, deepened, and imprinted by the Holy Spirit in the sacrament of confirmation. Then for sins after baptism, the sacrament of confession can restore to grace those who

---

33   Jn 1:1–4; Jn 9–15; Jn 16–18. See also Duns Scotus, *Quodlibetal Questions*, q. 8, a. 3, 8.48 & 55.
34   Thus marriage is a sacramental image of the Trinitarian life whereby two persons generate a third. For this reason marriage is sacred and its rights inviolate.
35   Rom 12:2.
36   1 Thess 5:23–24; 1 Pet 1:14–2:5.
37   Mt 16:17; Jn 6:44; 1 Cor 12:1, 3; 2 Cor 5:7; 1 Jn 4:2–3; Heb 11:1. This is why apostasy is a sin and why theologians and ministers of the word are held accountable for what they teach. Heb 13:17; Mt 18:6; Lk 16:2.
38   Mt 28:19; Jn 3:5; Acts 2:38; Rom 6:3–11; 8:17; 1 Cor 6:15, 19; 1 Cor 12:13, 27; 2 Cor 5:17; Gal 3:27; 4:5–7; Eph 4:25; 1 Pet 2:5, 9; 2 Pet 1:4.

have committed mortal sins — those deliberate acts of a grave nature which offend against the commandments of God — as well as sanctifying those who commit venial (daily) sins. Finally, faith is increased and deepened through the Eucharist which, like confession, is also a repeatable sacrament, supplying all the graces and virtues according to the faith of the recipient. Because the whole Christ is really present in this sacrament as its substantial principle, he is able to give himself substantially to us, whereby we really partake of his life.

> Truly, truly, I say to you, unless you eat the flesh of the Son of man and drink his blood, you have no life in you; he who eats my flesh and drinks my blood has eternal life, and I will raise him up at the last day. For my flesh is food indeed, and my blood is drink indeed. He who eats my flesh and drinks my blood abides in me, and I in him. As the living Father sent me, and I live because of the Father, so he who eats me will live because of me. This is the bread which came down from heaven, not such as the fathers ate and died; he who eats this bread will live forever.[39]

This is fundamentally because through this sacrament one receives Christ substantially, as we have said.

> Therefore, brethren, since we have confidence to enter the sanctuary by the blood of Jesus, by the new and living way which he opened for us through the veil, that is, through his flesh, and since we have a great priest over the house of God, let us draw near with a true heart in full assurance of faith, with our hearts sprinkled clean from an evil conscience and our bodies washed with pure water. Let us hold fast the confession of our hope without wavering, for he who promised is faithful.[40]

The author of Hebrews refers to this grace of faith as "knowledge of the truth" and "the substance of things hoped for, the conviction

---

39 Jn 6:53–58. Eastern Orthodox, Roman Catholics, and Anglo-Catholics as well as Lutherans interpret these words literally.
40 Heb 10:19–23.

of things unseen,"[41] which deliberate, grave sin can render void, subjecting us to the judgment. However, "if we confess our sins, he is faithful and just, and will forgive our sins and cleanse us from all unrighteousness."[42] Therefore, "in everything God works for good with those who love him, who are called according to his purpose."[43] Furthermore, we "are sure that neither death, nor life, nor angels, nor principalities, nor things present, nor things to come, nor powers, nor height, nor depth, nor anything else in all creation, will be able to separate us from the love of God in Christ Jesus our Lord."[44] All this grounds our affirmation that our faith is certain.[45]

Hope. However, the path of faith is sometimes experienced as being without light or direction. We believe and trust in God, but often we do not perceive or understand his ways: "O the depth of the riches and wisdom and knowledge of God! How unsearchable are his judgments and how inscrutable his ways! For who has known the mind of the Lord, or who has been his counsellor?"[46] However, an intrinsic part of faith is trust as we have seen. And trust contains an element of hope, since we can with confident faith place our trust in Christ, whom God has sent, and in his promises. And insofar as we believe that Christ is faithful and true to his promises, so we are able to place our hope in them.[47] Thus, hope is a theological virtue given to us along with faith.

"Hope is the theological virtue infused by God into the will, by which we trust with complete certitude in the attainment of eternal life and the means necessary for reaching it, assisted by the omnipotent help of God."[48] Hope resides in the will, having as its proper object the good of everlasting life and beatitude, and, as its proper function, trust in the mercy of God. Thus, hope is grounded in faith

---

41 Heb 10:26; 11:1.
42 1 Jn 1:9; Jas 5:15–16.
43 Rom 8:28.
44 Rom 8:38–39.
45 See Tanquerey, *A Manual of Dogmatic Theology* (New York: Desclée, 1959), 2:228–30; Denzinger, *Enchiridion Symbolorum*, 1789–94.
46 Rom 11:33–34.
47 1 Pet 1:3–9, 21.
48 Aumann, *Spiritual Theology*, 258.

which is the substance (*hypostasis*) of things hoped for. Faith gives substance to hope because faith is grounded in the revelation of God in Jesus Christ.[49]

> But when the goodness and loving kindness of God our Savior appeared, he saved us, not because of deeds done by us in righteousness, but in virtue of his own mercy, by the washing of regeneration and renewal in the Holy Spirit, which he poured out upon us richly through Jesus Christ our Savior, so that we might be justified by his grace and become heirs in hope of eternal life. The saying is sure.[50]

We desire everlasting life, not merely because we want to live forever — neither in this sinful world nor in hell is everlasting life a satisfying prospect for humankind. Rather, we desire the heavenly state because our souls are made to find our fulfillment in the beatific vision of God, when we shall behold him face to face.[51] "There shall be no more anything accursed, but the throne of God and of the Lamb shall be in it, and his servants shall worship him; they shall see his face, and his name shall be on their foreheads. And night shall be no more; they need no light of lamp or sun, for the Lord God will be their light, and they shall reign for ever and ever."[52] Because faith in Divine Revelation has placed this prospect as our hope we are strengthened to persevere to the end; hence the virtue in hope.

Because hope is a virtue it can sanctify us. It unites us to God by detaching us from worldly goods. It preserves us from discouragement, inspires us, and sustains us. Hope begets in us holy desires, especially the desire to possess God. It impels us towards this goal encouraging us in our good works. Energized by hope and with eyes on the eternal crown we learn to subdue our bodies and grow in self-control.[53] Hope gives us confidence in God which in turn makes us tranquil and peaceful even amidst ridicule, calumny, persecution, sickness, or misfortune. It facilitates our final perseverance: "Let us

---

49 Tit 1:1–3.
50 Tit 3:4–8.
51 1 Cor 13:12.
52 Rev 22:3–5.
53 1 Cor 9:24–27.

hold fast the confession of our hope without wavering, for he who promised is faithful."[54]

Charity. Charity (*caritas, agape*) is the theological virtue by which we love God above all things for his own sake in the way in which he loves himself, and our neighbor as ourselves for the sake of God.[55] It is the greatest of the theological virtues.[56] Agape is *not* eros (human psychophysical attraction) but love divinized and raised to its highest level. One might say that it is a love transformed by Divine Love itself: for we love in God and through God. Therefore, it is a mystical love, the fruit of communion with the reality of God. It is the only love of which Our Lord speaks.[57]

Love finds its Object beautiful.[58] Faith having already revealed to the soul the splendor of God in Christ Jesus, and hope having made him her constant desire, so, from within the soul who has found in Christ her treasure, love emanates from the other two virtues. For where one's treasure is, there is one's heart.[59] As one's faith expands and deepens and as one's hope becomes sure and steadfast, so one's love for Christ is facilitated, and everything becomes suffused with its ambience. For it is impossible to entertain two conflicting feelings, two principles, within the soul.

Because charity is Divine Love, it takes its form from the Spirit of God, "for love is of God, and he who loves is born of God and knows God."[60] Therefore, the motive of charity is not the particular good received from God nor any good one hopes to receive, but God himself as infinite beauty. We love God for who he is, for the excellence and glory of his Being. This is the highest state of love and it is supernatural: we cannot love what we cannot know, and we ourselves can only know God proportionally through the analogy of being. Even Jesus could speak to the people only through parables and

---

54 Heb 10:23.
55 Tanquerey, *The Spiritual Life*, 568.
56 1 Cor 13:13.
57 Nowhere in the Gospels does Jesus ever speak of *eros*, neither is it to be found anywhere in the rest of the New Testament.
58 Song 1:15.
59 Mt 6:21.
60 Jn 4:7.

metaphors.⁶¹ Therefore, in order to know God immediately, beyond formal concepts or analogies, it is necessary that one receive direction from a superior principle, viz., the Holy Spirit. This is why Jesus promised to the apostles that the Holy Spirit was to be given to them who would lead them into all truth.⁶²

Fundamentally, there is only one commandment and one truth: "*I am* the Lord your God."⁶³ Everything condenses into this. Therefore, love for God is the very form of all the virtues, since all creation takes its ordering from the Creator, who created all things in one act of love and who sustains all things in that love. To love the creature according to its form, to love our neighbors accordingly as they share our likeness formed in the image of God, to love Christ as the incarnate Son of God, and to love God the Father as the ultimate Principle of all that is, follow naturally from this sole commandment. Therefore, all things are loved for God's sake and God is loved for himself. From this come all virtue and the moral and spiritual life: that supernatural organism which is our new birth. Thus love is the form of all the virtues "which binds everything together in perfect harmony."⁶⁴

Now this charity with which we love is no other than the Spirit of the Son in our hearts, whereby we cry "Abba! Father!"⁶⁵ As the Spirit of God proceeds as the Love of the Father for the Son and the Love of the Son for the Father, so the Holy Spirit has the same essence which the Father communicates to the Son and by which the Son images the Father. The Father (as it were) is the generative Principle (*principium*), the Son is the Image (*idea, logos*), and the Holy Spirit is the Life (*pneuma*) of one Being in Act: three relations (*hypostases*) in one and the same Divine Substance (*substantia*).⁶⁶ God is pure Act, and in acting knows himself and loves himself as known. And thus

---

61 Mt 13:10–17; Mt 34–35; Jn 10:6; 16:25.
62 Jn 14:16–17; Jn 25–26; Jn 15:26; 1 Jn 4:13.
63 Ex 20:2; Deut 5:6.
64 Col 3:14.
65 Gal 4:6.
66 *Summa Theol*. I, q. 27, a. 2; q. 27, a. 2, obj. 2; q. 27 aa. 3 & 4. See also Thomas Aquinas, *Contra Errores Graecorum*, in *Theological Texts*, ed. Thomas Gilby (London: Oxford University Press, 1955), I, n. 98; Gilles Emery, *Trinity in Aquinas* (Ypsilanti, MI: Sapientia Press, 2003), 145–46, 219–21, 230–33.

comprehending himself, he expresses, conceives, and produces within himself his coeternal Word of wisdom and light: his only beloved Son, immaterial, immanent, and simple; radiant in majesty, beauty, and truth. The Father eternally loves the Son in Being; and the Son lovingly reveals the Father, as a real, complete, and well-defined image of God, perfectly expressing his Divinity. And since the Holy Spirit — true, eternal, and illimitable God — is the hypostasis of both this fecundative, generative love (from the Father) and this effulgent, glorifying love (from the Son), when we are receptive to the Holy Spirit, we are transformed in that personal communion which is the life of the Trinity dwelling in us. Thusly does Divine Charity constitute us in holiness, sanctifying us in the truth: a mystery which is as wonderful as it is ineffable.

Charity unites to God our whole soul with all its faculties and powers: "It unites the *mind* to God through the esteem conceived for him and the frequent thought of him. It unites the *will* by its perfect submission to the Divine Will. It unites the *heart* by the subordination of all our affections to the Divine Love. It unites our *energies* by dedicating them all to the service of God and of souls."[67] The effect of all this is that we grow in spiritual freedom since our love for creatures becomes properly ordered to our love for God which is not servile, but filial, that of a son or daughter happy to be doing God's work, joyfully bearing all things for his sake. Indeed, it is St Paul who tells us how love sanctifies, in those memorable words from 1 Corinthians:[68]

> Love is patient and kind; love is not jealous or boastful; it is not arrogant or rude. Love does not insist on its own way; it is not irritable or resentful; it does not rejoice at wrong, but rejoices in the right. Love bears all things, believes all things, hopes all things, endures all things. Love never ends…

Finally, love pre-eminently sanctifies when everything is done for the love of God, since it makes all that we do into a prayer. When

---

67 Tanquerey, *The Spiritual Life*, 572.
68 1 Cor 13:4–8.

we offer to God our heartfelt thanks in all that we do, or receive, or suffer at his hands, then we shall gain much merit.[69] God does not ignore our sighs and groans, but weaves them into an imperishable crown. "For God is not so unjust as to overlook your work and the love which you showed for his sake in serving the saints."[70] Whereas if we should have all the charisms, prophecies, knowledge, and even faith without love, it profits us nothing. Even if we do charitable works or acts of self-sacrifice, if we should do them without the love of God it merits nothing.[71] We simply cannot conceive "what God has prepared for those who love him,"[72] "for in all things God works for good with those who love him, who are called according to his purpose. For those whom he foreknew he also predestined to be conformed to the image of his Son.... And those whom he predestined he also called; and those whom he called he also justified; and those whom he justified he also glorified."[73]

From such love come the fruits of the Holy Spirit: love, joy, peace, patience, kindness, goodness, faithfulness, gentleness, and self-control. And with these come tranquility, modesty, poise and a profound humility as we realize in our depths the utter dependence of the soul's very existence upon the love of God.

The religious virtues

The religious virtues are: poverty, chastity, and obedience. As they belong to the life of the religious (monks, nuns, friars, sisters),[74] and since these are covered by the rules of their respective religious orders, we will not dwell on them here beyond the briefest remarks. For although these virtues impinge upon those who have separated themselves from the world, nonetheless, we too, as we grow in holiness, find that we also have less and less to do with the world. We too become captivated by the life of the Holy Trinity so that the

---

69 Mt 5:12, 19:29, 25:21; Lk 6:38; Rom 2:6; 1 Cor 3:8; Col 3:24; 1 Tim 4:8; Heb 10:35; 11:6.
70 Heb 6:10.
71 1 Cor 13:1–3.
72 1 Cor 2:9.
73 Rom 8:28–30.
74 The Church refers to those people remaining in the world as the faithful.

world loses its allure and we come to find ourselves as "strangers in a strange land."

These three religious virtues have one thing in common: devotion. To be wholly devoted to God is spiritual poverty, because one has relinquished, spiritually if not practically, all earthly things for Christ as did the apostles who had neither gold, nor silver, nor copper, nor bag, nor two tunics, nor sandals, nor staff, nor food but what they could beg, and no fixed lodgings.[75] To be single-mindedly devoted to God is chastity since he only is loved, purely with singleness of heart, above all things. To be humbly devoted to God is obedience since one no longer lives for one's own will, but solely for God's will. Thus, anyone who aspires to love God as God, who is above all things, will to some extent manifest these virtues, if not in a rule of life, then at least in one's heart.

THE SPARK OF DIVINE LOVE

All these virtues are the endowment of a moral and religious life. They presuppose that the beneficiary of these virtues and gifts is in a state of grace, since it is impossible for virtue to act upon a soul which is in a state of grave sin. Now no soul can be so *totally* depraved that there could be no goodness in that soul — nothing with which to work. For such a soul would lack even the goodness of its nature, i.e., the principle of its nature placed there by God. Now every being has the perfection of existence, as well as the perfection of being a particular being with its distinctive properties, or it would not have any identity: it would not be this particular distinguishable thing. For it to be a soul as such, it must have its own distinctive nature which God gave it. God sustains all things in being including the soul which is made in his image and likeness. God is not the author of evil. Moreover, nothing can be made to do what is not in its nature to do. Unless the soul possessed within it some formal good, it could never become virtuous. Such a soul would be incapable of even responding to prevenient grace. It follows that there is some formal, sufficient good in every soul, which

---

75   Mt 10:9–10.

Illumination

defines it and orders it as this soul with this (perfectible) nature given to us by God.

This basic goodness, which resides in even the most wicked, most corrupted soul, is called *scintilla*, from the Latin meaning spark. This scintilla occupies the highest point of the soul where God and the soul touch. At the locus of God's sustaining act, upon which the soul's existence depends and rests, is the highest principle of its being, and it is good. There is a scintilla of goodness in everyone, which is sufficient for conversion in those having the use of reason, and for salvation in the innocents.

This spark of goodness constitutes the human conscience, at least the conscience that has not been stilled. For it is indeed the case that through continuous sin, whereby the voice of conscience is deliberately ignored—especially if such sinful behavior is perpetuated over time—one's conscience will eventually become weakened, although not completely. Since conscience can be debilitated, even perverted, it follows that it is not infallible. In order for one to be secure in following the voice of one's conscience it must be correctly informed by the moral precepts. Since the individual ultimately has no choice but to rely upon one's conscience in any given moral judgment, each person is morally responsible to ensure that one's conscience is correctly informed. One's ignorance is not invincible here, since it is incumbent upon one's free choice to guard one's conscience.[76]

The principle which enables one to judge whether or not one's conscience is correctly informed is called *synderesis* (from Greek: *synterein*—to guard, keep safe). According to St Thomas it is a natural disposition or *habitus* by which one is able to recognize the first principles of the natural law.[77] Just as the speculative reason can judge the truth of certain rational principles as "a thing is identical with itself" or "what does not exist cannot act"; so the practical reason can also judge the truth of moral precepts such as "pursue the good and avoid evil" or "do unto others as you would have them do unto you." One can define synderesis, then, as an innate disposition or habit by which we are enabled rapidly and easily to apprehend the

---

76 Antonio Rosmini, *Conscience* (Durham: Rosmini House, 1989), 263.
77 *Summa Theol.* I, q. 79, a. 12.

primary precepts of the moral law.[78] Much debate occurred during the Middle Ages as to where this *habitus* is to be located. Some following St Thomas placed it in the intellect, while others, following St Bonaventure, placed it in the will. Suffice it to say for our purposes that, insofar as the person recognizes the ontological dignity that is in oneself, so one must grant that same dignity to others. This principle of reciprocity seems to underlie many of the moral precepts in the Bible: the Golden Rule, the *lex talionis*, the "love your neighbor like unto (*camocha*) yourself," and the "love [the stranger] as thyself, for you were strangers in the land of Egypt." In all these cases it is the recognition of identity, either in kind or in nature or in circumstance, which is invoked. It is easy to see, therefore, how the principle of distributive justice—of duties owed to one another—arises from this.

Synderesis, therefore, ultimately rests upon our ontological understanding of ourselves and of others as sharing the same dignity. For this reason it is inerrant and incorruptible, but the application of its understood principles to any given situation is far from infallible. This is why conscience can err, for even though the moral precepts may be seen to be clear and certain, nevertheless their application involves the faculty of judgment as to whether or not a particular action falls under the moral precept. For example, the precept "You shall not murder" is clear, certain, and universal, but one must judge when and under what circumstances the taking of a life is in fact the murder of an innocent human being. This is why conscience, in order to act wisely and rightly, must be constituted by the gifts and by the virtues and why Christ could say that without him we can do nothing.[79]

It is at the soul's summit where God touches her, infusing the spark (scintilla) of life and goodness to her, that synderesis is located. This *habitus* ordinarily flows from God's Truth into his image, which is infinitely removed from God in nature, yet intimately hidden in his Reality.[80] The human being, upon whom eternal Being continuously shines, must be an individual of a nature sufficiently formed to

---

78   Michael Maher, *Psychology* (London: Longmans, Green, 1900), 335. Cf. Deut 30:11–14; Rom 2:14–16.
79   Jn 15:4–8, 16.
80   Col 3:3.

intuit being according to the classical principle: *materiae dispositae advenit forma* (to matter disposed comes form). For it is the essence of Being to be intelligible and it is the nature of the Intelligible that it is communicative of form. All creation, indeed every creature, according to its capacity and nature, participates in this formal, organizing Intelligibility, which, like some vast eternal sun, everlastingly radiates its plenitude.[81]

Thus, the human animal, predisposed by nature, receives that intelligibility which Being — eternally in act — ceaselessly imparts, constituting it with an intelligent principle or soul. "Essentially intelligible, being cannot join itself to any subject without being understood; its being joined consists in its being understood. Being therefore has the power to create intelligences."[82] So *from the moment of conception,* "by a hidden law nature diffuses its work so that small vessels breathe, and *the vital spark is present* to those destined for it."[83] This nascent life is *of a kind* (*suppositum*) which is *already* image to the Intelligible: it is God himself who imparts this intelligibility to human nature which is informed thereby. At no moment is it ever otherwise. As the great English mystic, Mother Julian (Julienne) of Norwich, put it:

> Our soul *is made to be* God's dwelling-place; and the dwelling of our soul is God, which is unmade. A high understanding it is inwardly, to see and to know that God, who is our Maker, dwelleth in our soul. And a higher understanding it is, and more inwardly, to see and to know that our soul, that is made, dwelleth in God in substance. Of what substance, by God, we are what we are. And I saw no difference between God and our substance; but as it were all God. And yet my understanding took it that our substance is in God; that is to say, that God is God, and our substance is a creature in God.[84]

---

81 Mt 5:45; Gen 1:1–2; Ps 19:1–4; Rom 1:20; 1 Cor 15:40–41.
82 Antonio Rosmini, *Essence of the Human Soul*, 307–8.
83 Prudentius, quoted in ibid. Italics added.
84 Julian of Norwich, *Revelations of Divine Love*, trans. James Walsh (Wheathampstead: Anthony Clarke, 1961), 150. Italics added.

Thus our souls have their being in God and receive their image from him, making us like God.[85] Yet, since we are limited creatures, we are also unlike God. The principle of the analogy of being is grounded and actualized in this: *that we, as sharers of God's image, share his nature in a proportional manner.* The infinite God truly communicates being to his finite creatures which are sustained by him. We do not consist of God's substance, but subsist in him. We who are created in his image, out of nothing, must share in his perfections somehow, or we have no reality. For all perfections belong to God, and we share in them: "I saw that our kind [nature] is in God, wholly; in which he maketh diversities, flowing out of him, to work his will."[86]

However, those who are to be saved possess an inheritance that is kept "imperishable, undefiled and unfading"[87] and which cannot be marred by sin. Indeed "no one born of God commits sin; for God's seed (*sperma*) abides in him, and he cannot sin because he is born of God."[88] Such a person may venially sin[89] out of weakness or disquiet, but it is not possible for one in a state of grace deliberately to commit a mortal sin, *so long as one abides in Christ.*[90]

> In every soul which shall be saved there is a godly will that never assented to sin, nor ever shall. This will is so good that it may never will evil, but evermore, continually, it willeth good and worketh good in the sight of God. Our Lord willeth that we know this in faith and belief; and especially, that in truth we have all this blessed will whole and safe in our Lord Jesus Christ. For this same kind [i.e., nature], with which heaven shall be filled, must needs be according to God's righteousness, so knit and oned in

---

85 Ps 82:6.
86 *Revelations of Divine Love*, 156. See also Acts 17:28, 1 Cor 12:6; Phil 2:13; Heb 13:21.
87 1 Pet 1:3–5, 23.
88 1 Jn 3:9; Mt 7:18; 2 Cor 13:8; 1 Pet 1:23; 1 Jn 5:18. See also Jn 3: 3–8; Tit 3:5.
89 1 Jn 5:16–17.
90 1 Jn 3:6, 5:18. Cf. Jn 14:15, 15:4–10, 16:1. See also Ps 25:20–21, 86:2, 97:10, 119:9 and 11.

Illumination

him, that in it must be preserved a substance which never could nor should be separated from him.⁹¹

One may draw an analogy between synderesis and the Immaculate Conception. By a *singular grace* of God and in virtue of the merits of Jesus Christ, the Virgin Mary was preserved free from the stain of original sin. Yet the soul that is to be saved is also guarded in Christ Jesus who suffers none of his own to be lost.⁹² While Mary, who kept (*syneterei*) God's word in her heart,⁹³ has from her conception been kept Immaculate, so the will to consent to sanctifying grace is also guarded (*syneterei*) in the highest point (scintilla) of their souls.⁹⁴ Nowhere was Mary touched by any sin. But with us this is decidedly not so: we are *all* stained by Adam's fall. But in those "born of God" who, in his eternal foreknowledge, are to be saved — in that supreme point where their "life is hid with Christ in God" — there is a "seed," from God, which is preserved from wholeheartedly embracing sin, so they are enabled efficaciously, *though not irresistibly*, to consent to God's sanctifying grace.⁹⁵

* * *

We are united with God in Christ, knit to him in our faith working through charity given to us by the Holy Spirit, through whom and in whom all the virtues combine to perfect his body the Church throughout her members.⁹⁶ The Church has only to point to her great treasury of saints as evidence of this. We shall now turn to observe how the Holy Spirit moves in the lives of saints, where we too may savor that sublime union with God which faith accomplishes.

---

91 *Revelations of Divine Love*, 148.
92 Jn 6:39, 10:28, 18:9.
93 Lk 2:19.
94 See Ludwig Ott, *Fundamentals of Catholic Dogma* (Rockford, IL: TAN, 1974), 242–44; Denzinger, *Enchiridion Symbolorum*, 805, 825, 827.
95 Col 3:3; 1 Cor 1:7–8; Phil 1:6; 1 Thess 3:13, 5:23; Heb 10:26–31, 39. Everyone has been given sufficient grace to pray for efficacious grace (habitual or actual) as well as the grace of final perseverance. All those various opposing theories which attempt to reconcile grace and free will would at least concur with this. Cf. John Hardon, *History and Theology of Grace* (Ypsilanti, MI: Veritas Press, 2002), 278–79. See also Lutheran World Federation and the Catholic Church, *Joint Declaration of the Doctrine of Justification*, 25–26.
96 1 Cor 12:12; Eph 4:11–16.

CHAPTER 9

Union

They were stoned, they were sawn in two, they were killed with the sword; they went about in skins of sheep and goats, destitute, afflicted, ill-treated — of whom the world was not worthy — wandering over deserts and mountains, and in dens and caves of the earth.... Therefore, surrounded by so great a cloud of witnesses, let us also lay aside every weight and sin, which clings so closely, and let us run with perseverance the race that is set before us, looking to Jesus the pioneer and perfecter of our faith, who for the joy that was set before him endured the cross, despising the shame, and is seated at the right hand of the throne of God.[1]

THE HIGHEST STAGE OF THE RELIGIOUS life is the prayer of union. For most of us this state is a rare, fleeting, and superficial experience. However, for the perfect (*teleoi*)[2] it is their milieu. They dwell at that point where God sustains the soul—itself but a scintilla of light—like a tiny iridescent creature inhabiting an inexhaustibly bountiful sea. From there they draw their vitality, virtue, and wisdom. They no longer know themselves as isolated individuals straining to touch at finite points an indefinite horizon. Finding themselves continuously immersed in the Presence of God, they repose in the contemplation of him, the limitless source of all their life and light. Like Brother Lawrence who, while cloistered in the noise and clatter of his kitchen, enjoyed "an assurance that God is always deep within his soul, so that no doubt of it can arise, whatever may betide,"[3] everything is given to them, all belongs to them. Yet they never cease to confess

---

1 Heb 11:37–38, 12:1–2.
2 Phil 3:15; 1 Cor 2:6; Col 1:26–28. Cf. 1 Jn 2:12–14.
3 Brother Lawrence [Nicholas Herman of Lorraine], *The Practice of the Presence of God* (London: Allenson, 1906), 30–31.

in their finitude their humble dependence upon God's infinite goodness. "I abandon myself in his hands, that he may do with me what he pleases. This King, full of mercy and goodness, very far from chastising me, embraces me with love, makes me to eat at his table, serves me with his own hands, gives me the key of his treasures; he converses and delights himself with me unceasingly, in a thousand and a thousand ways...."[4]

They receive all things with equanimity, constantly adhering to God with loving devotion. "For he that is perfect is no longer merely rising gradually to this highest region in himself; he is established there; he is spiritualized and supernaturalized; he is now become truly an adorer in spirit and in truth."[5] Dead to the world, with eyes of devotion only for God, these untroubled saints are absorbed in the Wisdom that emanates through his Spirit. Like Mary sitting at the feet of Christ they have chosen the better part, leaving the administration of the household to Martha, her sister.[6] In the summit of their spirit they are serene and still, while the "house" of their souls may be left to attend to the pots and pans, or the poorest of the poor.

All their virtues are ordered and empowered by this loving devotion. In fact they cannot tell where their love ends and where God's love begins, for they love with the love of God which floods their souls, extending outwards, embracing all creation. Everything is done in God and for God, for love and with love, so that each virtue has its proper place and moment. Habitually docile to the inspirations of the Holy Spirit, self-effacing and self-composed, they faithfully fulfill their duties according to their diverse states in life. With nothing in their wills left to impede, faith, hope, and charity hold sway, informing all their actions. Perfectly centered, they act with ease and with readiness. They happily rejoice in the good fortune of others, and, just as joyfully, suffer if called to suffer. Indifferent to poverty or pestilence, they are resilient. Accepting of either blows or insults, they are courageous. They are spontaneous, free, and unpredictable.

---

4   *The Practice of the Presence of God*, 42.
5   Reginald Garrigou-Lagrange, *The Three Ways of the Spiritual Life* (London: Burns and Oates, 1942), 84.
6   Lk 10:38–42.

Union

Just as "the wind blows where it wills, and you hear the sound of it, but you do not know whence it comes or whither it goes; so it is with everyone who is born of the Spirit."[7] At once simple, wise, still, ecstatic, gentle, tireless, and peaceful; yet they are unconquerable and outspoken in the presence of evil. Scorned by the proud,[8] they are gladly heard by the ordinary.[9]

Although they seem too good to be true, the Church has been built upon such holy persons as these. During the first centuries many had fled the corruption and dissolution of the towns, living in poverty in the wilderness, praying, and directing those who would return to the world. Later some of these founded monasteries and convents, hospitals, orphanages, and hospices for the poor. Others counselled kings and advised popes. Great schools of philosophy and universities were established by them. They illuminated manuscripts, composed plainchant, advanced architecture, cultivated agriculture, investigated nature, and contemplated the heavens. They plumbed the depths of human psychology to a greater extent than has ever been realized since secular psychology (ironically) abandoned the study of the soul (*psyche*). They invented the concept of charity, providing food and shelter for the unfortunate and relief from disease, plague, and famine:

> The pagan writer Lucian (130–200) observed in astonishment, "The earnestness with which the people of this religion help one another in their needs is incredible. They spare themselves nothing for this end. Their first lawgiver put it into their heads that they were all brethren!" Julian the Apostate, the Roman emperor who made a futile, if energetic attempt in the 360s to return the empire to its earlier paganism, conceded that the Christians outshone the pagans in their devotion to charitable work. "While the pagan priests neglect the poor," he wrote, "the hated Galileans [that is, the Christians] devote themselves to works of charity, and by a display of false compassion have established and given effect to their pernicious errors. See

---

7 Jn 3:9.
8 Prov 1:22, 14:6, 21:24.
9 Mk 12:37.

their love-feasts, and their tables spread for the indigent. Such practice is common among them, and causes contempt for our gods."[10]

* * *

There are thousands of great saints known to the Church, and there are countless ordinary holy men and women unknown by the Church who also have lived exceptionally virtuous lives. In order better to illustrate the third way, the way of union, we would do far worse than to allow the lives and words of a few of these saints to witness for themselves. We have chosen from across the centuries five who exemplify a variety of the more outstanding virtues of the life of union with God: St Francis of Assisi, St John of the Cross, St Thérèse of Lisieux, St Teresa of Calcutta and St Maria Goretti.

THE POOR MAN OF ASSISI[11]

Francis was born in 1182 in the fortress town of Assisi situated in the hills of Umbria. He was baptized Giovanni, the son of Pietro Bernardone, a wealthy textile merchant, and Pica, a knight's daughter from Provence. He was the first to be given the nickname Francesco (frenchy), presumably because he loved to recite the *chansons de geste* which his mother would sing in the Provençal dialect to the young child upon her knees. His education was of the slightest, as he himself freely admits,[12] since he preferred to carouse with a group of young men of whom he was the *chef provocateur*. Indulged by his mother and dominated by his father, Francis became a dandy and a prankster who "miserably wasted and squandered his time almost to the twenty-fifth year of his life," as his biographer, friend, and disciple, Thomas of Celano, laments.[13]

---

10 Woods, *How the Catholic Church Built Western Civilization*, 180.
11 The following authors were consulted: Almedingen, Bedoyere, Celano, Chesterton, St Francis. See bibliography.
12 "Letter," in *The Writings of St Francis of Assisi*, trans. Benan Fahy (London: Burns & Oates, 1964), 107.
13 Thomas de Celano, *The Francis Trilogy*, vol. 1, *The Life of St Francis* (New York: New City Press, 1998), 23.

Union

In 1202 during an abortive foray as a self-styled knight, Francis was captured and imprisoned in the neighboring town of Perugia, with which Assisi was constantly feuding. After he had spent a year in the squalor of prison, Francis contracted a fever and was released, only to return home traumatized and disillusioned. He would wander listlessly from room to room leaning on a stick. Attempts by his companions to tempt him back into their former frivolities failed to interest him. Although his sense of courtly manners obliged him to provide — from his father's means — sumptuous banquets for his friends, his heart was never in it and he would often withdraw to spend hours meditating alone in woodlands and grottos.

Three years passed in this dark night when, in 1205, he and his companions had been inducted to join Walter de Brienne at Apulia for a crusade. But just a day into the journey a recurrence of the fever decided him to return to Assisi. On the way Francis encountered a leper and, though repulsed, embraced and kissed him. From then on he would often visit their colonies to give them money and would tend to them and bless them, grateful for the opportunity to serve God in this way.

One day, Francis chanced upon a ruined chapel at San Damiano. Stopping to pray he suddenly heard the crucifix above the altar seem to say: "Restore my house which is in ruins." Taking this literally Francis returned home and took a swath of expensive cloth from his father's shop, which he sold along with his horse, and then rushed back to donate the proceeds to the aged priest at San Damiano. The priest refused the tainted money, so Francis carelessly tossed the coins on a windowsill.

When Bernardone heard of this he was enraged. Forming a posse, he went to San Damiano to bring his son to account. Francis fled and hid in a nearby cave for a month, sustained by the aged priest. Eventually Francis was spotted trudging down the street of Assisi. His father immediately imprisoned him in his house, but Pica released him while Bernardone was away on business. Again Francis fled to San Damiano. However, his father, intending to disinherit him, had him brought before the Bishop. Kneeling before the Bishop, Francis replied: "Not only the money, my Lord, for that indeed belongs to my father, but my clothes also I return to him." And standing there naked he said: "Now in all honesty I can say at last 'Our Father who art in heaven' and no longer my father, Pietro Bernardone." The year was 1207.

Francis returned to San Damiano and became a mendicant. After begging stones and mortar he rebuilt the chapel. Then he directed his efforts to another ruined chapel called the *Portiuncula*. On the 24th of February, 1209, during Mass at the newly restored church, Francis heard the Gospel reading from Matthew 10:8–10: "Heal the sick, raise the dead, cleanse lepers, cast out demons. You received without paying, give without pay. Take no gold, nor silver, nor copper in your belts, no bag for your journey, nor two tunics, nor sandals, nor a staff; for the laborer deserves his food."

> "This is what I want," he said, "this is what I seek, this is what I desire with all my heart." The holy father, overflowing with joy, hastened to implement the words of salvation, and did not delay before he devoutly began to put into effect what he heard. Immediately, he took off the shoes from his feet, put down the staff from his hands, and, satisfied with one tunic, exchanged his leather belt for a chord.... As for the other things he heard, he set about doing them with great care and reverence.[14]

This text became the basis of the great Franciscan order to be called *Minores*. The first to join the order was an old friend Bernardo da Quintavalle; then two other companions, Peter and Giles. When the order increased to twelve, Francis travelled to Rome in 1210 to obtain official sanction from Pope Innocent III to live the Gospel ideal of poverty in imitation of Christ. On Palm Sunday in 1211, a young girl named Clare, from a noble family, stole away at night with a companion, Bona, to meet with Francis in the *Portiuncula*, where they formed, together with her sister, Catherine (who joined later), an order of nuns to be established at Sant'Angelo in Subasio. Then, having dispatched missionaries, Francis journeyed to Damietta in Egypt, vainly attempting to convert Saladin's nephew, Sultan

---

14 Ibid., 42.

Malik-al-Kamil. After a trip to the Holy Land and a second trip to Rome, he returned to the *Portiuncula* to draft the Rule for his order. His final years were spent preaching, praying, ministering to the poor and the lepers, and presiding over the Chapters.

Then in August of the year 1224 (having resigned four years earlier as Superior of the order), Francis along with Brothers Leo, Angelo, and Masseo, decided to make a retreat on the mountain of La Verna. For several weeks Francis remained alone praying in a cave, while the three companions resided in a nearby hut. Towards the end of this time Francis saw a vision of "a man, having six wings like a Seraph, standing over him, arms extended and feet joined, affixed to a cross."[15] The vision was "beautiful beyond comprehension" and Francis was wrought with sorrow at the suffering of the figure. Then his own "hands and feet seemed to be pierced through the middle by nails, with the heads of the nails appearing on the inner part of his hands and on the upper part of his feet . . . his right side was marked with an oblong scar, as if pierced with a lance."[16] Later Br. Leo would testify to this by his own hand: "Two years before his death Blessed Francis kept Lent on Monte Verna (in honor of St Michael the Archangel) . . . and the hand of God was upon him by the vision of a seraph, and the impression of the stigmata upon his body."[17]

Francis was so debilitated by the ordeal that he had to be carried back to Assisi. His remaining months were passed in extreme suffering, and though virtually blind, he labored on with joy. He died at the *Portiuncula* on October 3, 1226, with Clare and many others in attendance. Two years later, he was canonized by Gregory IX.

* * *

Brother Leo referred to St Francis as the "Mirror of Perfection." Certainly he reflected many virtues, the most striking of which was poverty, into which the saint had a profound insight. For St Francis

---

15   Ibid., 103.
16   Ibid., 104.
17   Note which Leo signed on an autograph left by St Francis, kept in Assisi. Quoted in E. M. Almedingen, *Francis of Assisi: A Portrait* (London: The Bodley Head, 1967), 158. The stigmata were also confirmed the day after the saint's death by Brother Elias, second vicar-general of the order.

poverty was his Lady, as he was her liege. By declaring his allegiance to Lady Poverty he knew that she would bring him to the Lord. Poverty was the condition of the Son of Man who had "nowhere to lay his head"; and through poverty Francis would make himself completely dependent upon Christ as his only treasure: "This should be your portion, because it leads to the land of the living. And to this poverty, my beloved brothers, you must cling with all your heart, and wish never to have anything else under heaven, for the sake of our Lord Jesus Christ."[18] Freely embraced, poverty is rich in the virtues, for with it come humility, wisdom, piety, simplicity, fortitude, patience, and self-discipline. The more the soul abandons itself to God, the more the soul receives of God. By emptying oneself of all that obstructs, of everything that might claim one's loyalties, one is left alone with God: rich beyond measure. Yet Francis is not to be admired merely because he stripped himself of all his possessions. Being poor in spirit,[19] worldly possessions already held no value for him. This is why his holiness seemed so easy: his spirit was an arrow aimed at a single target.

One day as Francis and Br. Leo were trudging through the snow and slush on the way from Perugia to the *Portiuncula*, he noticed that Leo was vexed sorely by the cold. Desiring to cheer him up and seeing an opportunity to instruct, Francis said: "Friar Leo, although the friars minor in every land set a great example of holiness, nevertheless take note that therein is not perfect joy." Then at stages the saint would continue to eliminate other things that did not constitute perfect joy: giving sight to the blind, causing the deaf to hear, raising the dead, possessing all knowledge, speaking an angelic language, or converting all the infidels. After two miles of this, Leo said in wonder: "Father, I pray thee in the name of God to tell me wherein is perfect joy." St Francis replied: "When we shall have returned frozen, soaked with rain and befouled with mud, and our brother doorkeeper should not recognize us, refusing us admittance, and if, after persistent knocking he should drive us away with blows

---

18 Francis of Assisi, "Rule of 1223," in Almedingen, *Francis of Assisi: A Portrait*, ch. 6.
19 Mt 5:3.

and insults, or if, after pleading with him he should throw us into the snow and beat us mercilessly, then, if we shall bear all these things patiently and cheerfully, for the love of Christ, O Friar Leo, note that here is perfect joy. For in all the other gifts we cannot glory because they are from God; but willingly to bear reproaches, suffering, and injuries for Christ's sake, this, our own, is our gift to him. As the Apostle says: 'I would not glory save in the cross of our Lord Jesus Christ.'"

Because St Francis was truly poor, his generosity and magnanimity of soul (always apparent from the beginning) were set free. More than once he exchanged his own threadbare habit for one even more tattered than his, or gave his last morsel of food to a starving beggar. Belonging to no place, he was able to embrace every place, blessing each village he entered with the words "Peace to you, good people." Being truly humble he esteemed everyone, never rejecting anyone in need.

In his simplicity, St Francis resembled God whose Being is absolute simplicity. And being simple, he was close to nature. Since God was his Father and he was a creature dwelling among God's creatures, he loved all creation as his family. So in his "Canticle" Francis could praise "Brother Sun, by whom the day is constantly enlightened," or "Sister Earth, our Mother, by whom we are sustained, and fed and governed." He gave thanks for Sister Water, "humble, chaste and precious," which cleansed him, and for Brother Fire, "beautiful, jocund, robust and strong," which illuminated the night and gave him warmth. Enraptured with the miracle of all that he surveyed, having preached to the larks and having admonished a wolf, having embraced lepers, and, at the last, asking to be stripped of his only possession, his habit, St Francis peacefully welcomed Sister Death.

THE MYSTIC DOCTOR[20]

While St Francis had written little and his life was full of instruction, with St John of the Cross, the reverse was true: his great lessons emerged from his poetry and commentaries. And though the saint of

---

20 The following authors were consulted: Sencourt, Slattery, Wojtyła, and St John of the Cross. See bibliography.

Assisi had had little education, St John was considerably more learned. Born in Fontiveros in Old Castile, in June 1542, Juan de Yepes was the youngest of three sons. His father, Gonzalo, came from a noble family who had disowned him when he married beneath himself. However, Gonzalo died when John was but two. Reduced to penury, his mother, Catalina, sought to secure financial assistance from her husband's family, but was rejected by them. Having also suffered the death of a son, she eventually settled in Medina del Campo, where John entered a school for the poor.

His gentleness and patience and the compassion he showed towards the sick caught the interest of one Don Alonso Alvarez, administrator of the local hospital for the poor. Don Alonso became his sponsor, and at the age of seventeen, John enrolled at the Jesuit school where he studied grammar, rhetoric, Latin, and Greek. He also immersed himself in the Spanish classics. Meanwhile, he continued to work in the hospital.

Finally, aged twenty-one, John entered the Carmelite order, attracted by their spirit of contemplation and devotion to the Virgin Mary. He received the name Brother John of St Matthew and after a year's novitiate was sent to the Carmelite student house in Salamanca. There he studied philosophy and theology. In the year 1567 he was ordained a priest and gave his first Mass at Medina. It was there that he met St Teresa of Jesus who had come from Avila to Medina to found the second of her reformed Carmelite communities. Inspired by her reforms, John accompanied her to Valladolid, where she intended to found another community.

St. Teresa's reforms were designed to take the Carmelites in a more contemplative and prayerful direction. More austere, disciplined, and cloistered than her parent order, they became known as discalced from their habit of not wearing shoes. Needless to say, such reforms fomented hostility which eventually caught up with John himself. On the night of December 2, 1577, a group of Carmelites assisted by men-at-arms arrested him, incarcerating him in the monastery in Toledo. It was here that he composed much of *The Spiritual Canticle* as well as some poems. John escaped, however, the following August.

He was sequestered in a monastery in El Calvario where he became vicar, but within a year moved to the town of Baeza as rector of its university. He also served as spiritual director to a community of nuns, then prior of a monastery in Granada, and in 1585 vicar provincial of Andalusia. During this time he founded seven new monasteries and produced the *Ascent of Mount Carmel*, *The Dark Night*, and the *Living Flame of Love*. After holding other offices such as councilor to the vicar general of the Discalced Carmelites, in 1591 he resigned from all offices and retreated to Ubeda suffering from febrile oedemas in his skin and subcutaneous tissues.

Although not comely in appearance, being short, thin, and bald, St John endeared himself to all he met. Compassionate, witty, gentle, and discerning, university professors and unlettered shepherd's wives alike were drawn to his confessional. Tirelessly he would work among the poor in hospitals and then cut stone in the quarry for his monasteries. Requiring little sleep, he spent most of the night praying. He cherished his Bible and would often be found in seclusion meditating on its contents. People were moved by his recollectedness at the altar. On one occasion during Holy Week he suffered so intensely from Christ's passion that he was unable to leave the monastery to hear confession. And when illness caused him to retire, rather than choose Baeza where he was known and respected, he chose Ubeda where he was unknown and mistreated by the prior. Eventually his legs became ulcerated and a large tumor formed on his back. Realizing the end was near he called for the prior to beg his pardon for all the trouble his illness had caused. On 14 December, 1591, he died in the odor of sanctity. His last words were from the Psalms: "Into your hands, O Lord, I commend my spirit."

* * *

Profoundly beautiful and spiritually sublime, the writings of St John of the Cross are designed to bring the reader to that supreme state of prayer which is spiritual union with God. This is the end for which we were created; for God, being perfect Form and Supreme Good, is to be loved absolutely and completely with all our being. We need no commandments to love him, to serve him or seek him. Once we confess his existence the very perfection and magnificence of his Being compel us to seek him. The intellect cannot rest until it comprehends Truth, and the will is dissatisfied until it unites with the Good.

Thus, the first major theme we discover in the writings of St John is that the purpose of human existence is transformation into God or, as we have noted with regards to the gifts, to become perfect through participation in the perfection of God.

> Thus it should be understood that the desire for himself that God grants in all his favors and unguents and fragrant anointings is a preparation for other more precious and delicate ointments, made more according to the quality of God, until the soul is so delicately and purely prepared that it merits union with him and substantial transformation in all its faculties.[21]

All the graces which God gives us are to lead us to this end. Indeed, the whole of creation is subject to this purpose: to bring it and us to God.[22] Here we glimpse a deeper reason as to why suffering is embodied within creation. Not only is the universe limited and therefore necessarily imperfect, not only was humanity allowed to fall in order to gain an incomparably greater gift than it would otherwise have had, not only has God so orchestrated things as to bring about the greatest and most magisterial good, but suffering in itself serves a glorious purpose for the individual: union with God. Suffering is inevitable, as we have seen, but spiritual persons can see the wisdom in God's creation and know how to secure the Good,[23] while worldly individuals, ever complaining and without comprehending, flee into their fleeting pleasures,[24] both justly receiving what they desire.

> Oh, what a miserable lot this life is! We live in the midst of so much danger and find it so hard to arrive at truth.

---

21 John of the Cross, *The Living Flame of Love*, in *Collected Works*, stanza 3:28.
22 Rom 8:19–23.
23 Mt 5:11, 10:22; Lk 21:19; Jn 15:13; Acts 14:22; Rom 8:17–18, 36; Rom 12:1, 14, 21; 2 Cor 12:15; Gal 6:17; Phil 2:17–18, 3:10–11; 2 Thess 1:4–5; 2 Tim 1:8; 1 Pet 2:21, 4:1, 4:13; 1 Jn 3:16.
24 Rom 1:24–32.

> The clearest and truest things are the darkest and most dubious to us, and consequently we flee from what most suits us. We embrace what fills our eyes with the most light and satisfaction and run after what is the very worst thing for us, and we fall at every step. In how much danger do humans live, since the very light of their natural eyes, which ought to be their guide, is the first to deceive them in their journey to God, and since they must keep their eyes shut and tread the path of darkness if they want to be sure of where they are going and be safeguarded against the enemies of their house, their senses and faculties.[25]

We seek God because we love him, and we love him because he is Love itself. However, since God is incomprehensible to the intellect and opaque to all the senses, therefore, God *is* a dark night to the soul. The virtue which takes us through this dark night is faith working through love given to us by the Holy Spirit. This is the second and most central theme in the writings of St John.

> ... to be prepared for this divine union the intellect must be cleansed and emptied of everything relating to sense, divested and liberated of everything clearly intelligible, inwardly pacified and silenced, and supported by faith alone, which is the only proximate means to union with God. For the likeness between faith and God is so close that no other difference exists than that between believing in God and seeing him. Just as God is infinite, faith proposes him to us as infinite. Just as there are three Persons in one God, it presents him to us in this way. And just as God is darkness to our intellect, so faith dazzles and blinds us. Only by means of faith, in divine light exceeding all understanding, does God manifest himself to the soul. The greater one's faith the closer is one's union with God.[26]

---

25 John of the Cross, *The Dark Night*, in *Collected Works*, Bk. 2, ch. 16, sec. 12.
26 John of the Cross, *The Ascent of Mount Carmel*, in *Collected Works*, Bk. 2, ch. 9, sec. 1.

For St John, faith has a twofold function which brings us to God: purgative and unitive. We examined the purgative function of faith in Chapter 7 where we found that our faith in God causes us to seek God with all our being by directing our lives towards him and stripping ourselves of all that offends the Divine Goodness. We saw that this gives rise to the virtues which also make us like God in our moral and spiritual character, i.e., holy. Nonetheless, we remain in the dark night because God is *substantially* unknowable to us, both intellectually and sensually. And it is precisely this dark night of faith which purifies us. Provided that one's intention is single, then faith will spontaneously work its purgative function especially in a world in which pain is inevitable!

But faith has a unitive function as well, since it is a supernatural gift. The life of faith is the very presence of God in the soul making himself known to us, to which we lovingly respond. Faith comes through hearing the word of Christ.[27] And Christ is God's Word to us. Therefore, it is the intention, as the formative principle of faith, that is the attribute which unites us to God. This intentionality (conation) within faith predisposes us towards God because it says "yes" to the Word of God that expresses his substantial nature. "The conclusion . . . is that in and through faith the intellect truly attains to the 'substance' of revealed truths and hence is truly united with the divine essence in a manner corresponding to the exigencies of the intellect enlightened by faith."[28] Thus, by contemplating the life, works, and teachings of Jesus Christ one comes to know him and to love him. One's faith in him grows and one becomes increasingly predisposed towards him *who is God revealed*. The intentionality of faith predisposes us to receive all that Christ has to give us, and he desires to give us nothing less than his very Self. "I do not pray for these only, but also for those who believe in me through their[29] word, that they may all be one; even as thou, Father, art in me, and I in thee, that they may be in us, so that the world may believe that thou has sent me."[30]

---

27 Rom 10:17.
28 Karol Wojtyła [John Paul II], *Faith According to Saint John of the Cross* (San Francisco: Ignatius Press, 1981), 246.
29 That is, the word of the apostles and their successors.
30 Jn 17:20–21.

The third major theme in St John is the transforming nature of charity upon the soul. The soul is truly transformed, not in substance but in its character and understanding, because its natural but limited activity has been absorbed into the Divine Life, in which it participates, and is elevated in all her faculties. The term John uses to describe this is spiritual marriage, which he has taken from the Song of Songs.

> This spiritual marriage is... a total transformation in the Beloved, in which each surrenders the entire possession of self to the other with a certain consummation of the union of love. The soul thereby becomes divine, God through participation, insofar as is possible in this life.... As a result she usually experiences an intimate spiritual embrace, which is a veritable embrace, by means of which she lives the life of God. The words of St Paul are verified in this soul: *I live, now not I, but Christ lives in me* [Gal. 2:20]. Therefore, since the soul lives in this state a life as happy and glorious as is God's, let each one consider here, if this be possible, how pleasant her life is. Just as God is incapable of feeling any distaste, neither does she feel any, for the delight of God's glory is experienced and enjoyed in the substance of the soul now transformed in him.[31]

In this state of union the soul is serenely and blissfully living the Spirit of God. Nothing disturbs this delight since, as St John says, the soul feels the glory that God, who is living in her, radiates; and God's glory is never disturbed. Moreover, this change takes place in the soul and not in God, since God is substantially unchangeable, because no perfection is lacking to him. It follows that, at the moment when God dwells in souls through the gift of supernatural faith which makes them participants in his life, this union is already consummated as far as God is concerned.[32] At the apex of every believing soul there is a point (*scintilla*) where God dwells in bliss and serenity directing the life of every Christian. The reason that many Christians are not conscious of this union is that they live

---

31 John of the Cross, *The Spiritual Canticle*, in *Collected Works*, stanza 22:3, 5.
32 Jn 14:23; Eph 3:17-19; 1 Jn 2:24; Rev 3:20; 21:3.

from their lower natures, i.e., because their attentions and efforts are directed to the world and because they have not corrected those habits, thoughts, and attachments which distract and misdirect their energies, thereby dissociating them from that prayerful union. Many Christians readily confess they only have to stop and become still and they will sense that center where God serenely sustains (*synderesis*) them, pouring grace into their hearts. Our delight is to dwell there permanently, so that in all things we are always pleasing to him. The spiritual life is but one of recollection (*anamnesis*), and the entire focus of John's spiritual direction is to place us in that dark night where our lives are already "hid with Christ in God."[33]

SPIRITUAL CHILDHOOD[34]

Marie Françoise Thérèse was the last of nine children born to Louis and Zelie Martin. Four of these children died at an early age. The remaining five all entered the religious life: one to the Visitation Convent at Caen, the other four to the Carmel at Lisieux. Thérèse was born at Alençon on 2 January, 1873, and was baptized two days later. Just four years later, her mother died, and the entire family moved to Lisieux where Thérèse passed her childhood.

In her autobiography, Thérèse states that upon her mother's death her childlike gaiety deserted her. Fortunately her life with her father and sisters was affectionate and devout so that from her earliest days she had wanted to follow her sisters into the cloister. When Thérèse was only fourteen she asked to enter the Carmel, but was refused. Since appeals to the local priest and bishop had also failed, Thérèse, her sister Céline, and her father decided to travel to Rome to seek a dispensation from Pope Leo XIII that she might enter Carmel when she was fifteen. The pope said to her, "You will enter if it is God's will." Disappointed they returned home via a visit to the shrines of St Clare and St Francis at Assisi. However, on New Year's Day in 1888 she received a letter from the prioress that

---

33 Col 3:3.
34 The following authors were consulted: Combes, Johnson, Slattery, and St Thérèse of Lisieux. See bibliography.

she would be received into the Carmel after Lent on April 9. On 8 September, 1890, she professed her final vows.

Her days at the Carmel were occupied with domestic duties in the laundry, kitchen, sacristy, and infirmary, punctuated by the liturgy of the hours, Mass attendance, spiritual reading, and personal prayers. In 1894 the prioress, Mother Agnes (who was also her biological sister), asked her to record her childhood memories. The following year Thérèse offered herself to God as a victim soul and a year later she suffered her first hemorrhage. In June 1897 she was moved to the infirmary where she completed her autobiography. She died aged twenty-four on 30 September, her eyes alight with supernatural joy. Her final words were: "I do not wish to suffer less. Oh, how I love Him! My God, I love Thee."

Immediately upon its publication in 1898 her life story, *L'Histoire d'une âme,* became a best seller and made an otherwise unknown nun an object of devotion. Thérèse was canonized by Pope Pius XII in 1925 and made co-patroness of France together with Joan of Arc. So popular was this saint who was affectionately known as "the Little Flower" that St John Paul II declared her a Doctor of the Church.[35]

* * *

St. Thérèse's "little way" rests upon the simple truth that we are all children of our heavenly Father: that true devotion to God rests upon a childlike, unconditional, loving trust in his care. At once innocent and humble, this attitude offers to God the devotion which says "Abba, Father,"[36] and is clearly reminiscent of Jesus's teaching: "Truly, I say to you, whoever does not receive the kingdom of God like a child shall not enter it."[37] St Thérèse, herself, describes how she discovered this path:

> I will find a little way to Heaven, very short and direct, an entirely new way. We live in the age of inventions now, and the wealthy no longer have to take the trouble to climb the stairs; they take a lift. That is what I must find, *a lift* to

---

35 Her parents, Louis and Zélie, were beatified by Pope Benedict XVI on 19 October 2008.
36 Rom 8:15, Gal 4:6.
37 Mk 10:15.

> take me straight up to Jesus, because I am too little to climb the steep stairway of perfection. So I searched the Scriptures for some hint of my desired *lift* until I came upon these words from the lips of Eternal Wisdom: "*Whosoever is a little one, let him come to Me.*"[38] I went closer to God, feeling sure that I was on the right path, but as I wanted to know what he would do to a "little one" I continued my search. This is what I found: "*You shall be carried at the breasts and upon the knees; as one whom the mother caresseth, so will I comfort you.*"[39] My heart had never been moved by such tender and consoling words before![40]

Just as St Francis embraced poverty as his way to union with God, and St John of the Cross entered into the dark night of faith to find union with God, so St Thérèse also grasped that we do not require a set discipline or rule in order to become holy. Rather, we must *become* what we already are in the highest point of our souls — that holy creature sustained by God — simply by accepting our status as children of a heavenly Father and living accordingly. It is this that is so revolutionary, since it reaffirms that God is not distant from us, but very close within us as the very principle of our being. In the words of another great spiritual writer and director, St Francis de Sales:

> The human reason — or rather, the human soul in so far as it is rational — is truly the temple of almighty God, where he is chiefly fain to dwell ... it has an apex, the highest point in the spiritual faculty of reason. No light of human reasoning functions there; the mind simply knows, the will simply acts, forcing the soul to acknowledge and submit to the truth of God, and to his will. For although faith, hope and charity lavish their heavenly impulses on practically all the soul's faculties, reasonable as well as sensitive, although they bring those faculties to submit to the rightful authority of the theological virtues — yet

---

38 Prov 9:4.
39 Is 66:12–13.
40 Thérèse of Lisieux [Thérèse Martin], *The Story of a Soul* (London: Burns and Oates, 1951), 135.

their special domain, where clearly those virtues naturally belong, is the soul's highest point.[41]

This is the scintilla, that spark which is guarded by God from consenting to any sin, where God touches the soul, tenderly speaking her name.[42] At this point, where the Eternal contacts the temporal, we are one with God; our task is to dwell there.

And St Thérèse has shown us a simple way to do so — by offering to God all the little things in our life: all that we do, suffer, or enjoy.[43]

> Love proves itself by deeds, and how shall I prove mine? *The little child will scatter flowers* whose fragrant perfume will surround the royal throne, and in a voice that is silver-toned, she will sing the *canticle of love*.
>
> So, my Beloved, shall my short life be spent in Your sight. I can prove my love only by scattering flowers, that is to say, by never letting slip a single little sacrifice, a single glance, a single word; by making profit of the very smallest actions, by doing them all for love.
>
> I want to suffer, and even rejoice for love, for this is my way of scattering flowers. Never a flower shall I find but its petals shall be scattered for you; and all the while I will sing, yes, always sing, even when gathering my roses in the midst of thorns; and the longer and sharper the thorns may be, the sweeter shall be my song!

The distinguishing feature of this little way is that it is, itself, the very thing it strives to become, viz., our loving dependence upon the Father in whom we subsist and from whom come all our blessings.

We are living the mystery of fall and redemption. Our rebellion against God severs us from that nature eternally communicated to us by God in act. But Jesus, "the pioneer and perfecter of our faith,"[44]

---

41 Francis de Sales, *Treatise on the Love of God* (Bangalore: SFS Publications, 1982), 26–27.
42 Jer 14:9; 15:16. This point, which is God's creative act, cannot be corrupted or we would cease to exist.
43 Thérèse, *Story of a Soul*, 192.
44 Heb 12:2.

has reconciled us with God, who now dwells in the apex of our souls, so that we might boldly rejoice in our status as children of a loving heavenly Father. Love reconciles and unites; and souls concretize this union when they lovingly choose to unite every instant of their lives with the Eternal Will. Just as the loving union of the Father and the Son brings forth the creative Spirit of God; just as the loving union of the Christ with his bride, the Church, generates the Spirit of Truth in the Church; and the loving, innocent union of a man and a woman naturally brings forth life;[45] so the union of God with the soul propagates charity in one's person.

Nature and grace are not contraries. Love communicates being since God *is* Being in act. Through the act of love we both come into existence and *are constituted* with the capacity to love. By loving God in all that we do and suffer, we approximate the Divine Nature. This is the analogy of being in its actuality, for in loving we are breathing the Divine Fire which ignites that little spark in our small souls. "God is love, and he who abides in love abides in God, and God abides in him. In this is love perfected with us, that we may have confidence for the day of judgement, because *as he is so are we in this world*."[46] In the words of St Thérèse:[47]

> I long to fly and imitate the eagles, but all I can do is flutter my small wings. I am not strong enough to fly. What will become of me? Must I die of sorrow at finding myself so helpless? Never! It will not trouble me in the very least. Surrendering myself with daring confidence, I shall simply stay gazing at my Sun until I die. Nothing will frighten me, neither wind not rain, and should the Star of Love be blotted out by heavy clouds so that nothing but the night of this life seems to exist, then will be the time for *perfect joy*, the moment to push my confidence to the furthest bounds; I shall take good care to stay just where I am, quite certain that beyond the somber clouds my beloved Sun is shining still!

---

45 Eph 5:31–32.
46 1 Jn 4:16–17.
47 Thérèse, *Story of a Soul*, 194.

THE POOREST OF THE POOR[48]

Mother Teresa was born Agnes Gonxha Bojaxhiu in Skopje, Macedonia, on August 27, 1910, of Albanian parents. There were three children, one boy and two girls. She attended the local government school, but at the age of twelve, feeling strongly the call of God, she joined the Sodality run by the Jesuits. There she learned about the Bengal Mission from letters regularly sent to the school by missionaries in Calcutta. Inspired to become a missionary to spread the love of Christ, young Agnes volunteered for the Bengal Mission.

When she was eighteen Agnes left her parental home in Skopje and joined the Sisters of Loreto, an Irish community of nuns with missions in India. After a few months' training in Dublin she was sent to India to begin her novitiate in Darjeeling. On 6 January she became a teacher at St Mary's High School in Calcutta. On May 24, 1931, she took her initial vows, choosing the name Teresa after "the little one" of Lisieux. For several years she taught geography, then after taking her final vows on 24 May, 1937, she became principal of the school and was also placed in charge of the Daughters of St Anne, the Indian religious order attached to the Loreto Sisters.

On 10 September, 1946, while travelling on a train to Darjeeling, Teresa heard the call of God — "a call within a call" — to go among the poorest of the poor. In January 1948 she requested permission from her superiors to leave the convent school and devote herself to working among the poorest of the poor in the slums of Calcutta. This request was conveyed to Rome and approved. The following August, Mother Teresa abandoned the Loreto habit for her blue and white sari. After a three-month intensive course in nursing at the American Medical Missionary Sisters in Patna, she returned to Calcutta. Virtually without funds, she depended on Divine Providence, and in December began an open-air school for slum children in Moti Jheel. Soon she was joined by voluntary helpers, and financial support was also forthcoming, enabling her to expand her work. She became an Indian citizen during that year.

---

48 Authors consulted: Desmond Doig and Malcolm Muggeridge. See bibliography.

On October 7, 1950, Mother Teresa received permission from the Holy See to start her own order, "The Missionaries of Charity," whose primary task was to love and care for those persons who were unloved and unwanted: "whose living conditions were incompatible with the dignity of the human person, and who are deprived, materially, spiritually or socially, in relation to their neighbors."[49]

Those she helped were often in distressing conditions: men with faces half eaten away or whose flesh fell from their backs when they were raised, babies abandoned in rubbish piles, bodies wasted by hunger to virtual skeletons or covered in open sores, those too weak to lift a limb, the deformed, the choleric, those found dying in the sewers. All were taken to her centers, cleaned, fed, attended to, but always treated with dignity and compassion. About these Mother said: "The greatest disease today is not leprosy or tuberculosis, but rather the feeling of being unwanted, uncared for and deserted by everybody. The greatest evil is the lack of love and charity, the terrible indifference towards one's neighbor who lives at the roadside assaulted by exploitation, corruption, poverty and disease."[50] And again: "We help the poor die with God. We help them to say sorry to God. It is between them and God alone. Nobody else.... We just help them to make their peace with God because that is the greatest need—to die in peace with God."[51]

> Be kind and merciful. Let no one ever come to you without coming away better and happier. Be the living expression of God's kindness: kindness in your face, kindness in your eyes, kindness in your smile, kindness in your warm greeting. In the slums we are the light of God's kindness to the poor. To children, to the poor, to all who suffer and are lonely, give always a happy smile—give them not only your care, but also your heart.[52]

---

49 Taken from the *Constitutions* of the Missionaries of Charity.
50 Malcolm Muggeridge, *Something Beautiful for God* (London: Collins, 1971), 73–74.
51 Desmond Doig, *Mother Teresa: Her People and Her Work* (Glasgow: Collins Fount, 1988), 140.
52 Muggeridge, *Something Beautiful*, 69.

In 1965 the Society became an International Religious Family by a decree of Pope Paul VI. After that Mother Teresa opened centers in Caracas, Venezuela; Colombo, Ceylon; Tabora, Tanzania; and Rome. In the year before her death, her Order ran 755 homes in 125 countries. During that year the Missionaries of Charity fed half a million of the hungry in five continents, treated a quarter of a million sick, taught over 20,000 slum children, and managed homes for the mentally destitute, lepers, AIDS patients, the crippled, alcoholics, and drug abusers. They also operated crèches, shelters, soup kitchens, and tuberculosis sanatoriums.

Mother Teresa received several awards for her work with the needy, including the 1971 Pope John XXIII Peace Prize, India's Jawaharlal Nehru Award for International Understanding in 1972, and the Nobel Peace Prize in 1979. Mother Teresa died peacefully on September 5, 1997, bequeathing a legacy of selfless service to those in want. She was eighty-seven.

In 2002, St John Paul II recognized the healing of an Indian woman as the miracle required to beatify Mother Teresa. The healing, which had occurred on the first anniversary of her death, involved a Hindu woman who suffered from a huge abdominal tumor. Members of the Missionaries of Charity prayed for their founder's intervention to help her. When she awoke the next morning, the tumor was gone. Her doctor, Dr R. N. Bhattacharya, also a non-Christian, said, "I did not find any reason that without an operation a tumor of such size would disappear overnight." An exhaustive investigation by the Congregation, backed by expert medical and scientific testimony, confirmed the miracle. Mother Teresa was beatified on October 19, 2003, by Pope St John Paul II.

In 2008, a Brazilian man, Marcilio Haddad Andrino, was dying from brain abscesses. His wife, Fernanda, prayed to Mother Teresa for help. He was sent to hospital to have the abscesses drained, but before they could do so he awoke from his coma completely cured. Mother Teresa was canonized by Pope Francis on 14 September, 2016.

* * *

Like other saints, Mother Teresa suffered the dark night of the soul described by St John of the Cross; but in her case, the dark night lasted for decades. In 1956, she wrote: "Such deep longing for

God — and ... repulsed — empty — no faith — no love — no zeal." "In my soul I feel just that terrible pain of loss," she wrote in 1959, "of God not wanting me — of God not being God — of God not existing." This interior trial, known to only a few of her most intimate associates, continued until her death.

The fact that she experienced such an intense trial shows that she was extremely advanced in the spiritual life. This was not the obscurity of unbelief, which has never known the light. Rather it follows upon the way of illumination when the love of God has already flowed into one's soul, so that its withdrawal leaves the soul "poor, abandoned, and unsupported by intellect, will, or memory, left to the darkness of pure faith, in sorrows, afflictions, and longing for the love of God."[53]

When souls are placed in such a dark night, their afflictions are terrible. They often feel that God has rejected them and abandoned them in this darkness forever, believing they neither have nor ever will have of themselves anything deserving God's love. They feel abhorrent to God and grieve inconsolably at having merited such rejection. So oppressive is this night that they cannot even raise their minds to God, or discover any consolation, savor, or affection from him, neither in prayer nor in the Mass. The soul simply feels that God no longer hears her prayers.

God only places in this dark night of the soul those souls who have already passed through purgation and illumination. This night is normally a prelude and preparation for spiritual union with God. The reason why all consolation and favor have been removed is to place the soul in a state of pure faith weaned from intellectual forms and from all sensual and spiritual attachments: that locus where God is directly communicating his gift of himself to the soul.

In time, aided by the priest who acted as her spiritual director, Mother Teresa did indeed conclude that these painful experiences helped her to identify not only with the forsakenness that Jesus Christ felt during his crucifixion, but also with the abandonment that the poor faced daily. In this way she hoped to enter, in her words, the "dark holes" of the lives of the people whom she tended:

---

[53] See John of the Cross, *The Dark Night*, Bk. 2, ch. 4, sec. 1. This state is clearly described in Lam 3:1–20 and Ps 88.

Union

Without suffering, our work would just be social work, very good and helpful, but it would not be the work of Jesus Christ, not part of the Redemption. Jesus wanted to help by sharing our life, our loneliness, our agony, our death. Only by being one with us has he redeemed us. We are allowed to do the same; all the desolation of the poor people, not only their material poverty, but their spiritual destitution, must be redeemed, and we must share it, for only by being one with them can we redeem them, that is, by bringing God into their lives and bringing them to God.[54]

ST. MARIA GORETTI[55]

Luigi and Assunta Goretti were poor agricultural workers, simple but possessing a deep faith which they transmitted to their children. They had six surviving children (the first having died in infancy): Angelo the eldest, then Maria who was born on 16 October, 1890, followed by two more brothers, Alessandro and Mariano, and two sisters, Ersilia and Teresa. Because of poverty and distance, the children never attended school. Instead they learned the faith from their parents.

Luigi initially farmed a tiny plot of land in a small village in the Ancona region of Italy while the children shared responsibilities in the household or in the fields. However, the farm could not support the growing family; so admitting defeat, Luigi became a sharecropper on an estate some twenty miles from Rome. The family had to share lodgings in an old cheese dairy with one Giovanni Serenelli, a widower, and his teenage son, Alessandro. However, Serenelli was a drifter and his drinking made him belligerent. His son was a loner and moody, spending most of his time reading salacious crime magazines. Neither of them attempted to accommodate living with the Gorettis. In fact Assunta had to do for them as well as her own.

In 1901, when Maria was nearly eleven, her father died from malaria, which he had contracted from the nearby marshes. Assunta had to

---

54 Muggeridge, *Something Beautiful*, 67–68.
55 This account comes from Glynn Mac Niven-Johnston, *Maria Goretti: Teenage Martyr* (London: Catholic Truth Society, 1997).

substitute for her husband in the fields, for by this time the family was deeply in debt. This laid a heavy burden upon Maria, who had to take over her mother's domestic duties as well as her own. It also meant that Maria was left alone at times with Alessandro, who attempted to insinuate himself into Maria's affections. On several occasions he asked for sexual intimacies, but Maria, of course, refused. He became increasingly insistent, even threatening to kill her if she resisted. Maria was terrified and sought to avoid him, since she was too frightened and ashamed to relate to anyone what was happening. Instead, she took refuge in prayer.

However, on 5 July, 1902, while everyone was occupied with tasks away from the lodgings, Alessandro, now in his twenties, seeing his opportunity, grasped an awl and rushed upon Maria, dragging her into the kitchen. Again he demanded sexual favors from the eleven-year-old girl. "No," Maria said, "God does not want this. If you do this you will go to hell." He had desired her consent, but this time when she refused, he became enraged. In a state of frenzy he plunged the needle-sharp instrument into her repeatedly, slashing and stabbing at her. She cried out: "I'm dying. God help me." As she tried to crawl away, Alessandro panicked, grabbed her by the throat, and stabbed her in the back. Having finally silenced her, he threw the awl behind some furniture and locked himself in his room pretending to be asleep.

Maria's baby sister was awakened by the clamor, and her crying alerted the others including Giovanni and Assunta. When they came upon Maria, she was still alive and was able to tell them some of what had happened. The doctor and police were called to the scene and Maria was rushed to the hospital while Alessandro was hurried to the local jail manacled between two horses.

The doctors did everything they could, but her injuries were too extensive: all her internal organs including her heart were damaged. The doctors made her comfortable and called for the parish priest. At her request she was placed in a bed near a picture of Our Lady hanging on the opposite wall. Although in terrible pain she spoke only of her assailant: "Poor Alessandro. He is going to go to hell. Poor Alessandro." When the priest came at last, he described to her Christ's death and his forgiveness, asking if Maria also forgave Alessandro. She said she forgave him with all her heart and that she wanted him to be with her in heaven. She was asked if she would like to be made a child of Mary, which filled her with joy. The medal was placed around her neck and she was given last rites. After a period of fever and delirium she died in the afternoon of 6 July, 1902. Later, the parish priest recorded that "she wholeheartedly pardoned her murderer and died in the arms of the Lord."

Alessandro was eventually brought to Rome to stand trial. Cynical and arrogant, he showed no remorse and denied any blame. Forced by the evidence to admit his guilt, he then pleaded insanity. Then he said he killed Maria in order to obtain security of care in the state prison system. However, he was found guilty of murder and because of his age sentenced to thirty years in prison. For eight years he remained defiant. Once he castigated a visiting priest: "This is all your fault. I would have had her but for you and your church."

Shortly afterwards Maria appeared to Alessandro in a dream. She was dressed in white and was quietly picking lilies in a garden. Having gathered a large bouquet she offered them to him. When he received them they began to glow like the flames of a candle, and in the dream he understood with certainty that she had completely forgiven him.

From that moment Alessandro began to change. He became a model prisoner and was eventually released four years early for good behavior with the agreement of Assunta, whose permission had to be obtained under Italian law. Upon his release from the prison in Sardinia (1928), he found employment as a builder. As soon as he earned enough money he returned to Italy nine years later. His first act was to visit Maria's grave. Then he sought out Maria's mother, who was working at the presbytery as housekeeper, to ask her forgiveness. Assunta affirmed immediately that for Maria's sake she did indeed forgive him, since Maria had already done so.

As Christmas was approaching, Alessandro accepted the priest's invitation, at Assunta's request, to stay at the presbytery for a few days. At Midnight Mass Assunta led Alessandro to the altar rail to receive Holy Communion at her side. The scene raised a commotion among the congregation, so Alessandro turned to them and confessed: "I have committed a great sin and I ask your forgiveness."

By this time the cause for Maria's beatification had already begun and Alessandro was interviewed extensively. The details of Maria's death emerged from his own testimony. He said, "I knew I was breaking the law of God. I killed her because she refused. She had never encouraged me in any way — not by a word or a smile. The fault was all my own." Later Alessandro became a gardener in an isolated monastery where he stayed, shunning publicity and sensation-seekers, until his death in 1969, aged eighty-two. His final words were, "I'm going to be with Maria."

After a comprehensive examination of her life and sanctity based upon the collected testimonies of those who had known her, as well as that of Alessandro, and the required two miracles,[56] Maria Goretti, having been declared a martyr, was beatified in 1947 and canonized on 24 June, 1950. Half a million people were present at the ceremony held in the open air, including the president and prime minister of Italy. Her mother was also there with her family and standing at her side was Alessandro Serenelli.

* * *

Evil is inevitable given the necessary imperfection of a finite world and the iniquity wrought by human disobedience.[57] But saints such as Maria Goretti are able, through God's infinite grace, to embrace evil and, by uniting it with the sufferings of Christ, participate proportionally in his redemptive work, since Christ himself has transformed suffering, giving it a redemptive power which is inexhaustible and infinite in merit. The essence of atonement (reparation) is that Divine Love which, by taking our alienation upon itself, transforms it into reconciliation.[58] The extension of the life of the Trinity into our world through the self-emptying of the Incarnation is itself an act of redemption.[59] The willing suffering of sin by him who knew

---

56   One involved the complete restoration of a crushed foot of a workman who had invoked Maria's intercession. The other comprised the complete and instantaneous healing of a woman seriously ill from pleurisy, who had also invoked Maria's aid.
57   See chapter 3.
58   Prov 16:6.
59   Phil 2:5–8.

no sin and his offering of it to the Father is an act of reparation, of reconciliation. To accept estrangement in love is to transform it into something new. When we absorb evil in this way we also do reparation for it, because by our willing acceptance it is transformed into that love which reconciles: the love which is also the life of the Trinity, which the Son freely surrenders to the Father and the Father begets in the Son. And even though only the Son has been able to reconcile humanity through his perfect offering, nevertheless, whenever we suffer the effects of evil and make our offerings in the same spirit, then we too are enabled in ourselves willingly to "complete what is lacking in Christ's afflictions for the sake of his body, that is, the Church."[60] Therefore, in uniting our afflictions with his we do not add anything to what his sufferings have merited for the Church, but we are able to do what Christ cannot do, namely offer God what is uniquely ours—our will. As St Francis said to Br. Leo about the nature of true joy: "For in all the other gifts we cannot glory because they are from God; but willingly to bear reproaches, suffering, and injuries for Christ's sake, this, our own, is our gift to him. As the Apostle says: 'I would not glory save in the cross of our Lord Jesus Christ.'" By his cross Christ has bestowed meaning and dignity upon our sufferings which, through the merits of Christ's passion, death, and resurrection, can procure intercession for others. By turning our adversities into a prayer we are united in the apex of our souls, through faith, with the sufferings of Christ, also making our prayers a fragrant offering to God.[61]

This is why St Paul can say to the Church "I rejoice in my sufferings for your sake,"[62] since God does not ignore our sighs and groans, but out of the honor he holds for his Son, accepts our offering too.[63] This is only fitting, otherwise struggle and sacrifice lack all meaning. But it is the self-abandonment of the Son to the Father that gives dignity to our personal crosses. They are the mark of our union with Him.[64] "When we cry, 'Abba! Father!' it is the Spirit himself bear-

---

60 Col 1:24.
61 Rom 12:1; Heb 13:15; 1 Pet 2:5.
62 Col 1:24.
63 1 Pet 2:19, 3:14 and 17–18, 4:14, 5:9–10.
64 2 Cor 4:7–12; Gal 6:17; Phil 3:10–11.

ing witness with our spirit that we are children of God and fellow heirs with Christ, provided we suffer with him in order that we may be glorified with him."[65] Our patient perseverance and the willing offering of our trials to God the Father images the sacramental nature of the relationship of the Son with the Father, and, in like manner, transforms the alienation of sin into the love that reconciles, making every cross a sacrament. "Suffering more than anything else, makes present in the history of humanity the powers of the Redemption. In that 'cosmic' struggle between the spiritual powers of good and evil, spoken of in the Letter to the Ephesians,[66] human sufferings, united to the redemptive suffering of Christ, *constitute a special support for the powers of good,* and open the way to the victory of these salvific powers."[67] St Maria Goretti, although but a child, gave personal and heroic witness to this truth: that the more menacing the specter of evil, the greater the salvific merit with which the Cross of Christ crowns our loving endurance. And in this is revealed the ultimate and spiritual answer to the meaning of human suffering.

CONCLUDING SUMMARY

The thin but certain truth — that we think of being in general — has led us to the conviction that beneath this contingent existence there dwells a Substantial Being who is necessary, infinite, immaterial, almighty, and eternal; who radiates goodness, truth, and beauty which inform all creation (including the quantum states of our neuro-physiology) and extend even to the eudaemonistic ordering of human affairs. None of this threatens common sense, for this is simply the grail of any science: the unification of knowledge.

Yet this diaphanous notion of being affords no access to substance in itself, but of form only. In this light, we looked upon Jesus who proclaimed for himself the distinction of having proceeded from his Heavenly Father as the pre-existent Logos, which indwells and

---

65 Rom 8:17.
66 Eph 6:12–18.
67 John Paul II [Karol Wojtyła], *Salvifici Doloris* (Homebush, NSW: Society of St Paul, 1984), 69.

informs his sacred humanity. In Christ Jesus, eternal Wisdom has passed among us, perfumed with magisterial grace, tenderness, and forgiveness, innocence, verity, goodness, and beauty. Jesus is the quintessential reflection of Wisdom delighting to be among her children. Such resplendence of Form has incarnated in *no other*. Jesus *is* God's Word. But this Word is no mere analogy, since God is one, simple, and immaterial Reality; so that no sooner does Divine Wisdom take human form than Jesus ardently proffers himself for our sanctification. Thus does Being impart being. For in the outstretched arms of the crucified Son, the love of God is for us displayed.

But the confession that Jesus is the Son of God, bringing salvation in his name, is the gift of faith. Believing in him, we also confess the "one, holy, catholic, and apostolic Church" which Christ founded, built upon the rock of St Peter (Cephas) whose successors have continued to proclaim a unified teaching and tradition, handed down unchanged since the apostles, in harmony with the Scriptures. And Jesus has breathed upon his apostles the Holy Spirit who has led this Church into his Truth — and his Truth remains one, so faith is certain.

Truth is also a living Spirit in whom we are invited to participate, receiving proportionally of his life. For along with this union, which the intentionality of faith effects, comes a vital and deepening intimacy with God, since faith has connected us to that point in our souls where he dwells, loving us into being. This communion becomes the wellspring of all virtue and holiness, since all perfections stream from God, radiating his Beauty. Being receptive to all that graces our souls, we are thus conformed to him in the highest point of our natures. God, who is all beatitude and light, providentially guards a tiny spark in the apex of the soul, which is the soul's nature and its good, and which is sufficient (potentially) to bring all persons to saving and certain Truth, but which, in those who are to be saved, the gift of faith formally (actually) renders efficacious for salvation. Refuse this grace and we separate ourselves from his Spirit, thereby extinguishing even the light of our own truth.

Not willing to crucify the Love which forms us, we, emulating the saints given to us by God, strive to evidence in our lives also the fruits of supernatural virtue by living from this Spirit that animates our souls — for Uncreated Love infuses those who are whole-heartedly abandoned to his will. Since God acts unimpeded in those whose will is now his will, they become his responsive instruments. With nothing to obstruct or hinder Love's operation, the whole person loves God and his creatures with and in the very Spirit that proceeds from both the Father and the Son. Because the Father does everything for the glory of his Son, those who are quickened by his Spirit also glorify the Son in all they do or suffer, since these are the works of God in them. They then become pleasing to the Father, who loves the image of the Son formed in them. And they, likewise, return this love to the Father through the self-giving of his Son in them, so that all they accomplish or endure becomes a sweet oblation to God. Since God himself now works without ceasing in the soul of the person united to Him, all one's works, however small, become more meritorious (for oneself, but also for others) by virtue of the Love which is living and working within.

God's light is the light of the soul, and in his Being we have our being. The sanctified soul, having recovered her simplicity, reflects the image of God like a mirror and enjoys the vision that all things come from God, sharing proportionally in his perfection. Absorbed in God, the soul cannot distinguish anything in itself which is not from God. All is holy. The certain principle of its cognition, the light of being, proceeds from the Divine self-knowing Who imparts intelligibility to all things. All its affections are immersed in his Holy Love. Only conation — that existential impulse which is at the heart of the person's intentional activity, but which is ignited by the spark of Divine Love — remains one's own. Yet it too freely submits to God. Thus transformed, one becomes as one with God, through participation: by his Will one acts, in his Light one comprehends, with his Spirit one is made holy, and within the Immensity of the Godhead one is kept safe — that Spiritual Marriage whereby God gives himself to the soul and the soul surrenders to him in loving union. Then life becomes a perpetual prayer — one's cross a triumph — and all existence betrays a hidden grace.

Such sanctity would be unachievable were it not for Christ's gift of the Church, his Bride, and her sacraments which strengthen us,

Union

infusing grace into our hearts, safeguarding us in his certain truth. The Church has only to point in evidence to its treasury of saints, who put the world to shame, but who show us the way to a holy life: a life that receives all from God and relinquishes all to him in love.

* * *

We have examined the Reality, Wisdom, and Spirit of God and found them to be profound mysteries, grounded as they are in one Substantial Being, *never* in nothing. However, that other mystery, death, need not be a dark night for one who has, by the grace of God, placed one's faith in Christ Jesus. In him we also have our hope, which is well placed because of who he is. Once again faith is certain. Therefore, we are confident that so long as we persevere to the end in our love for him, however inadequately—and it can never be enough—by the grace of God we will one day understand, and then we shall no longer think being, merely, for we shall see him as he is.

BIBLIOGRAPHY

Allday, Jonathan. *Quarks, Leptons and the Big Bang*. Boca Raton, FL: CRC Press, 2017.

Almedingen, E. M. *Francis of Assisi: A Portrait*. London: The Bodley Head, 1967.

Alter, Robert and Frank Kermode. *The Literary Guide to the Bible*. London: Fontana, 1987.

Anderson, Digby, ed. *Decadence: The Passing of Personal Virtue and its Replacement by Political and Psychological Slogans*. London: Social Affairs Unit, 2005.

Anderson, N. *Jesus Christ: The Witness of History*. Leicester: IVP, 1985.

Aquilina, Mike. *The Mass of the Early Christians*. Huntington: Our Sunday Visitor, 2007.

Aquinas, Thomas. *Summa Contra Gentiles*. Edited by Joseph Rickaby. London: Burns and Oates, 1905.

———. *Summa Theologica*. Vol. 19 of *The Great Books*. London: Encyclopaedia Britannica, 1952.

———. *Theological Texts*. Translated by Thomas Gilby. London: Oxford University Press, 1955.

Aristotle. *On Interpretation*. Vol. 8 of *The Great Books*. London: Encyclopaedia Britannica, 1952.

Armstrong, Dave. *A Biblical Defense of Catholicism*. Manchester, NH: Sophia Institute, 2003.

Arnold, Matthew. *Fire and Sword: The Reformation*. Saundersfoot, Wales: St Anthony Communications, 2002. CD.

Arndt, William F. and Wilbur F. Gingrich. *A Greek-English Lexicon of the New Testament and Other Early Christian Literature*. Chicago: University of Chicago Press, 1979.

Ashby, W. Ross. *An Introduction to Cybernetics*. London: Methuen, 1956.

Augustine of Hippo. *The City of God*. Vol. 18 of *The Great Books*. London: Encyclopaedia Britannica, 1952.

———. *The Trinity*. New York: New City Press, 1991.

Aulin, Arvid. *The Cybernetic Laws of Social Progress*. Oxford: Pergamon Press, 1982.

Aumann, Jordan. *Spiritual Theology*. London: Sheed and Ward, 1984.

Badde, Paul. *The Face of God: The Rediscovery of the True Face of Jesus on the Holy Face of Manopello*. San Francisco: Ignatius Press, 2010.

Baggott, Jim. *Farewell to Reality: How Modern Physics Has Betrayed the Search for Truth*. London: Pegasus Books, 2013.

Barbour, Julian. *The End of Time*. London: Phoenix, 2003.

Barrett, C. K. *The New Testament Background: Selected Documents*. London: SPCK, 1961.
——. *The Gospel According to John*. London: SPCK, 1978.
Barrow, John D. *The Constants of Nature*. London: Jonathan Cape, 2002.
Barrow, John D. and Frank J. Tipler. *The Anthropic Cosmological Principle*. Oxford: Oxford University Press, 1989.
Barth, Karl. *Evangelical Theology*. London: Weidenfeld and Nicolson, 1963.
Bauckham, Richard. *Jesus and the Eyewitnesses: The Gospels as Eyewitness Testimony*. Grand Rapids: William B. Eerdmans, 2006.
Bedoyere, Michael de la. *Francis: A Biography of the Saint of Assisi*. London: Catholic Book Club, 1962.
Bennett, Janice. *Sacred Blood, Sacred Image: New Evidence for the Authenticity of the Shroud of Turin*. San Francisco: Ignatius Press, 2005.
Bennett, Jonathan. *Linguistic Behavior*. Cambridge: Cambridge University Press, 1976.
Bennett, Rod. *Four Witnesses: The Early Church in Her Own Words*. San Francisco: Ignatius Press, 2002.
Berselli, Constante and Giorgio Gharib. *In Praise of Mary: Hymns from the First Millennium of the Eastern and Western Churches*. Slough: St Paul, 1981.
Berwick, Robert C. and Noam Chomsky. *Why Only Us: Language and Evolution*. Cambridge: MIT Press, 2016.
Blasi, Fulvio Di. *God and the Natural Law*. South Bend, IN: St Augustine's Press, 2006.
Blosius, Ludovicus. *A Book of Spiritual Instruction*. London: Burns and Oates, 1955.
Boethius, Severinus. *Consolation of Philosophy*. Translated by V. E. Watts. London: Folio Society, 1998.
Bohm, David. *Wholeness and the Implicate Order*. London: Ark, 1983.
Bouyer, Louis. *A History of Christian Spirituality*. Vol. 1, *The Spirituality of the New Testament and the Fathers*. Tunbridge Wells: Burns and Oates, 1968.
Brandmüller, Walter. *Light and Shadows: Church History amid Faith, Fact and Legend*. San Francisco: Ignatius Press, 2009.
Brisson, Luc and Walter Meyerstein. *Inventing the Universe*. Albany: State University of New York Press, 1995.
Bruce, F. F. *Commentary on the Book of the Acts*. Grand Rapids: William B. Eerdmans, 1977.
——. *The Canon of Scripture*. Glasgow: Charter House, 1988.
Bultmann, Rudolph. *Jesus and the Word*. New York: Scribner's, 1958.
——. *The History of the Synoptic Tradition*. New York: Harper and Row, 1963.
Carroll, Warren H. *A History of Christendom*. Vol. 3, *The Glory of Christendom*. Front Royal, VA: Christendom Press, 2000.

———. *A History of Christendom*. Vol. 4, *The Cleaving of Christendom*. Front Royal, VA: Christendom Press, 2000.
Catechism of the Catholic Church. London: Geoffrey Chapman, 1994.
Caussade, Jean Pierre de. *Self-Abandonment to Divine Providence*. London: Burns and Oates, 1948.
Celano, Thomas de. *The Francis Trilogy*. New York: New City Press, 1998.
Chaitin, Gregory. "A Random Walk in Arithmetic." *New Scientist*, March 24, 1990, 30–32.
Chalk, Frank and Kurt Jonassohn. *The History and Sociology of Genocide*. New Haven: Yale University Press, 1990.
Charles, R. H. *Apocrypha & Pseudepigrapha of Old Testament*. Oxford: Oxford University Press, 1913.
Cheetham, Nicolas. *The Keepers of the Keys*. London: Macdonald & Co., 1982.
Chesterton, G. K. *St Francis of Assisi*. London: Hodder & Stoughton, 1934.
Childs, Brevard S. *The New Testament as Canon*. London: SCM, 1984.
Colombière, Claude de la. *Trustful Surrender to Divine Providence*. Rockford, IL: TAN, 1983.
Combes, L'Abbé Andre. *St Thérèse and Suffering*. Dublin: Gill and Son, 1951.
Copleston, Frederick. *A History of Philosophy*. Vol. 2, *Augustine to Scotus*, New York: Paulist Press, 1977.
———. *A History of Philosophy*. Vol. 4, *Descartes to Leibniz*, New York: Paulist Press, 1977.
———. *A History of Philosophy*. Vol. 6, *Wolff to Kant*. New York: Paulist Press, 1977.
Courtois, Stephane, Nicolas Werth, Jean-Louis Panné, Andrzej Paczkowski, Karel Bartosek, and Jean-Louis Margolin. *The Black Book of Communism*. Harvard: Harvard University Press, 1999.
Coutances, Jean-Michael. *Carthusian Spiritual Exercises*. London: Burns and Oates, 1913.
Cowan, B. P. *Classical Mechanics*. London: Routledge & Kegan Paul, 1984.
Craig, William. "The Replacement of Auxiliary Expressions." *Philosophical Review* 65 (1956): 38–45.
Davies, Paul C. W. *The Accidental Universe*. Cambridge: Cambridge University Press, 1982.
———. *God and the New Physics*. London: J. M. Dent & Sons, 1983.
———. *Quantum Mechanics*. London: Routledge & Kegan Paul, 1984.
———. *Superforce*. London: Heinemann, 1985.
———. *The Cosmic Blueprint*. London: Heinemann, 1987.
Davies, Paul and John Gribben. *The Matter Myth*. London: Penguin Books, 1992.
Dawson, Christopher. *The Formation of Christendom*. San Francisco: Ignatius Press, 2008.

Denzinger, Heinrich. *Enchiridion Symbolorum*. Edited by C. Rahner. 30th ed. Fitzwilliam: Loreto, 1955.

Descartes, René. *Meditations*. Vol. 31 of *The Great Books*. London: Encyclopaedia Britannica, 1952.

D'Espagnat, Bernard. *On Physics and Philosophy*. Princeton: Princeton University Press, 2006.

Dodd, C. H. *The Interpretation of the Fourth Gospel*. Cambridge: University Press, 1953.

Doig, Desmond. *Mother Teresa: Her People and Her Work*. Glasgow: Collins Fount, 1988.

Drane, John. *Introducing the New Testament*. Sydney: Lion Publishing, 1986.

Dubay, Thomas, S. M. *The Evidential Power of Beauty: Science and Theology Meet*. San Francisco: Ignatius Press, 1999.

Duhem, Pierre. *Medieval Cosmology: Theories of Infinity, Place, Time, Void, and the Plurality of Worlds*. Chicago: University of Chicago Press, 1987.

Duran, Alphonsus Maria and Paul Mary Vota. *Why Apologize for the Spanish Inquisition?* London: Miles Jesu, 2000.

Emery, Gilles, O. P. *Trinity in Aquinas*. Ypsilanti, MI: Sapientia Press, 2003.

Eusebius Pamphilus. *Ecclesiastical History*. Translated by C. F. Cruse. Massachusetts: Hendrickson, 1998.

Fanti, Giulio and Pierandrea Malfi. *The Shroud of Turin: First Century after Christ!* Singapore: Pan Stanford Publishing, 2015.

Feyerabend, Paul. *Against Method*. London: Verso, 1988.

———. *Farewell to Reason*. London: Verso, 1987.

Fforde, Matthew. *Desocialisation: The Crisis of Post-Modernity*. Cheadle Hume: Gabriel, 2009.

Francis of Assisi. *The Writings of St Francis of Assisi*. Translated by Benan Fahy. London: Burns & Oates, 1964.

Frend, W. H. C. *The Rise of Christianity*. London: Darton, Longman and Todd, 1984.

Fritzsch, Harald. *Quarks: The Stuff of Matter*. London: Penguin Books, 1983.

Gardner, Michael. *The Ambidextrous Universe*. Harmondsworth: Pelican, 1970.

Garrigou-Lagrange, Reginald. *The Three Ways of the Spiritual Life*. London: Burns and Oates, 1942.

Gonzalez, Guillermo and Jay Richards. *The Privileged Planet*. Washington DC: Regnery, 2004.

Grenz, Stanley J. *The Named God and the Question of Being*. Louisville: Westminster John Knox Press, 2005.

Grisez, Germain. *God? A Philosophical Preface to Faith*. South Bend, Indiana: St Augustine's Press, 2005.

Guarducci, Margherita. *The Primacy of the Church of Rome*. San Francisco: Ignatius Press, 2003.

Guibert, Joseph de. *The Theology of the Spiritual Life*. New York: Sheed and Ward, 1953.
Habermas, Gary R. *Ancient Evidence for the Life of Jesus*. New York: Nelson, 1984.
Hall, Alexander W. *Thomas Aquinas and John Duns Scotus: Natural Theology in the High Middle Ages*. New York: Continuum, 2007.
Hampson, Norman. *The Enlightenment*. Harmondsworth: Penguin Books, 1990.
Hannom, James. *God's Philosophers: How the Medieval World Laid the Foundations of Modern Science*. London: Icon Books, 2009.
Hardon, John, S. J. *History and Theology of Grace*. Ypsilanti, MI: Veritas Press, 2002.
Havener, Ivan. *Q: The Sayings of Jesus*. Wilmington: Michael Glazier, 1987.
Heisenberg, Werner. *Physics and Philosophy*. London: Penguin Books, 1989.
Hindley, Geoffrey. *A Brief History of the Crusades*. London: Robinson, 2003.
Hoare, Rodney. *The Turin Shroud is Genuine: The Irrefutable Evidence*. London: The Souvenir Press, 1994.
Holland, Tom. *Millennium*. London: Little, Brown, 2008.
Holzner, Joseph. *Paul of Tarsus*. London: Scepter, 2008.
Hutson, H. H. "Form Criticism in the New Testament." *Journal of Bible and Religion* 19 (1951): 130–33.
John of the Cross. *The Collected Works of St John of the Cross*. Translated by Kieran Kavanaugh and Otilio Rodriguez. Washington DC: ICS Publications, 1991.
John Paul II [Karol Wojtyła]. *Salvifici Doloris*. Homebush, NSW: Society of St Paul, 1984.
Johnson, Vernon. *Spiritual Childhood*. London: Sheed and Ward, 1953.
Josephus, Flavius. *The Antiquities of the Jews*. Translated by William Whiston. Massachusetts: Hendrickson, 1993.
Julian of Norwich. *Revelations of Divine Love*. Translated by James Walsh. Wheathampstead: Anthony Clarke, 1961.
Kamen, Henry. *The Spanish Inquisition*. London: Phoenix, 1998.
Kant, Immanuel. *Critique of Pure Reason*. Vol 42 of *The Great Books*. London: Encyclopaedia Britannica, 1952.
Kelly, Edward F., Emily Williams Kelly, Adam Crabtree, Alan Gauld, Michael Grosso and Bruce Greyson. *Irreducible Mind: Toward a Psychology for the 21st Century*. Lanham: Rowman & Littlefield, 2010.
Kelly, Thomas A. F. *Language, World and God*. Blackrock: Columba Press, 1996.
Kereszty, R. A. *Jesus Christ*. Staten Island, NY: Alba House, 2002.
Kline, Morris. *Mathematics: The Loss of Certainty*. Oxford: Oxford University Press, 1980.

Knight, Kevin, ed. *New Advent: Fathers of the Church,* http://www.newadvent.org/fathers.
Koestler, Arthur. *The Sleepwalkers.* Harmondsworth: Penguin Books, 1982.
Ladd, G. E. *New Testament and Criticism.* Grand Rapids: William Eerdmans Publishing, 1983.
——. *I Believe in the Resurrection of Jesus.* London: Hodder & Stoughton, 1975.
Lanslots, D. I. *The Primitive Church.* Rockford: TAN, 1980.
Lawden, D. F. *An Introduction to Tensor Calculus, Relativity and Cosmology.* New York: John Wiley & Sons, 1982.
Lawrence, Brother [Nicholas Herman of Lorraine]. *The Practice of the Presence of God.* London: Allenson, 1906.
Leo of Assisi. *The Mirror of Perfection.* Translated by Countess Constance de la Warr. London: Burns and Oates, 1902.
Lerner, A. Ya. *Fundamentals of Cybernetics.* New York: Plenum, 1975.
Lewis, C. S. *The Problem of Pain.* Glasgow: Fount, 1986.
Lonergan, Bernard. *Insight.* Toronto: University of Toronto Press, 1992.
Longman, Tremper, III. *Literary Approaches to Biblical Interpretation.* Grand Rapids: Academie Books, 1987.
Lutheran World Federation and the Catholic Church. *Joint Declaration of the Doctrine of Justification.* London: CTS, 2001.
Luther, Martin. *The Bondage of the Will.* Translated by Henry Cole. Grand Rapids: Baker Book House, 1976.
Lynch, E. K. *The Scapular of Carmel.* Washington, NJ: World Apostolate of Fatima, 1955.
Lyons, John. *Chomsky.* Glasgow: Collins Fontana, 1979.
MacNiven-Johnston, Glynn. *Maria Goretti: Teenage Martyr.* London: Catholic Truth Society, 1997.
Maher, Michael. *Psychology.* London: Longmans, Green, & Co., 1900.
Majid, Shahn, ed. *On Space and Time.* Cambridge: Cambridge University Press, 2008.
Malebranche, Nicholas. *Dialogues on Metaphysics.* Translated by Willis Doney. New York: Abaris Books, 1980.
——. *The Search After Truth & Elucidations.* Translated by Thomas M. Lennon and Paul J. Olscamp. Columbus: Ohio State University Press, 1980.
——. *Treatise on Nature and Grace.* Translated by Patrick Riley. Oxford: Clarendon Press, 1992.
Maritain, Jacques. *Approaches to God.* Translated by Peter O'Reilly. London: Allen & Unwin, 1955.
——. *A Preface to Metaphysics.* London: Sheed and Ward, 1945.
——. *The Degrees of Knowledge.* London: Centenary Press, 1937.

Marx, Karl and Frederick Engels. *The German Ideology.* Vol. I: *Critique of Modern German Philosophy According to its Representatives Feuerbach, B. Bauer, and Stirner.* Moscow: Progress Publishers, 1976.
McGrath, Alister. *The Twilight of Atheism.* London: Rider, 2004.
McHugh, John A. and Charles J. Callan, trans. *Catechism of the Council of Trent.* London: Herder, 1945.
Mendelson, Elliot. *Introduction to Mathematical Logic.* New York: D. Van Nostrand, 1979.
Mercier, Désiré-Joseph. *A Manual of Modern Scholastic Philosophy.* London: Kegan Paul, 1938.
Merleau-Ponty, Maurice. *Phenomenology of Perception.* London: Routledge & Kegan Paul, 1962.
Merton, Thomas. *New Seeds of Contemplation.* New York: New Directions, 1961.
Metzger, Bruce M. *A Textual Commentary of the Greek New Testament.* Princeton: United Bible Societies, 1971.
Mills, Robert. *Space, Time and Quanta.* New York: W. H. Freeman, 1994.
Montagnes, Bernard. *The Doctrine of the Analogy of Being according to Thomas Aquinas.* Translated by E. M. Macierowski. Milwaukee: Marquette University Press, 2004.
Morerod, Charles. *Ecumenism and Philosophy.* Ann Arbor: Sapientia Press, 2006.
Morrison, F. *Who Moved the Stone?* Bromley: STL, 1983.
Muggeridge, Malcolm. *Something Beautiful for God.* London: Collins, 1971.
Nagel, Ernest. *The Structure of Science.* London: Routledge & Kegan Paul, 1971.
Nagel, Ernest and J. R. Newman. *Gödel's Proof.* London: Routledge, 1989.
Neidorf, Robert. *Deductive Forms.* New York: Harper & Row, 1967.
Newton-Smith, W. H. *The Rationality of Science.* Boston: Routledge & Kegan Paul, 1981.
Nisbet, Robert. *Twilight of Authority.* London: Heinemann, 1976.
Northrop, F. S. C. "The Method and Theories of Physical Science in Their Bearing upon Biological Organization." In *Great Ideas in Modern Science*, edited by R. W. Marks. New York: Bantam, 1967.
Oakley, Francis. *The Crucial Centuries: The Mediaeval Experience.* London: Terra Nova, 1979.
O'Carroll, Michael. *Theotokos: A Theological Encyclopedia of the Blessed Virgin Mary.* Wilmington, DE: Michael Glazier, 1988.
O'Connor, James T. *The Hidden Manna.* San Francisco: Ignatius Press, 1988.
Osborne, G. R. *The Resurrection Narratives: A Redactional Study.* Grand Rapids: Baker, 1984.
Ott, Ludwig. *Fundamentals of Catholic Dogma.* Rockford, IL: TAN, 1974.
Pelikan, Jaroslav. *Jesus through the Centuries.* New York: Harper & Row, 1985.

Penrose, Roger. *Fashion, Faith and Fantasy in the New Physics of the Universe*. Princeton: Princeton University Press, 2016.
——. *The Emperor's New Mind*. London: Vintage, 1990.
——. *The Road to Reality*. London: Jonathan Cape, 2004.
Pernoud, Regine. *Those Terrible Middle Ages: Debunking the Myths*. San Francisco: Ignatius Press, 2000.
Perrin, Norman. *The Resurrection Narratives*. London: SCM, 1977.
Petit, François. *The Problem of Evil*. New York: Hawthorn Books, 1959.
Phillips, R. P. *Modern Thomistic Philosophy*, vol. 2. Westminster, MD: Newman Press, 1957.
Pieper, Josef. *The End of Time*. San Francisco: Ignatius Press, 1999.
Pitre, Brant. *The Jewish Roots of the Eucharist*. West Covina, CA: St Joseph Communications, 2006. DVD.
Plato. *Symposium*. Vol. 7 of *The Great Books*. London: Encyclopaedia Britannica, 1952.
Ratzinger, Joseph (Benedict XVI). *Jesus of Nazareth*. Vol. 1. London: Bloomsbury, 2007.
——. *Jesus of Nazareth*. Vol. 2, *Holy Week*. London: CTS, 2011.
Read, Piers Paul. *The Templars*. London: Phoenix, 2001.
Redford, Joseph. *Bad, Mad or God?* London: St Paul's, 2005.
Reumann, John. *Jesus in the Church's Gospels*. Philadelphia: Fortress, 1985.
Roberts, Alexander, James Donaldson and Arthur Cleveland Coxe, eds. *Ante-Nicene Fathers*, vol. 1. Buffalo, NY: Christian Literature Publishing, 1885.
Robinson, John A. T. *Redating the New Testament*. London: SCM, 1976.
Rohl, David. *The Lost Testament. From Eden to Exile: The Five-Thousand-Year History of the People of the Bible*. London: Century, 2002.
Rosmini, Antonio. *Conscience*. Durham: Rosmini House, 1989.
——. *Essence of the Human Soul*. Durham: Rosmini House, 1999.
——. *Maxims of Christian Perfection*. London: Darton, Longman & Todd, 1962.
——. *Principles of Ethics*. Durham: Rosmini House, 1989.
——. *The Essence of Right*. Durham: Rosmini House, 1993.
——. *Theodicy*. 3 vols. London: Longmans, Green, 1912.
——. *The Origin of Ideas*. London: Forgotten Books, 2015.
——. *The Origin of Thought*. Durham: Rosmini House, 1989.
——. *The Problem of Ontology: Being as One*. Durham: Rosmini House, 1998.
Saint-Jure, Jean Baptiste. *The Knowledge and Love of Our Lord Jesus Christ*, in *Trustful Surrender to Divine Providence*. Rockford, IL: TAN, 1983.
Francis de Sales. *Treatise on the Love of God*. Translated by Vincent Kerns. Bangalore: SFS Publications, 1982.
Schillebeeckx, Edward. *Jesus: An Experiment in Christology*. London: Collins, 1974.

Schurer, Emil. *A History of the Jewish People in the Time of Jesus*. New York: Schocken Books, 1961.

Scotus, John Duns. *De Primo Principio (A Treatise on God as First Principle)*. N.p.: Kessinger Legacy Reprints, 2004.

——. *God and Creatures: The Quodlibetal Questions*, edited by Felix Alluntis and Allan B. Wolter. Princeton: Princeton University Press, 1975.

——. *On Being and Cognition: Ordinatio 1:3*. Edited and translated by John van den Bercken. New York: Fordham University Press, 2016.

——. *Philosophical Writings*. Edited by Allan Wolter. Cambridge: Hackett, 1987.

Sencourt, Robert. *Carmelite and Poet: A Framed Portrait of St John of the Cross*. London: Hollis and Carter, 1943.

Sider, Theodore. *Logic for Philosophy*. Oxford: Oxford University Press, 2010.

Slattery, Peter. *The Springs of Carmel*. Homebush, NSW: St Paul, 1990.

Smolin, Lee. *The Trouble with Physics*. London: Penguin Books, 2006.

Spitzer, Robert J. *New Proofs for the Existence of God*. Grand Rapids: Eerdmans, 2010.

Stapp, H. P. *Mind, Matter, and Quantum Mechanics*. New York: Springer-Verlag, 1993.

——. *Quantum Theory and Free Will: How Mental Intentions Translate into Bodily Actions*. New York: Springer International, 2017.

Stark, Rodney. *Bearing False Witness: Debunking Centuries of Anti-Catholic History*. London: SPCK, 2017.

——. *God's Battalions: The Case for the Crusades*. New York: Harper Collins, 2009.

Stein, Robert H. *The Synoptic Problem*. Grand Rapids: Baker Book House, 1987.

Stevenson, J., ed. *A New Eusebius: Documents Illustrating the History of the Church to AD 337*. London: SPCK, 1987.

——, ed. *Creeds, Councils and Controversies: Documents Illustrating the History of the Church AD 337–461*. London: SPCK, 1986.

——. *The Catacombs: Rediscovered Monuments of Early Christianity*. London: Thames & Hudson, 1978.

Tanquerey, Adolphe. *A Manual of Dogmatic Theology*. 2 vols. New York: Desclée & Co., 1959.

——. *The Spiritual Life: A Treatise on Ascetical and Mystical Theology*. Rockford: TAN, 2000.

The Little Flowers of St Francis. Translated by W. Heywood. London: Methuen, 1924.

Thérèse de Lisieux [Thérèse Martin]. *The Story of a Soul*. London: Burns and Oates, 1951.

Travis, Stephen H. "Form Criticism." In *New Testament Interpretation*, edited by I. Howard Marshall. Grand Rapids: William B. Eerdmans Publishing, 1985.
Tresmontant, Claude. *The Hebrew Christ: Language in the Age of the Gospels*. Chicago: Franciscan Herald Press, 1989.
Vermes, Geza. *Jesus the Jew: A Historian's Reading of the Gospels*. Philadelphia: Fortress Press, 1981.
———, ed. *The Dead Sea Scrolls in English*. Harmondsworth: Penguin Books, 1987.
Vincent, Marvin R. *Word Studies in the New Testament*. Grand Rapids: Eerdmans, 1946.
Walsh, Michael. *The Triumph of the Meek*. San Francisco: Harper & Row, 1986.
Waltke, Bruce K. "Oral Tradition." In *Inerrancy and Hermeneutic*, by Harvie M. Conn. Grand Rapids: Baker Book House, 1988.
Ward, Peter and Donald Brownlee. *Rare Earth*. New York: Copernicus, 2004.
Watson, R. I., *The Great Psychologists*. Philadelphia: J. B. Lippencott, 1963.
Wenham, J. *Redating Matthew, Mark, and Luke: A Fresh Assault on the Synoptic Problem*. London: Hodder and Stoughton, 1991.
———. *The Easter Enigma*. Exeter: The Paternoster Press, 1984.
Wiener, Norbert. *The Human Use of Human Beings*. New York: Avon Books, 1967.
William, Michael. *The Genesis of Political Correctness: The Basis of a False Morality*. N.p.: Michael William, 2016.
Williams, Thomas, ed. *The Cambridge Companion to Duns Scotus*. Cambridge: Cambridge University Press, 2003.
Wilson, Ian. *The Shroud: The 2000-Year-Old Mystery Solved*. London: Bantam Press, 2010.
Wojtyła, Karol (Pope St John Paul II). *Faith According to Saint John of the Cross*. San Francisco: Ignatius Press, 1981.
Woods, Thomas E. *How the Catholic Church Built Western Civilization*. Washington, DC: Regnery Publishing, 2005.
Wright, N. T. *The Resurrection of the Son of God*. London: SPCK, 2003.
Zagoskin, Alexandre. *Quantum Mechanics: A Complete Introduction*. Hachette, UK: Teach Yourself Books, 2015.

INDEX

Accidental modifications, 218
Accidents, 9n12, 13, 43, 98n7, 186, 187n126, 218
Acheiropoietos, 147
Act, 4, 20, 26, 39–40, 70, 204–5
Acts of the Apostles, 105
Albigensian Crusade, 192
Alexius Comnenus I, Emperor, 190
Analogy of being (*analogia entis*), xi, 18, 40–41, 44, 67, 85–86, 89, 95–96, 205, 227, 232, 240, 262
    Participatory, 204
    Predicative, 44
Anthropic principle, 51n40, 52, 64, 70
Antioch, 168, 172–73, 181, 190
A priori, 5n4, 30, 34–37, 46, 53, 57–58, 61–62, 137
Apulia, 247
Aquinas, St Thomas, 4, 40n16, 41, 44n22, 233n66
    Five ways of, 19
Aristotle, 5, 15n23, 29n56, 59, 183–84
Assisi, 77, 185, 246–47, 249–50, 258
Atheism, 30, 45
Auxiliary expression, 98

Bacon, Francis, 97
Bauckham, Richard, xii, 103–4, 108–9, 120
Beauty, x, 3, 22n39, 28, 31, 65, 67–68, 73, 85–86, 95, 197, 203, 232, 234, 272–73
Bernard, of Clairvaux, St 191
Bernardo da Quintavalle, 248
Bernardone, Pietro, 246–48
Bhattacharya, Dr. R. N., 265

Big Bang, 14, 20n32, 21n35, 49–50, 52, 63, 97
Black hole, x, 14, 49n36
Black Legend, 190
Body of Christ, 181, 186–87
Bohm, David, 46n29, 58–59
Borde Guth Vilenkin Theorem, 63n64
Brienne, Walter de, 247

Cairo, 191
Calcutta, 246, 263
Canticle of the Creatures, 251
Carmelite, 252–53
Catacombs, 175, 177
Categories, 30, 34–38, 48, 53, 58, 62, 109
Catholic Church, 171–73, 182n108, 197, 208n45, 241n95
Causality, 13, 15, 32, 34–35, 38–39, 59
Caussade, John Pierre de, 213n60, 215n65, 216n67
Celano, Thomas de, 246
Chaitin, Gregory, 97n5
Chartres, School of, 183
Chi-rho, symbol, 170
Claire de lune, 18
Clare, 185, 248–49, 258
Clement of Alexandria, 120n95, 180
Clement of Rome, Bishop, 105–6, 167–68, 172
Clermont, Council of, 190
Coenaesthesia, 29n56, 65
Compton wavelength, 48
Confession, 116, 157n12, 161, 170, 173, 188, 228–29, 232, 253, 273
Constantine, Emperor, 170

Contingency, contingent, 21n36, 35n8, 37, 58, 64
Contradiction, principle of, 5, 7, 12, 32
Craig, William, 98, 141n49
Criteriology, 6, 10, 16
Criterion of truth, 8, 29
Crusades, *see also* Albigensian Crusade, 190–91
Cyprian of Carthage, Bishop, 170–71, 175, 180

Damietta, 191, 248
Daniel, book of, 113n62
Darjeeling, 263
Dark night of the soul, 265–66
Daughters of St Anne, 263
Decadence, 221
Descartes, René, 10–11, 58
D'Espagnat, Bernard, 36n11, 46n29, 47, 56n51, 58n54, 59, 60n57, 61n61
Didache, 172, 179
Dignity, *see* person, 74, 77, 89, 118, 182, 185, 218–19, 225, 238, 264, 271
Duty, 216, 218–21

Edward, of England, Lord, 191
El Cid, 190
Enlightenment, the, ix, 34, 221
Enoch, Book of, 111, 112n56, 113n61, 121
Ephesus, Council of, 178
Eucharist, 164, 172–73, 179–81, 186–87, 209, 15, 225, 229
Eudaemonism, 80, 272
Eusebius, 104n22, 107n28, 120n96, 168, 173n71
Evil, x, 11, 30, 66, 68–72, 74–80, 82–84, 90–91, 150

Fallacy, of affirming the consequent, 99, 141n49
Feedback, positive and negative, 82
Form criticism, 101–4
Formal principle, idea, 14, 53, 70–71, 203, 218
Francis de Sales, 260, 261n41,
Francis of Assisi, St, 77, 246, 249–50
Frederick II, 191–92
Free will, 41, 60n57, 72–73, 76, 151, 200, 213, 217, 219, 241n95

Galileo Galilei, 184–85
Gelasius I, Pope St, 171
Giles, 248
God
    Existence of, ix–x, 17, 19, 23, 29, 36, 60, 89, 153, 207
    Personal nature of, 25
    Providence of, 79, 87–88, 111, 154–55, 215–16, 263
    Simplicity of, 26
    Transcendental properties of, 25–26, 36–37, 44, 217
    Trinity of, 204, 206, 224n20, 228, 234
Gödel's theorem, 6, 62, 63n64, 98, 100
Golden Altar of Incense, 134
Good, the, 44, 73–74, 78, 80, 86, 88, 90, 150, 217, 219, 254
Goretti, Maria, St, 246, 267, 270, 272
Gospels, dates of, 104–5, 108
Grace, *passim*, 32n3, 39n15, 113n62
Grand Inquisitor, 189
Graviton, 47
Gravity, 47–49, 51–52
Gregory VIII, 191
Guarducci, Margherita, 169

Index

Habitus, 237–38
Hanina ben Dosa, 137
Hippolytus, 181
Hobbes Thomas, 40
Holiness, 201–2, 206, 212–13, 216, 221, 234–35, 250, 273
Holy Spirit, 119, 125, 158, 162, 165–66, 170, 172, 176–77, 181, 203–5, 207–12, 222–23, 228, 233–34, 241, 244, 255, 273
Honi the Circle Drawer, 137
Hubble's constant, 49n36, 51
Hume, David, 34–35, 88
Hypothetical construct, 42, 98, 102, 104

Idealism, 10, 42, 53–54, 60n60, 64
Identity, principle of, 5–7, 12, 18, 23, 32–33, 69, 97, 98n7
Ignatius of Antioch, St, 168, 173, 176, 180
Immaculate Conception of Mary, 241
Innocent III, Pope, 191, 248
Intelligible, intelligibility, 9, 38, 65, 70, 102, 218, 239
Irenaeus of Smyrna, Bishop, 104n22, 107n28, 108n34, 120n95, 169, 176–77

Jaki, Stanley, 52
Jerusalem, 91, 105, 113, 129, 141, 145–46, 181, 190–91
Jesuits, 183, 263
Jesus Christ, ix, xii, 96–97, 123, 139, 148, 150, 154, 157n12, 161, 172–74, 180–81, 193, 207, 231, 240–41, 250, 266
  Divine, 111, 114, 117, 178
  Head of Church, 155, 164
  King, 113, 149
  Lamb of God, 128, 136, 148, 150, 154, 192
  Logos, 205–6, 233
  Lord of the Sabbath, 119, 132–34, 148
  Real presence in Eucharist, 180
  Resurrection of, 136, 143
  Savior, 166, 172, 180, 202, 209, 231
  Son of God, 110–11, 113–17, 119, 135, 140, 148, 176, 192, 197, 233, 273
  Temple, 132–35, 149
  Word, 123, 126, 178, 204n29, 256
John of the Cross, St, 185, 206n35, 246, 251–57, 260, 265, 266n53
John Paul II, Pope St, 256n28, 259, 265, 272n67
Julian of Norwich, 239n84

Kamen, Henry, 188, 190n135
Kant, Immanuel (Kantian), 30, 33–42, 44–46, 53, 57–60, 62, 64, 97, 137, 150

Lamb of God, see Jesus Christ
Last Supper, see also Passover, 124, 127–29, 131, 134, 156, 159, 179
Least means, law of, 79
Leibniz, G.W., 13n19, 34, 68
Leo, Brother, 249–51, 271
Leo XIII, Pope, 258
Lewis, C.S., 186
Linguistics, 33
Little way, 259, 261
Locke, John, 34–35
Logic, 5–6, 8, 10, 29–30, 36n9, 60–61, 79, 99–100
Logos, see Jesus Christ
Louis IX, 191
Lucian, 245
Luther, Martin, 40–42, 45, 173–75, 211n58

Malebranche, Nicholas, 9n13, 15n23, 65n66, 73n9, 86–87
Malik al Kamil, Sultan, 249
Marx, Karl, 40, 221n11
Mary Blessed Virgin and Mother of God, 157–59, 170, 175–79, 185, 210–12, 241, 252
Materiae dispositae advenit forma, 239
Mathematics, 5–6, 34, 36, 46, 62, 79
McCabel, 51
Miller-Tichy, proof, 100, 141n49
Minores, 248
Missionaries of Charity, 264
Modus ponens, 99
Modus tollens, 6–7, 29, 101
Mohammedans, 190
"Montanus," 190
Moslems, 188, 190
Muratorian Canon, 105–6, 108

Nagel, Ernest, 43
Nero, Claudius, Emperor, 104, 106n26, 167–68
Neurons, 58
Neusner, 133–34
Neutrino, 54
Neutron star, 33, 70
Newton, Isaac, 34, 36, 49n36, 58
Nicaea, Council of, 178
Nietzsche, Friedrich, 30, 40
Northrop, F.S.C., 99, 100n12
Noumenal, 36–38, 61

Ockham, William of, 33, 101n15
Ockham's razor, 11
Ontologism, 10
Organizing principle, 10, 14, 33, 46, 53, 57, 218, 239
Origen, 107n28, 169–70
Oviedo, Sudarium of, 144–47

Passover, 128–29, 135, 156
Paul, St, 105–7, 135, 140–43, 160–62, 166–71, 180, 209, 226, 257, 271
Paul VI, Pope, 265
Penance, 161, 164, 173, 206, 209
Penrose, Roger, 46–47, 50, 64n65
Permian extinction, 68
Perseverance, 200, 202, 207, 272
Person, nature of, 218–19
  Dignity of, 182, 264
Perugia, 247, 250
Peter, companion of St Francis, 248
Peter, St, *see also* Primacy of Peter, 105–7, 116, 143, 157–60, 162, 166–67, 169–70
Photons, 47, 52–55
Physics, x, 5–6, 11, 33–34, 47, 51, 55–60, 62–63, 95, 101, 183
Pica, 246–47
Pilgrimage, 169–70, 191
Planck, length, 47
Planck, time, 50–51, 88
Poincaré, Henri, 61
Political correctness, ix, 221
Portiuncula, 248, 250
Postmodern(ism), ix–xii, 9–10, 42, 62, 221
Prayer, xi, 88–89, 177–81, 209–10, 225, 234, 253, 266–68, 271
Primacy of Peter, 166–168
Privation, 71–72, 80, 84–85, 90, 95, 150
Proposition (of book), 5–7, 29–30
Provence, 191, 246
Psalms of Solomon, 113
Psychology, 183, 245
Purgation, 201–2, 222, 266

Q document, 98n10, 99, 114n69
Quantum entanglement, 54, 56, 88, 213

Quantum mechanics, 55n47, 62, 64, 79
Quantum physics, x, 55, 56n50, 58, 63, 95, 98n6
Quarks, 47–50, 83
Qumran, 113

Raison d'etre (reason of being), 11, 220
   Extrinsic, 12–15, 22n39, 25, 32
   Intrinsic, 12–14, 46, 70–71, 218–20,
Real presence, *see* Jesus
Reason, 11–15, 29–30, 34–36, 69, 89, 150–51, 153, 203, 219, 227, 237, 260
Reconquest, 190
Reductionism, 65
Referent, 33, 46, 63, 98–101
Relativism, 30, 164, 222
Reliability, principle of, 98
Resurrection, *see* Jesus Christ
Rights, 199, 218–20
Robinson, John A.T., 107
Rosmini, Antonio, Bl, 36–39, 60n58, 65n66, 72n8, 79–80, 219n5, 237n76, 239n82

Sabbath, 119, 132–34, 148
Sacrament, blessed, *see also* Eucharist, xi, 214, 228–29, 272
   of the present moment, 214–16
Sacraments of the Church, 164, 209
Sanctification, 89, 198, 203, 206, 209, 273
San Damiano, 247–48
Saint-Jure, Jean Baptiste, 214n61
Sanhedrin, 117–18, 135
Savior, *see* Jesus Christ
Schillebeeckx, Edward, 136–37
Scholastic(ism), 34, 57–58

Science and the Church, 16, 97, 183–84
Scintilla, 237–38, 241, 257
Scotus, John Duns, Bl, 9n12, 14n20, 17n25, 20n33, 25n47, 27n49, 31n2, 40, 57, 224n20
Secularism, 222
Septuagint, 173–74
Serenelli, Alessandro, 267, 270
Simeon bar Kosiba (bar Kochba), 137
Similitudes of Enoch, 121
Sitz im Leben, 102–3, 114
Sola scriptura, 155
Soul, 37, 64–65, 71, 138, 155, 174, 204–11, 224–28, 236–40, 257, 260–65
Space, 16, 34–37, 47, 49n36, 54, 56–58
Space-time, 14, 16, 47, 50, 96, 140n47
Spain, 106, 146, 185, 188–90
Spanish Inquisition, 188–90
Spin, 43, 47
Spiritual life, 77, 202, 205, 209, 218n2, 222–23, 233, 258, 266
Stigmata, 249
String theories, 63n64
Substance, 11, 13–16, 26, 30, 36–38, 43, 65, 84, 89–90, 187, 203–4, 219, 239–41
Sub tuum, 177
Suffering, 68–69, 78, 81, 84, 167, 254, 270–72
Syballine Oracles, 113, 176
Synderesis, 237–38, 241, 258

Teresa of Calcutta, St, 246, 263–66
Tertullian, Quintus, 173, 175, 181
Theodicy, 68–69
Theotokos, 177–79
Thérèse de Lisieux, St, 246, 258–62

Time, 7, 16, 34–37, 50–58, 79
Transcendental
   Dialectic, 36
   Properties of God, 25–26
Transubstantiation, 186–87
Turin, Shroud of, 144–48
Turks, 190

Umbria, 246
Urban II, Pope, 190–91

Verisimilitude, 100
Vermes Geza, 110, 113 n64

Virtue, xi, 77–78, 84, 91, 157, 202, 205, 211–16, 221–33, 236, 244
   Cardinal, 211, 222–26
   Religious, 211, 235–36
   Theological, 211, 223, 226–28, 230, 232, 260
   Charity, 211, 213, 232–34, 244–45
   Faith, 147, 215
   Hope, 211, 223, 226, 229–32

Women in the Medieval Church, 185
Wright, N.T., xii, 138

www.ingramcontent.com/pod-product-compliance
Lightning Source LLC
Chambersburg PA
CBHW020350170426
43200CB00005B/122